DISASTER

DISASTER

HURRICANE KATRINA AND THE
FAILURE OF HOMELAND SECURITY

CHRISTOPHER COOPER
ROBERT BLOCK

Times Books
Henry Holt and Company
New York

Times Books
Henry Holt and Company, LLC
Publishers since 1866
175 Fifth Avenue
New York, New York 10010
www.henryholt.com

Distributed in Canada by H. B. Fenn and Company Ltd.

Library of Congress Cataloging-in-Publication Data
Cooper, Christopher, 1961–
    Disaster : Hurricane Katrina and the failure of Homeland Security / Christopher Cooper
    and Robert Block.—1st ed.
        p. cm.
    Includes index.
    ISBN-13: 978-0-8050-8130-5
    ISBN-10: 0-8050-8130-5
    1. Hurricane Katrina, 2005. 2. United States. Dept. of Homeland Security. 3. United States.
Federal Emergency Management Agency. 4. Emergency management—Gulf States. 5. Disaster
relief—Gulf States. I. Block, Robert (Robert Jeffrey), 1960– II. Title.

    HV6362005.G85 C66 2006
    976'.044—dc22

                                                                                        2006045557

Henry Holt books are available for special promotions and premiums.
For details contact: Director, Special Markets.

First Edition 2006

Designed by Meryl Sussman Levavi

Printed in the United States of America
10 9 8 7 6 5 4 3 2 1

To Remi and Jack, who respond to my small tempests and calamitous disasters with effortless aplomb. And to my mother, who typed my first term paper and predicted I'd be a writer one day. And to the city of New Orleans, which deserves to be rebuilt, not as an act of charity but an act of contrition.

CC

For my wife, my son, and my father: they inspire me and never fail to make me smile. And for the first responders, all the men and women who disregard danger to help those lives impacted by disasters large and small. They are truly the better angels of our nature.

RB

DISASTER. It strikes anytime, anywhere. It takes many forms — a hurricane, an earthquake, a tornado, a flood, a fire or a hazardous spill, an act of nature or an act of terrorism. It builds over days or weeks, or hits suddenly, without warning. Every year, millions of Americans face disaster, and its terrifying consequences.

On March 1, 2003, the Federal Emergency Management Agency (FEMA) became part of the U.S. Department of Homeland Security (DHS). FEMA's continuing mission within the new department is to lead the effort to prepare the nation for all hazards and effectively manage federal response and recovery efforts following any national incident. FEMA also initiates proactive mitigation activities, trains first responders, and manages the National Flood Insurance Program.

—Mission Statement,
Federal Emergency Management Agency

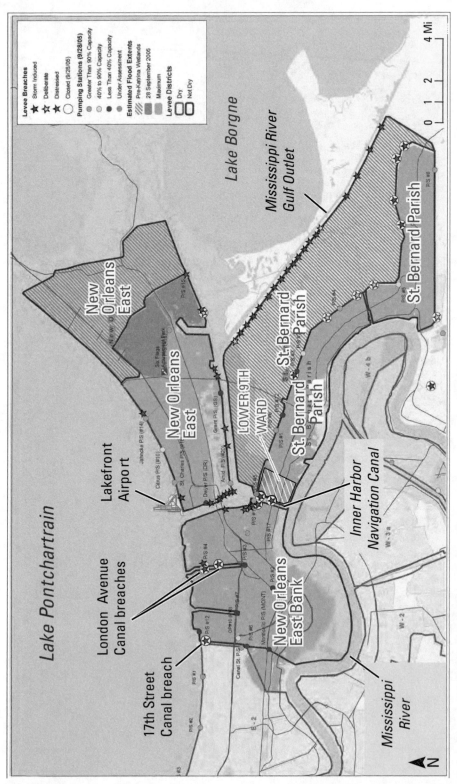

Source: Courtesy of the U.S. Geological Survey

Contents

Part Three
FLOTSAM AND JETSAM

Authors' Note

Shortly before Hurricane Katrina hit the Gulf Coast, five state emergency managers took a tough message to a meeting in Washington with Michael Jackson, the deputy secretary of homeland security. In plain language, the group told Jackson that the Department of Homeland Security's obsession with terrorist attacks had undermined the nation's readiness for natural disasters and ironically had made the country more vulnerable to calamity, not less. Jackson dismissed their concerns with a wave and a smile. He said the department knew what it was doing. "Trust but verify," Jackson said.

In a matter of days it would become clear that Jackson was simply wrong. Hurricane Katrina crashed into Mississippi and Louisiana with unbridled fury, and by nearly every account, the federal response was an abject failure. It's hard to imagine how the Department of Homeland Security, the sprawling colossus that was supposed to make the country safe, could have failed so spectacularly.

September 11, 2001, was supposed to have been the signal disaster that "changed everything" and brought the policies, processes, and structure of the U.S. government into alignment as a powerful counterweight to every menace hurled at this country by God and man. In the words of its designers, the Department of Homeland Security was to be the embodiment of federal might, sharpened to a fine point. It would be a "good" bureaucracy, designed to coordinate all federal disaster efforts into a single, focused, modern machine. But this proved not to be the case at all.

In the aftermath of Katrina, federal officials would trot out all manner of excuses for the department's glaring failures, many of which have come to be accepted as fact. City and state officials were said to have been unprepared and had fiddled when they should have evacuated New Orleans in advance of the lumbering storm. Washington officials often said that Katrina was a double disaster—a strong blow from the storm itself, followed twenty-four hours later by a catastrophic flood. The Bush administration said it had pre-staged an unprecedented amount of supplies in the region, but the magnitude of the hurricane proved far more intense than even the most pessimistic of doomsday scenarios. And the federal government's information-gathering agencies would complain that they had an incomplete, inaccurate picture of what was occurring in the ruined, drowned city.

In fact, none of these assertions turned out to be true. Hurricane Katrina wasn't the storm of the century; it didn't deal New Orleans a direct blow, and winds in the city were not as strong as in many outlying areas. City and state officials had managed to evacuate some 90 percent of the city in advance of the storm—a rate unprecedented in the annals of disaster response. Hurricane Katrina didn't present a double disaster—indeed, many of the floodwalls collapsed below their rated strength, in advance of the storm's passage. Federal officials laid in an insufficient quantity of supplies. And perhaps most important, in the immediate aftermath of the storm, pertinent, accurate, real-time information flowed in great waves through government agencies from all manner of responsible sources. And yet in many instances this information sat unused, unread, and even dismissed by the very people charged with ensuring that timely news about disasters made its way to the top levels of the federal government.

Perhaps the most unsettling element to the Hurricane Katrina disaster is the way it happened—not as a silver shadow streaking across the sky but as a massive, lumbering tempest that signaled its intentions days before following through. There were no dramatic fireballs, no sudden flashes of light, no buildings that fell to vapor over the course of an hour or so. Hurricane Katrina traveled toward its destination at roughly walking speed, giving federal officials days to plot a counterstrategy. If intelligence drives Homeland Security's disaster-response planning and execution, few calamities provide better advance intelligence than a hurricane. Storm surges can be modeled, wind speed can be measured, and landfall is a predictable event. Yet, as Katrina moved through the Gulf of Mexico, the department reacted with far less determination than it had during a myriad of false terrorist alarms in the months and years before. Indeed, in 2004 the agency had included a hurricane strike in New Orleans in its pantheon of most-feared disasters, right up there with a nuclear attack and a plot to sabotage the nation's food supply. Yet as Katrina approached, Washington seemed to go dark in the face of clear catastrophe.

And in the storm's aftermath, the Department of Homeland Security moved at a snail's pace, giving lie to its very reason for being. All of the problems that Homeland Security's creation was supposed to have resolved—the interagency jealousies, the tangles of red tape, the inherent inability to "connect the dots"—seemed to be even worse. Instead of streamlining Washington's ability to perform, the department clogged it up with new layers of bureaucracy and stovepipes of information.

This book is a chronicle of a disaster foretold. It is a story of federal hubris in the face of strident warnings that came from all manner of emergency responders, who had watched helplessly for years as Bush administration officials summarily dismantled the Federal Emergency Management Agency and remade it into a cadre of debris janitors and political hacks. And it is a warning to every American that despite endless reassurances from the federal government that this country is now safer than it was before September 11, 2001, there is in fact little to support such rhetoric beyond good intentions.

This is a story about what went wrong during Hurricane Katrina from the top down rather than the bottom up. No real attempt is made in these pages to present a chronicle of the misery that was heaped upon the citizens of New Orleans, many of whom were among the city's most vulnerable. This is neither an oversight nor an attempt to minimize the very real suffering that occurred in New Orleans in the days, weeks, and months after the storm hit. The people of New Orleans suffered terribly in the aftermath of Katrina, and their plight, ably chronicled in a variety of publications, is both heartbreaking and horrible.

This book is also not a chronicle of heroic rescues or the brave men and women who brought succor to the miserable and headed off what would have been a far worse disaster had they not stepped up to the challenge. Trained and untrained, professional and volunteer, many people seized the opportunity to do the right thing in this disaster, and they performed valiant deeds that saved the lives of untold thousands. Many of these great deeds occurred in spite of Washington's activities, not because of them. They are a shining testament to the iron backbones and warm hearts of first responders everywhere.

This book also makes no attempt to document every weft and warp of the local response to Hurricane Katrina or to catalog every mistake that state and city officials made. Local leadership during the immediate aftermath of Hurricane Katrina was wobbly in many respects; the administrations of Governor Kathleen Blanco of Louisiana and Mayor Ray Nagin of New Orleans were clearly and demonstrably overwhelmed from almost the moment the storm struck, if not before. But this situation, like the catastrophic effects of the storm itself, was recognized by the federal government far in advance. Louisiana is one of the most impoverished states in the Union, and as New Orleans congressman William Jefferson noted later, "Even if the storm had totally missed us, we'd need federal help just to rake up the leaves."

Finally, this book makes no attempt to rehabilitate the reputation of any officials—at the local, state, or federal level. Their actions and decisions speak for themselves.

In the end, this book attempts to show that New Orleans, while uniquely fragile geographically and confusingly exotic culturally, is just an average place in the scale of risk. A hurricane is an average threat, and New Orleans is a place like any other—inherently vulnerable to calamity, be it from an overturned freight train, an overseas terrorist plot, a raging forest fire, or a temblor that rocks the Richter scale. If, after four years and billions of dollars spent on preparedness, Homeland Security can't handle a hurricane, it is likely to struggle when faced with any manner of other disasters. The preparation for and response to Hurricane Katrina should disturb all Americans. If New Orleans is vulnerable, so are we all.

Christopher Cooper and Robert Block

May 2006
Washington, D.C.

Part One

PRELUDE
TO DISASTER

1

THE PERFECT STORM

The perfect storm is as predictable as it is inexorable. Born in the Atlantic Ocean, it hits Puerto Rico and Hispaniola and Cuba, and it grows bigger as it moves through the warm waters of the Gulf of Mexico. Though there is plenty of time to flee, many residents along the Gulf Coast stay put. And just as predicted, this storm makes a straight track for the tiny camp town of Grand Isle, Louisiana, obliterates it, and moves north toward New Orleans.

The hurricane moves upriver for nearly sixty miles, leaving catastrophe in its wake. It passes right over New Orleans, and as it does, the storm tilts nearby Lake Pontchartrain like a teacup and dumps it into the city. A quick rush of brackish water drenches New Orleans and leaves it sitting in as much as twenty feet of water. And then the hurricane is gone, and everything lies in ruins.

The perfect storm is big enough to make New Orleans a certain kind of hell, but not so big that it makes first responders throw their hands up in despair. The floodwater is the worst of it—it collects in the lower parts of the city and takes weeks to pump out. As it sits, the water becomes a thick and fetid mash of household chemicals and dead things and gasoline that bubbles from the tanks of thousands of submerged automobiles and service stations. The water makes some people ill, but the worst is the complication it adds to the rescue efforts.

All told, the water and wind brought by the hurricane damage some 250,000 homes and turn a million residents into vagabonds, many of whom are now utterly dependent on the government for food and shelter. The storm kills tens of thousands of people outright and leaves the city virtually uninhabitable, downing all communications systems and paralyzing the infrastructure. After the storm passes, looting breaks out. And thousands of dazed and dying survivors sit on their roofs in the semitropical sun awaiting rescue. Though the tales of heroic rescue are numerous and inspiring, many people perish, waiting for help that doesn't come.

Some call Hurricane Katrina the perfect storm. It wasn't. The perfect storm, which the Federal Emergency Management Agency (FEMA) calls Hurricane Pam, exists only on a computer screen, the creation of a small federal contractor located in a nondescript office park on the outskirts of Baton Rouge. Developed in the spring of 2004 over a period of fifty-three days and at a cost of $800,000, Hurricane Pam is a low-tech affair, nothing more than a simulated computer storm surge that plays out on a monitor accompanied by a stack of descriptive documents that catalog the damage the storm wrought when it made its fictitious landfall.

Hurricane Pam is a training exercise, designed to get local and federal disaster responders thinking about how they might deal with the aftereffects of a catastrophic storm that hit New Orleans. Louisiana is lousy with emergency disaster plans, and its various government agencies have invested millions of dollars cooking them up. The city of New Orleans has one specifically for hurricanes, as do all of the parishes (counties) along the coast. Inland, the rest of the state's sixty-four parishes have created generic plans to deal with a wide variety of calamities, natural and man-made. Not to be outdone, about twenty state agencies have disaster plans. Some have several.

The federal government, as well, has dumped hurricane plans on the state over the years, and they are all hundreds of pages long, thick with appendixes and crammed with dense, jargon-filled prose. Most of them were cooked up in Washington by small teams of bureaucrats; a few were created without any local input at all. Most sit unread in disaster offices throughout southern Louisiana. In the office of Jesse St. Amant, the longtime emergency preparedness director for Plaquemines Parish, the collection of disaster plans on his long, low bookshelf stretches for several feet.

St. Amant's favorite federal plan is Response 95. Unveiled by FEMA in May 1995, the plan's debut was spoiled when a wandering rainstorm dumped twenty inches of water on the city of New Orleans as the exercise was taking place. This rainfall "of biblical proportions," as the local newspaper described it, swamped the city in waist-high stormwater. Though FEMA struggled mightily to fill a hotel ballroom downtown with local disaster planners, it was forced to cancel the event when the area's first responders phoned in hasty regrets. "I told FEMA that real life always trumps an exercise," St. Amant said with a chuckle.

As the head disaster planner for what is unarguably Louisiana's most vulnerable parish—Plaquemines juts eighty miles into the Gulf of Mexico and is completely surrounded by low-lying marsh—St. Amant believes Response 95 may have been the biggest bust of all, since any potential readership it might have achieved was washed out with the spring rain in New Orleans. But nearly all of the scores of state and FEMA training documents met a similar fate: The common practice among governmental bodies in Louisiana was to accept such studies without comment, agree to adopt them by unanimous vote, and store them on a shelf, along with the budget books and other effluvia of local bureaucracy. "Nobody ever actually reads them," St. Amant said.

But the Hurricane Pam scenario was a plan with a twist. Officially called the Southeast Louisiana Catastrophic Hurricane Plan, the Pam exercise made the readers—local emergency responders—authors as well. Instead of sitting first responders down in a ballroom and playing a cookie-cutter "wargame" scripted by some Washington contractor, Pam took a bottom-up approach, inviting the participants to take a crack at writing their own game plan for coping with the "Big One," down to the grittiest detail. Though guided by FEMA, the plan was created by the men who would wear the hip waders and man the flatboats, the medics and doctors who would operate the triage centers, and the cops and city workers who would be out on the street in a real disaster. Pam was what is known in the emergency response business as a planning exercise, where participants are fully briefed about a catastrophe and then draw up a blueprint for how they would cope. The rules were simple: Players can only make plans with the resources they possessed at the moment. For example, if a firehouse had five engines but two were always rotated out of service for maintenance, then the firefighters could only plan to respond with three. Anything else was unrealistic and destined to fail.

Although Pam was billed as part of a new drive by Washington for "catastrophic planning" in a bad new world of international terrorism, the impetus for the exercise was really Hurricane Georges, a rather puny hurricane when it hit the Gulf Coast in September 1998. Though small, Georges killed beyond expectations, taking some 600 lives as it rampaged through a procession of Caribbean islands before tacking into the Gulf of Mexico and taking dead aim at New Orleans. But just before making landfall, Georges defied forecasters and swung sharply to the east, veering into Biloxi, Mississippi, and causing scattered damage from New Orleans to Mobile.

If ever a city dodged a bullet, New Orleans did when Georges veered east. The hurricane prompted a massive and chaotic evacuation and would have been a serious killer had it hit New Orleans on the perfect path it had been taking. Georges made Louisiana disaster officials realize they were woefully unprepared for the "Big One" of Gulf legend. The city hadn't been hit square by a hurricane for more than a generation, and its first responders were beyond rusty.

Georges had laid bare the fundamental insufficiency of the state's emergency hurricane plan: There was no coordination between state agencies and parishes, as local governments followed their own plans for dealing with the storm. Some parishes called for mandatory evacuations while others did not, some parishes opened shelters while others failed to do so, and each parish had an idea for when it was proper to tell citizens to evacuate, which it didn't bother to communicate to any other parish. The result was gridlock—both literally and figuratively. There had to be a better way.

The father of Hurricane Pam may well have been a man named Colonel Michael L. Brown (no relation to the man with the almost identical name who headed FEMA in 2005), the former deputy director of emergency preparedness in Louisiana. In August 2000, Colonel Brown had written a twenty-page letter to James Lee Witt, the FEMA director at the time, requesting money for a plan that would simulate the effects of a massive hurricane hitting New Orleans and would help locals develop a "post-devastation" schematic for rescuing survivors and cleaning up. To this point, improbable as it may seem, the federal government had no plan on hand that specifically focused on dealing with the aftereffects of a catastrophic hurricane.

"We know that a Category 3, 4 or 5 hurricane striking the mouth of the Mississippi River at New Orleans would be a disaster of cataclysmic proportion," Brown wrote in his letter to Witt. After reciting the expected destruction—seventeen feet of water in New Orleans streets, up to 5,000 dead, as many as 300,000 people stranded in their homes—Brown got to the point: The state of Louisiana was in no position to respond to such a cataclysm, and that would likely mean death for many citizens. "In the aftermath of such a catastrophe, there will be an offshoot of life-threatening situations that will swiftly deplete our resources and absorb whatever limited time we might have to rescue those who survive," Brown said. "We believe that the level of response required to sustain, protect and rescue survivors during such post-hurricane devastation is well beyond what we conceptualize as 'the worst-case scenario.'"

In quick and terse fashion, Brown sketched a rough outline of what was needed. There would be a scenario presented of a mock hurricane, a storm that would hit New Orleans in just the right spot to create catastrophe. With this scenario in hand, disaster officials would present it to first responders and stage a series of conversations, where they assessed the damage, mounted a coordinated search-and-rescue effort, identified shelters for evacuees, and moved down the line to recovery. And throughout the exercise, participants would be challenged to answer the practical questions of disaster response for themselves, instead of being handed the answers from on high. How would emergency responders communicate? How long would rescue teams work before taking a break and who would take their place? Where would they get boats, and from whom? Who would provide food and water? Brown's exercise aimed to answer these questions in the most minute and granular fashion. And the answers would come through discussion and argument with locals and state responders, not from Washington officials 1,100 miles away.

The FEMA brass liked the idea. They wrote a few letters, chewed on it a bit. And Brown's idea went nowhere.

The following year, a new administration set up in Washington, and Brown tried again, resending his letter to Witt's successor, Joseph Allbaugh, shortly before the 2001 hurricane season began. Only this time he sent it through the state's powerful U.S. senator, John Breaux. But again, nothing happened. Then came the terrorist attacks of September 11, 2001, and the danger of natural disasters got eclipsed by the threat of Islamic jihadist madness. Once more Brown's idea fell by the wayside.

After 9/11, the vogue in disaster management, not surprisingly, became terrorist events of the darkest sort that could be imagined: nuclear suitcases detonated on crowded streets, poison-gas attacks with crop dusters, mail sabotage with biological agents, suicide bombers targeting shopping malls—what were known as "low-probability, high-consequence" events. As concrete barriers went up around Washington office buildings, bureaucratic obstacles flew up around spending money on preparedness that wasn't connected to a shadowy terrorist threat. A congressionally mandated series of terrorist drills, carried out in desultory fashion before 9/11, now grew to stratospheric levels of grandness. Hurricane planning went out the window, unless a state was able to disguise it as terrorist training—as some states did.

The Department of Homeland Security, which was created by Congress in 2002 and swallowed FEMA along with about two dozen other federal agencies, started cooking up disaster exercises far more spectacular and lavish than the relatively modest plan Colonel Brown was championing down in Louisiana. They were sequels to the congressionally mandated Top Officials exercise, or TOPOFF, a $3 million, classic large-scale, military-style drill in May 2000 that had featured lavish pyrotechnics and complicated physical maneuvers. It called for staging a full-scale mock terrorist attack that unfolded simultaneously in three different cities. In the first city, Denver, terrorists staged a biological attack using a plague agent, while Portsmouth, New Hampshire, experienced an assault with mustard gas. Meanwhile, in Washington, D.C., terrorists exploded a bomb that was laced with nuclear material. The elaborate exercise, involving one thousand officials, was at the time one of the biggest ever conducted outside of the Pentagon. But it would look like a nickelodeon compared to the Technicolor extravaganza of its sequel, TOPOFF2, staged by the Department of Homeland Security in May 2003, when terror fears were at their zenith. Carried out with eight thousand state, local, and national officials and costing a whopping $16 million, TOPOFF2 put the dirty bomb in Seattle and socked Chicago with the biological plague. It featured live explosions, fake news segments, and the use of hundreds of "victims" moaning realistically in the streets and in hospital emergency rooms.

TOPOFF2 was a primarily a stage show. But it highlighted serious problems. An internal government report of the five-day drill said that the nation's emergency-response system was hampered by the failure of government agencies to share information, by uncertainty over the chain of command, and by confusing new government procedures. The upshot: America may be not much better prepared to deal with a big terrorist attack than it was before 9/11. "Fortunately, this was only a test," said the report. "However, if a real incident occurs before final procedures are established, such unnecessary confusion will be unacceptable." The report added that because the drill was simulated, "the full consequences of the confusion"—including the possibility of needless civilian deaths—"were not observed."

FEMA was a reluctant participant in the TOPOFF2 exercise. First, TOPOFF2 was run by a hated rival agency, the Office of Domestic Preparedness, which was also part of the new Homeland Security behemoth. But more important, FEMA officials viewed it as overscripted and too top-down in its approach to the response. Moreover, it didn't address the more likely scenario of a calamity caused by Mother Nature.

Later in 2003, FEMA began to revisit the subject of the New Orleans hurricane scenario, which many in the agency believed was desperately needed but still unfunded by the Department of Homeland Security. But this time, an official from the White House's Homeland Security Advisory Council sat in on these meetings, and he heard the agency's frustration over not having the resources to exercise a killer hurricane scenario. "He was astonished that as of that date we had not completed this type of plan and [he] promised to do what he could," said Sean Fontenot, a Louisiana disaster official. Four months later, FEMA got the money for its bottom-up disaster-planning experiment. The agency let a contract in May 2004, and began work immediately on what would become Hurricane Pam.

Oddly enough, the White House's interest in staging the exercise rose directly out of its obsession with Osama bin Laden.

In December 2003, just over two years after the twin attacks on New York and Washington, President Bush called on the Department of Homeland Security to draw up a list of priority concerns. The White House was eager to show that this lumbering department it had just created was capable of prioritizing and focusing on disasters that presented the greatest risk to the nation. The aim of the project was to identify the worst disasters that could happen and then come up with a plan of preparation.

The result was a series of "Planning Scenarios," a fifty-five-page list of fifteen doomsday events that could visit the United States and cause major fatalities. In keeping with the Bush administration's focus on terrorist attacks, twelve of the fifteen scenarios dealt with shadowy international groups bent on doing the nation harm. For the purposes of these scenarios, the shadowy group was called "the Universal Adversary," and it was imbued with capabilities that exceed those of many countries.

In Scenario 8, the Universal Adversary ruptures a train tanker carrying chlorine gas by detonating a small bomb underneath it. The resulting leak kills 17,500 people and hospitalizes 100,000 more. In Scenario 13, the same group uses anthrax to spike food simultaneously at a West Coast packing plant and at an orange juice factory in the South. After the food is distributed, some 300 people die. In Scenario 7, it releases sarin nerve gas in an office building, killing 6,000 people. And in Scenario 5, the Universal Adversary commandeers a crop duster and sprays a mustard gas mixture over a packed college football stadium.

Scenario 1 is the ultimate low-probability, high-consequence nightmare scenario. In this instance, the Universal Adversary builds and detonates a ten-kiloton nuclear device in Washington, D.C. The scenario begins with the theft of highly enriched uranium from a nuclear plant in the former Soviet Union. It ends Hollywood-style, with a mushroom cloud that blooms over the city and drifts slowly east-northeast. In this scenario, it is assumed that many first responders will die. "Decontamination, disposal and replacement of lost infrastructure will cost many billions of dollars," the planning document says. The scenario doesn't attempt to calculate the number of fatalities that will occur, but it does calculate that "an overall economic downturn, if not recession, is probable in the wake of the attack."

By contrast, Scenario 10 is less sexy yet far more probable. In this story line, a massive hurricane hits a major southern city, which also happens to be a popular tourist destination, just like New Orleans. A twenty-foot storm surge with accompanying rain overwhelms the local levee system and drowns low-lying areas. More than a thousand people die outright, in part due to a flawed evacuation scheme. Thousands more residents are left homeless. Local storm shelters are overwhelmed. A 95,000-ton oil tanker impales itself on a bridge and begins to leak. Municipal utilities fail, as do communications systems. Food and water are in short supply, and local 911 switchboards are overwhelmed by nuisance calls from people seeking lost pets.

"There are severe economic repercussions for the whole state and region," the planning document says. "The impact of closing the port ripples through the country. The loss of petrochemical supplies could raise prices and increase demand on foreign sources."

Guiding all of these scenarios was the Office of State and Local Government Coordination and Preparedness, a body within the Department of Homeland Security that doles out grant money to "detect, prevent and disrupt" terrorist attacks, but rarely deals with natural calamities. For the most part, these scenarios are simple script treatments. They do not describe a plan of response. They are simple "what if " story lines that would be familiar to any casual reader of airport potboiler novels.

The shortcomings of the scenarios deeply bothered Eric Tolbert, who was chief of FEMA's response division. Tolbert was an old-line disaster responder who had begun his career in the field as a paramedic and had worked his way up to being the state director of emergency management in his native North Carolina. Like many of FEMA's old guard, he believed the agency was spending too much time worrying about terrorist events—a relative rarity—and not enough time on the disasters that break out with far more regularity: the fires and floods and earthquakes that torment nearly every region of the country.

Tolbert and FEMA's new director, an Oklahoma lawyer named Michael D. Brown, had long been pressing the White House, Secretary of Homeland Security Tom Ridge, and Congress to spend money planning for real-world disasters—the natural ones that hit all the time and, most of all, the really big ones that hit rarely but with devastating consequences. In 2004, they got the money and permission to begin developing plans for the natural disaster scenarios on the national scenario list. The appropriation was a relative pittance—only a few million dollars out of Homeland Security's $31 billion overall budget. But it was a start.

And Tolbert had no doubt about where to start. "When I have a nightmare," he said, "it's a hurricane in New Orleans." And so the planning began.

Tolbert was hardly the only person having bad dreams about a storm hitting New Orleans. The city hadn't been hit dead-on by a hurricane since Betsy in 1965, and the last one to even seriously menace the city was Hurricane Camille in 1969, which hit the Mississippi shoreline about fifty miles east of New Orleans. In the last 120 years, the city has averaged one hurricane hit about every decade, and "with Camille hitting over 30 years ago, we are well overdue for a major one," Paul Trotter, the National Weather Service's local chief, told a reporter in May 2004.

Moreover, much of the city's vaunted levee system, mandated by Congress to provide no more than Category 3 hurricane protection, was untested. The U.S. Army Corps of Engineers, which was in charge of all New Orleans levees, had seen its local budget slashed repeatedly by the Bush administration—by some $80 million in 2005 alone. And millions of acres of surrounding wetlands—a natural buffer to storm surges—had melted away under intensive development by energy and shipping concerns.

In 2004, a University of New Orleans researcher predicted that even a hurricane of moderate strength would devastate the city, causing loss of life and property damage eclipsing that of even a major West Coast earthquake.

Hurricane Pam was intended to address a threat that was well known to everyone. FEMA brought together hundreds of people from dozens of federal agencies and the military to sit down with state troopers and school superintendents and volunteer firefighters to hammer out the details of response, drawing clear lines of authority and responsibility, and calculating just exactly what resources would be needed. Though the federal government paid for Hurricane Pam, the locals were the ones who brought the plan to life, hanging it with the minutiae of the first response, working through the logistics of evacuation and preparation, and crafting the government's initial reaction to a storm that everyone knew was coming.

Innovative Emergency Management Inc. (IEM), the Baton Rouge consulting company hired to build the computer models that brought Pam to life, deliberately avoided special effects. Rather, the company sought to turn disaster planning on its head by creating a believable scenario and then inviting the participants to grapple with its effects. The hurricane would be little more than a handout. The drama would unfold as disaster officials discussed how to cope. The officials would be segregated into groups to discuss smaller pieces of the disaster plan. Every day, leaders of these groups would deliver progress reports to top state and federal officials. All the sessions would be recorded and then transcribed and cleaned up. In the end, the free-flowing plan of action would appear in a three-ring binder, ready for review in advance of the next hurricane season.

Though low-tech was the guiding principle, a great deal of research went into making the Hurricane Pam scenario believable. The last thing the planners wanted was for the training sessions to break down into arguments over whether the hurricane as described would cause the damage as stated. IEM's technicians called in a levee expert from Louisiana State University and got him to help them design the perfect track for their New Orleans storm, one that would sink the city under a uniform, seventeen-foot storm surge that would reach deep inside southeast Louisiana and bring damage to thirteen parishes. The company also consulted with the National Weather Service until it got what it considered to be the perfect storm—a hurricane that approached from the southwest, tracked up the Mississippi River, and crossed to the east, passing directly over the city and soaking everything in rain.

Over fifty-three days, IEM built Hurricane Pam, focusing on the small details of an exercise that would involve as many as 270 disaster responders. Greg Peters, an IEM contract worker, noted that the company fussed relentlessly over its guest list. "You know, they'd sit around asking questions like 'Do we need someone from the phone company to be here?'" he said. "The answer was yes and so they'd move on: 'How about the Department of Transportation?' and so on."

But the center of the plan was always this perfect storm, a few "words and tables," as IEM's president and chief executive, Madhu Beriwal, put it—words and tables calculated to stand up to assault, should someone want to quibble with the scenario. Brad Tiffey, IEM's chief manager for the Hurricane Pam drill, worried endlessly about the storm's precise path. "It's funny how big of a difference five or ten miles can have on a hurricane's effect," he said. Ultimately Tiffey and his technical staff settled on a tried-and-true storm track, the one traveled by Hurricane Georges, the very real storm that had sparked the creation of Pam in the first place. The only difference was that this time the tempest did not veer to the east.

But Tiffey and his staff also recognized that Pam could not be too big or too overwhelming. "They wanted a plan to arise from all of this, not plot the Apocalypse," Peters said. So, as they fashioned their storm, IEM's technical staff departed from the Hollywood script but also from the traditional mind-set of disaster planners that the best way to practice is to present the absolute worst-case scenario. FEMA's original Pam disaster imagined a massive Category 5 hurricane bearing down on Louisiana with winds of 160 miles per hour and a twenty-foot storm surge. But the designers worried that in the face of such an unusually large hurricane, the locals "would throw up their hands and say, 'We can't cope with this,'" said Madhu Beriwal. So IEM took a different tack; it created a smaller storm, a Category 3 storm, which wrought plenty of havoc but did not leave the city vaporized. Notably, Hurricane Pam did not breach the city's flood protection system, though its storm surge easily overtopped the levees and swamped many city neighborhoods.

There was a second reason for making Pam milder than a super-storm. It would help bust the myth that the "Big One" was the only storm worth fretting over. "We decided to let the participants see that a slow-moving Category 3 could be just as devastating as anything out there," said Tiffey. In truth, only three Category 5 hurricanes have hit the continental United States since records have been kept. Smaller hurricanes are far more common and often just as deadly. And so it became that Pam was no monster tempest but a slightly oversized Category 3 storm, with winds of 125 miles per hour. What set Pam apart was the soaking amount of rain it carried (up to twenty inches in some spots), its lumbering speed, and its unerring track toward the most populated city in Louisiana. In the scenario, the National Weather Service predicts New Orleans will be hit by Pam, and that's exactly what happens.

Outside of the scenario, the plan was a skeleton that the players would fill out themselves. There were fifteen sections to the plan, covering everything from rescue efforts and medical care to clearing the city's streets of water and debris and handling hazardous waste spills. For each section, there was to be a workshop where locals would consult the scenario, draft a list of supplies and manpower, and then fire questions at each other, just as Colonel Michael L. Brown had envisioned it.

As the locals talked out the problems and refined their techniques in the workshops, IEM stenographers would be on hand to refine the ideas and put them into serviceable prose. The result would be a full plan of action for the "Big One" as well as a plan that could be employed for smaller disasters as well. And the plan would be a living document, adding lessons learned as future hurricanes hit and undergoing continual refinement and revision. Ultimately, IEM intended to feed the plan into a hurricane simulation program to see exactly how effective it was, which would in turn spark more refinements.

But most important, the Hurricane Pam plan would be absorbed by the very people who needed it most. "A lot of times people don't read the plan," Beriwal said. "The intent of this planning exercise was to engage."

On July 16, 2004, the first day of the exercise, the Louisiana Emergency Operations Center started filling with disaster officials. The building added an element of realism to the drill—it is a near-perfect storm center, filled with computers and phones and big plasma screens, as well as a stage area from which reports can be delivered. A smaller cadre of local officials attended these pre-landfall sessions, laying out evacuation plans and readying the Louisiana Superdome as the city's shelter of last resort, while an official from the National Weather Service issued faux bulletins and flashed slides on a projection screen. IEM activated the joint command center, where state and federal officials took daily briefings and coordinated the overarching plan of response. One of the most unusual experiments in disaster planning had begun.

On the third day of the exercise, the room filled to capacity as Pam made landfall while about 270 emergency workers looked on. Representatives from the Pentagon, the Coast Guard, and FEMA mixed with National Guard officers, state disaster chiefs, and emergency personnel from dozens of parishes and the adjoining states of Arkansas and Texas. Pam made its predicted low-tech landfall: The model played out on a projection screen as IEM employees handed out documents describing the havoc Pam had wrought on its slow churn through Louisiana. And then it was over.

One by one, IEM officials read out the damage tabulations. In the scenario, Pam's storm surge crashes into the city and easily tops its floodwalls. The gush of water, coupled with driving rain, fills New Orleans and the surrounding suburbs like a cereal bowl. The floodwater turns the city into a grim Venice, swelling its lone evacuation center well beyond what officials can immediately handle. About 50,000 seek shelter in the Louisiana Superdome before the storm hits; many thousands more come afterward. In total, some 500,000 area residents are left at least temporarily homeless.

New Orleans being a city of ambivalent evacuees who have grown used to watching hurricanes veer from predicted paths at the last minute, IEM assumed that evacuation rates would be low. In the scenario, only 65 percent of the metropolitan area evacuates, including a mere 34 percent from the city itself. Nearly 600,000 people decide to ride out the storm by IEM's projections—not an unreasonable figure, given Louisiana's evacuation track record. But riding out the storm proves foolish: 61,290 people in the thirteen-parish area perish due to wind or water. About 20,000 of that number are in New Orleans.

Pam destroys 462,000 housing units and 4,020 businesses; thousands of other buildings are damaged. The water smothers the city's drainage system, knocking out 80 percent of the drainage pumps, including many of the older ones that run on an obsolete electrical current and will be difficult to repair. By IEM's calculations, many of the pumps will be out of commission for six months. It will take almost a month to rid city streets of floodwaters.

Some 30 million cubic yards of debris clutter the city, which is sure to tax the available landfills and slow the search-and-rescue efforts. Survivors sit on roofs and in attics all over town. Local officials will need to make more than 200,000 rescue runs, which they are incapable of doing on their own. Nearly 60,000 hungry people sit in government-approved shelters.

There was an overriding caveat built into the Hurricane Pam scenario: No matter the rhetoric about who is in charge of recovery or who has responsibility for carrying out certain tasks, local officials would almost certainly be unable to fend for themselves. "The response capabilities and resources of the local jurisdiction . . . may be insufficient and quickly overwhelmed," the disaster scenario said.

After the damage readouts, the 270 officials broke into groups that were based on their specialty. A group charged with draining water out of New Orleans included officials from the Army Corps of Engineers and the local levee board, while a search-and-rescue planning team included officials from the U.S. Coast Guard and the Louisiana Department of Wildlife and Fisheries. There was a group in charge of shepherding food, water, and generators. Another group discussed temporary housing, while yet another laid plans for triage centers to take care of the thousands of injured.

And so what unfolded was something quite different from the usual "war game" exercise that FEMA and the Pentagon had always used to stage their drills. War games are far more scripted, high-concept exercises often played on very realistic mock sets. But the low-tech Pam generated tremendous passion, perhaps because it had such a real-life application.

In the search-and-rescue session, for example, participants figured that they would need 308 boats, 800 body bags, 400 flashlights, 150 paddles, and 12 spare bilge plugs for small craft. "I was like, whoa, fellas, twelve boat plugs? We're getting down in the weeds here," said Jesse St. Amant, of Plaquemines Parish. But getting down in the weeds was precisely the point: Madhu Beriwal believed that a great failure of FEMA's previous disaster plans was that they didn't have enough detail, precisely because they were cooked up by people in Washington who have no clue as to what a boat plug is, for instance, or how many might be needed.

It was the same in other sessions. The supply distribution group calculated it would need about 40,000 volunteers to staff local shelters, while Army Corps officials calculated that they would need to be able to deliver 1.53 million gallons of water and 5.5 million pounds of ice to the area each day. The debris removal group determined it would take around two years to clear all the ruination. And a group charged with drying out the city estimated that it would take two months to complete.

Rather than joining any specific group, FEMA officials attended all of them to lend advice and offer technical help. IEM was in every room as well, to record the conversations for its written plan and to keep the participants talking.

IEM employees were also there to enforce the cardinal rule, as outlined by Colonel Brown. "No fairy dust," he said, and what he meant was this: If a job called for 300 boats, participants would have to find those boats and not just wish them to exist. If planners needed fifteen semitrucks to haul generators to New Orleans, they had to identify where they would get them, or at least make a realistic guess at the source. "They were supposed to plan with the resources that were available or that could presumably be brought in," said Beriwal. "They were not supposed to be thinking that magically 1,000 helicopters would show up and do this."

In retrospect, there was fairy dust, much of it dispensed by FEMA, though most participants didn't realize it at the time. Greg Peters said the conversation would often stutter to a halt in the breakout groups over some question over basic supply: Who would provide a daily supply of, say, bottled water for the thousands of ex-pected evacuees or ensure that triage units would have ample sup-plies of bandages? "It happened a lot—the conversation would stop over something like generators or ice and a FEMA guy would say, 'Look, don't worry about that, we've got contracts in place, you'll get your million gallons of water a day or whatever,'" Peters said. "It was almost like they were bragging."

Indeed, the Hurricane Pam plan is shot full of FEMA's promises: bedding on hand for 100,000, mobile communications centers, even video uplinks to establish teleconferences over great distances. Later, when FEMA was actually put to the test, it would have trouble sup-plying even the most basic requests—flashlights, for instance, ap-peared to be beyond the capability of the agency, let alone the staggering amount of water and ice specified by the Army Corps of Engineers.

Despite FEMA's empty promises, the Pam exercise could be con-sidered at least a qualified success. That was due in large part to the fact that the locals had clearly read the plan, if not lived it. Peters and others said that the local officials got excited as they hammered out the details of their Pam response, carrying their discussions and ar-guments into the bars of Baton Rouge long after the sessions were over and rising in anger to defend a particular plan of action. "I know some of the search-and-rescue guys almost came to blows while I was there," Peters said.

Though Beriwal doesn't know whether fistfights broke out, she agrees with the premise that passion ruled. On the eighth and final day of the exercise, after the sessions were over and IEM workers huddled in the emergency operations center to begin talking over how to turn the drill into a document, Colonel Brown, the state's deputy disaster chief, ambled over to say his good-byes.

"He spoke to us about how meaningful and important the exercise was," Beriwal said, "and he was so overcome by emotion that he left the building. He didn't finish his sentence. He was crying."

Rather than an end unto itself, the Pam exercise was supposed to mark an initial dialogue, the start of a continuing discussion over how to cope with a disaster nearly everyone believed would soon befall New Orleans. Many of the elements of the Pam plan remain little more than bold-stroke sketches: The question of reentry to the city by returning residents was barely discussed, for example. Although follow-on workshops were held in November 2004 and July and August 2005, questions regarding temporary housing were never fully worked out. Local officials never got the opportunity to ask the hard questions about FEMA's prepositioned stockpiles of supplies. A discussion on the inevitable necessity of moving evacuees from short-term shelters such as the Superdome was given only the briefest of consideration in the Pam drill. And questions about securing the storm-wracked city from looters and lawbreakers went similarly unaddressed in the eight-day planning session. Even so, IEM did manage to cover some ground in the follow-on workshops. It nailed down details of temporary medical care, supply logistics, and temporary housing for storm victims.

But in a breathtaking display of penny-wise planning, FEMA canceled most of the follow-up sessions scheduled for the first half of 2005, claiming it was unable to come up with money for the modest travel expenses its own employees would incur to attend. FEMA officials have since said that the shortfall amounted to less than $15,000. "Homeland took the money from us so we couldn't take any steps at all to address the gaps," FEMA director Brown recalled.

Pam remains a work in progress and very much incomplete. Only about a third of its fifteen sections have gotten any attention at all from workshop groups. But in subsequent disasters in Louisiana, the locals have excelled in the areas that were covered during the Pam workshops. That's particularly true of evacuations, which improved markedly in the state following the Hurricane Pam drill.

Of course not even Pam imagined the ultimate doomsday scenario—the utter collapse of New Orleans's flood-control system. Indeed, very few of the doomsday documents that sparked the plan's creation mention the possibility that a storm surge could topple the city's levees.

2

WATER PORK

The state motto for Louisiana is "Sportsman's Paradise," but that sells the civil engineering community short. The state, and especially its southern part, is an engineer's paradise, the topography of the place being so unstable that even the simple act of spreading blacktop is shot through with complication.

The New Orleans metropolitan area offers a strong case in point. Shoehorned between a churning, fickle river and an angry, shallow lake that connects directly to the Gulf of Mexico, New Orleans, with its huge port and notoriously shifty soils, is literally engineered from the mud. In this subsea, subtropical city, buildings routinely sink and shift, concrete buckles dramatically, and virtually every drop of water that falls must be physically pumped to higher ground. What isn't below sea level is often water. The Lake Pontchartrain Causeway is, at twenty-four miles, the longest bridge in the nation, while the area's levee and drainage system is considered one of the most sophisticated in the world—decades in the making, it is not yet completed, and it has cost millions to construct and will take billions to complete. Protecting this city from flood is a Herculean task: It is little surprise that New Orleans is home to the nation's largest agglomeration of federal engineers.

In the New Orleans area, the construction of levees and flood protection structures is overseen and mostly financed by the U.S. Army Corps of Engineers, a job it began to assume in the 1920s and that it completely dominates today. With authority over 30,000 square miles of terrain and 2,800 miles of waterway, the modern Army Corps has a dual mandate to improve navigation while simultaneously protecting residents from storm and flood. The corps also serves as a fertile conduit for federal patronage: While many of its creations have been hailed over the years as wonders of modern engineering, a similar number of projects have been condemned by critics as the worst sort of taxpayer boondoggle—"water pork," as they call it in Washington.

The city of New Orleans alone is home to more than one hundred miles of hurricane protection—nearly thirty miles of river levee as well as all manner of floodwalls and dirt berms, along with more than two hundred floodgates, most of it overseen by the Army Corps. Just outside of the city are hundreds more miles of similar structures. In the city, the corps shares responsibility for the structures with two local organizations, the state-controlled Orleans Levee District, overseen by the eight-member Levee Board, and the Sewerage & Water Board, an agency controlled by the mayor. These three agencies often have different goals and priorities, and relations between them have been uneasy at times. A 2005 report by the National Science Foundation observed, "It was not always clear which agency had responsibilities for what" parts of the city's vast and elaborate drainage and flood control system. But basically it shakes down this way: The Sewerage & Water Board runs the drainage pumps, the Army Corps builds the levees, and the Levee Board maintains them, mowing the grass and painting the walls and making sure nothing springs a leak.

And when things go seriously wrong with this system, the line of responsibility is equally clear: If the problem extends beyond anything a few sandbags or a truckload of gravel won't remedy, the federal government takes control and provides a fix. Like most big infrastructure projects, there is a cost split: In most but not all cases, the federal government, through the Army Corps, pays 70 percent of the bill, and the local government pays 30 percent of the total. Through 2005, the federal government had paid $528 million to provide storm protection around the New Orleans area, and the state, largely by floating long-term bonds, had paid $210 million. The project to protect the area has been all but perpetual: Extending through two generations, it is expected to go on for a generation more. The project doesn't include the ongoing drive to keep the Mississippi River within its banks. That is separate and costs millions more. Nor does it include several other projects that exist for the pure benefit of shipping interests.

Before any project starts, the money has to be wrestled out of Washington, and this chore has traditionally fallen to the Louisiana congressional delegation. For decades, the delegation from this backwater of a state held tremendous sway over the purse strings on Capitol Hill, primarily through the ministrations of senior members such as Senators Russell Long, J. Bennett Johnston, and John Breaux, along with House members such as the late majority leader Hale Boggs, the former Appropriations Committee chairman Bob Livingston, and Billy Tauzin, who served as chairman of the Commerce Committee. These politicians dominated the process of bringing home water pork and were responsible for grabbing outsized amounts of money for the state, such as the $410 million they snagged for the corps' Orleans District in 1999. "In the past, there's no question Louisiana got more federal money per capita than any other state in the union except Alaska," said Tommy Boggs, the son of Hale and former congresswoman Lindy Boggs and a powerful Washington lobbyist himself.

Though much of the money these men brought home was put into noncontroversial public works programs, not all of it was spent wisely. One ongoing project that has drawn intense criticism over the years is the massive exercise to make the Red River in northern Louisiana a navigable waterway. The endeavor to turn this brush-choked tributary into a shipping channel has proved a tremendous exercise, involving the digging of a nine-foot-deep, two-hundred-foot-wide channel that runs 236 miles and connects the city of Shreveport in northwest Louisiana to the Mississippi River on the eastern side of the state. The Army Corps likes to say it had to "train the river into stable alignment," but it is a lesson the waterway has been slow to learn. Aside from its initial $1 billion cost, the river requires about $13 million worth of dredging every year. All told, some $2 billion has been plowed into this waterway, earning it a permanent entry in the "Pig Book," an annual compendium of congressional pork spending compiled by the nonprofit organization Citizens Against Government Waste.

Though it carries one-tenth of 1 percent of the nation's inland shipping traffic, the Red River Navigation Project soaks up about 2 percent of the money nationally that is devoted to such projects. And though it was opposed by a string of presidential administrations and has been roundly pilloried as the worst sort of federal excess, the waterway became operable in 1994, thanks to the almost singular efforts of Senator J. Bennett Johnston, chairman of the Senate Energy and Natural Resources Committee. When Johnston retired from the Senate in 1997, Congress renamed the section of the Red River he had fought so hard to remake. It's now called the J. Bennett Johnston Waterway. For its part, the corps long defended the project as economically viable, despite the fact that it has never carried more than a trickle of shipping traffic. The corps continues to defend the project today.

For the first 120 years of its existence, the Army Corps of Engineers had a standing mission: to expand and bring rigor to the nation's navigation system. But beginning in the late 1920s, the corps took on the additional role of overseeing flood control projects and protecting communities from disaster. Critics says the corps has never been completely comfortable with this dual role, and perhaps no project gives more credence to their argument than the construction of the Mississippi River Gulf Outlet (MRGO), a navigation project that even the corps now allows may have made the New Orleans region more vulnerable to a hurricane storm surge than it otherwise might have been.

The MRGO, known in shipping circles as the "Mister Go," was devised as a shortcut from downtown New Orleans to the Gulf of Mexico, cutting about forty miles off the Mississippi River route. But the time saved comes at a tremendous environmental cost—the seventy-six-mile-long, man-made navigation channel cuts through forty miles of virgin marsh and through four natural levees that offered the city a measure of protection from Gulf storm surges.

Completed in 1968, the MRGO has long been opposed by environmentalists and like-minded politicians, who say it provides a dangerous shortcut for hurricane storm surges. Some experts say the waterway even magnifies storm surges by creating a funnel that increases their height and ferocity. The corps has long denied that this is the case.

But even the corps can't deny the tremendous toll the MRGO has taken on Louisiana's storm-suppressing marshlands, which have withered in the years since it was built. The unstable banks of the man-made waterways are constantly collapsing, and a cut that originally was 650 feet wide has now ballooned to 2,000 feet in some spots. The waterway also allows salt water to intrude deep into Louisiana's interior marsh, killing off ancient cypress stands and reducing vast tracts of land to open water. This makes the city far more vulnerable to storm surges. Even the corps says that 2.7 miles of marsh will reduce a hurricane storm surge by at least a foot.

As a sop for storm-protection resources, the MRGO has proven just as rapacious. The channel, which has lost 87 percent of its traffic in the last thirty years and was servicing a paltry 2.7 ships a day in 2002, requires an average of $16 million per year to dredge and maintain. Worse, virtually every storm that comes close to the Louisiana coastline seems to silt in the waterway to the point that it is unusable. For example, in 1998 Hurricane Georges forced the corps to spend $37.5 million on dredging. The corps' annual dredging expenses for the MRGO are nearly enough to complete one of the seven hurricane protection projects the agency had on the books for the New Orleans area in 2005. All seven of those projects languished for lack of money.

For years, local officials have implored the corps to shut down the destructive and underused waterway. But the corps maintains the waterway is vital for shipping, and the request has always fallen on deaf ears.

In the past, federal money was plentiful enough in Louisiana to pursue projects of dubious worth, even large ones, while still having the money to build higher levees, install floodwalls, and improve drainage. That has been less true in recent years. Johnston and Breaux are retired, and the state's current senators have less than two terms of seniority between them. Many of its most experienced congressmen have retired as well, and the once-powerful Louisiana delegation hasn't been able to secure the pork it once commanded. Moreover, the Army Corps itself is stretched by the wars in Iraq and Afghanistan and by blooming federal deficits, prompting the White House and Congress to cut back on "earmarked" pet projects the corps has traditionally pursued. These days, even if Louisiana has legitimate needs, its congressmen "are gonna have to scrap for it," says Tommy Boggs.

In relative terms, Louisiana still receives an outsized share of pork—during its first years in office, the Bush administration gave the state $1.9 billion through the Army Corps. But the go-go days are clearly over. In fact, from 2000 to 2005, overall federal appropriations to the corps' Orleans District fell by 44 percent, prompting the agency to freeze hiring for its staff, many of whom were already on loan to the Iraq war effort. In 2005, the corps even had to cancel its annual employee picnic.

By 2005, the lack of cash was taking its toll on the hurricane defenses of the city and its suburbs. In eastern New Orleans, the back levee was subsiding and was thought to be as much as three feet below grade, meaning it would be no match for even a modest hurricane. In nearby St. Charles Parish, the levee system had several gaps, rendering the whole system ineffective. An uncapped, below-grade levee in neighboring St. Bernard Parish put its 67,000 residents at risk to a hurricane catastrophe.

And in the city of New Orleans, which is especially vulnerable to a storm surge, two massive pumping stations sat unprotected from high water, flanked by nothing more than small dirt berms. If a storm surge were to hit the city, just the flooding through these gaps could lead to the flooding of hundreds of houses. In May 2005, the corps had this to say about the chinks in the city's armor: "In Orleans Parish, two major pump stations are threatened by hurricane storm surges. Major contracts need to be awarded to provide fronting protection for them. Also, several levees have settled and need to be raised to provide the design protection. The current funding shortfalls in fiscal year 2005 and fiscal year 2006 will prevent the Corps from addressing these pressing needs."

In fact, the corps said it could spend $20 million at once on the city's hurricane protection project, if only it could get its hands on the money.

Instead, the trend from Washington has been anything but up. In 2003, the corps sought $11 million for New Orleans–area storm protection projects. The Bush administration countered with $3 million, which Congress bumped up to $5.5 million. In 2004, the corps requested $22.5 million, which the administration cut to $3.9 million and Congress topped up again to $5.5 million. The money didn't even pay the overhead. "This was insufficient to fund new construction contracts," the corps said at the time. Walter Maestri, Jefferson Parish's director of emergency management, spoke for a lot of local officials when he summed up the year's appropriation for hurricane protection. "It appears that the money has been moved in the president's budget to handle homeland security and the war in Iraq, and I suppose that's the price we pay," he told the local newspaper. In 2005, the administration proposed giving $3 million to the New Orleans project. "This will be insufficient to fund new construction projects," the corps again said.

But not all projects, however, went begging. In 2005, the corps received $14 million to dredge the MRGO and $11.6 million to dredge the J. Bennett Johnston Waterway. "We thought all the projects were important—not just levees," former senator Breaux told the *Washington Post* in the fall of 2005. "Hindsight is a wonderful thing, but navigation projects were critical to our economic survival."

New Orleans is a city of excesses and improbabilities, of neighborhoods built on swamps and million-dollar bridges that go nowhere and lavish development projects that just never seem to take off. But if there was one ongoing project that had long inspired confidence and pride in New Orleans, it was the city's elaborate drainage system, an intricate network of open and underground canals that moved storm water off the streets and into the river and the lake.

New Orleans is a terrible place to locate a city. Trapped between a raging river that often slopped its banks, a pair of shallow lakes, and a seemingly endless vista of marsh to the south, the "Isle of Orleans" (as its French founder dubbed it) was settled in 1699 and settled in 1718, and from the very beginning it was a struggle to make the place habitable. Almost as soon as New Orleans had streets it had a crude drainage system in place—a series of small ditches running through what is now the French Quarter that sent water downhill to a larger canal and on "back of town" to the swamps that rolled out toward Lake Pontchartrain.

People like to say New Orleans is all below sea level, but it isn't. Along the Mississippi River the land sits twelve feet above sea level, and a handful of low ridges cutting out perpendicular from the river are above sea level as well. But in general, the land dips as it heads from the river to Lake Pontchartrain and hits its lowest spots—about six and a half feet below sea level—as it nears the shoreline.

For the first two hundred years or so of the city's existence, ground elevation dictated development: People built on the high ground along the river and on the ridges that spread out like fingers toward the lake. Everything else was swamp. And because water always flows downhill, the swamp became the city's sewer, the repository for household filth and runoff from the storms that routinely swept the place.

But as the city developed, people built canals to the swamps and then through the swamps and then all the way to the lake. These canals were mostly ad hoc affairs, privately excavated and designed to drain specific neighborhoods and plantations. They went everywhere, unchecked by government.

By the turn of the nineteenth century, the city had expanded to take up most of the highest ground in the area, and a few municipal canals dominated the landscape. The biggest of these was the Orleans Canal, which is present on a map from 1833. The 17th Street Canal shows up on a map created about fifteen years later. And an 1895 map shows the London Avenue Canal. Today, these three "outfall" canals, which extend from what used to be the back swamp to the shore of Lake Pontchartrain, make up the backbone of the city's modern drainage network.

But it would be a long time before the city's drainage system worked with anything approaching safety or efficiency. The canals, clogged with animal carcasses and debris, were little more than stagnant incubators of fearsome diseases such as yellow fever and dysentery. They were also ineffective: For most of the century, the city's streets swam with waist-deep water, even following modest rainstorms. Because flooding was such a problem, many houses were ringed with small dirt levees to keep the flotsam of the street off the porch. But with no sewage system in place beyond crude privies, these little flood-control structures ensured that neighborhood yards were sumps of disease, and indeed, the city was swept by several fearsome epidemics in the late nineteenth century.

By the 1890s, the city and state could ignore the problems no longer. They created two agencies to improve conditions: the Sewerage & Water Board and the Orleans Levee District. One built drainage canals. The other built levees.

The job of the Sewerage & Water Board was made far easier by the development of the Wood Screw Pump in 1914. Developed by a local engineer named A. B. Wood, the devices were quickly adopted by the Sewerage & Water Board to move the filthy water from the city's streets through canals and into the lake and the river. And the business of building canals began in earnest: By the turn of the twentieth century, the city had about seventy drainage canals to take storm runoff and had embarked on the construction of a separate system to handle sewerage.

The Wood pumps did more than simply keep the streets dry—in conjunction with the canal system they allowed developers to drain the cypress swamps standing between the city and Lake Pontchartrain. It is no coincidence that New Orleans saw some of its most explosive growth in the first years of the twentieth century.

Running from Lake Pontchartrain through the center of New Orleans, past the manicured yards of the Lakeview district, to the edge of the working-class Seventh Ward neighborhood, the Orleans Outfall Canal today sits quiet and unseen by most of the town's residents. It is no recreational waterway; it is full of soupy, stagnant water on most days and its steep banks are overgrown with pokeweed and hackberry trees. When the rains come, the city's Pumping Station No. 7, which sits at the terminal end of the canal, kicks to life, sucking storm runoff from 4,000 acres of city roadway and pushing the churn northward down the channel, 2.4 miles to Lake Pontchartrain.

The two other outfall canals in the city—London Avenue and 17th Street—work in similar fashion: At one end is the main pumping station, and at the other end is the lake. The pumps suck runoff out of the city and push it north. In this upside-down place, north is downhill.

All three of these canals are buttressed by floodwalls, massive piles of earth, sheet piling, and reinforced concrete that look like just about the strongest structures known to man. They run through backyards and alongside streets and even across roads. To the unaccustomed eye, they seem ubiquitous and odd, like they might be part of a sprawling gulag. But the floodwalls provide the basic protection from hurricane storm surges, often the only things keeping catastrophe at bay. And though people have predicted for years they might one day be topped by a monster storm surge, hardly anyone has ever suggested the floodwalls might simply fall over in the face of a hurricane.

Ironically, the very system that keeps New Orleans streets from flooding also exposes the city to the biggest threat from an approaching hurricane. In a rainstorm, the New Orleans drainage system works brilliantly and the three outfall canals are models of efficiency, transporting billions of gallons of water into Lake Pontchartrain. But when a Gulf hurricane approaches, the possibility arises that the system might reverse itself: The outfall canals would become intake canals. Instead of stormwater moving out of neighborhoods and into the lake, a storm surge might enter the narrow race and blast through the middle of the city. Even a middling-sized hurricane could send a storm surge gushing over the canal floodwalls, if its aim were true enough. And the pumps at the end of the three canals would be no match for a rushing tidal current.

If this sounds like a disaster waiting to happen, it was; doomsayers had long predicted it. Indeed, in 1871, a city surveyor named W. H. Bell pointed out that the city's drainage system was designed exactly backward. He urged the city to place its pumps on the lakeshore, at the mouths of the canals, where they could block the entrances and protect against a storm surge. Otherwise, he said, "heavy storms would result in water backup within the canals, culminating in an overflow into the city."

Bell was ignored but in time was proved right; an unnamed hurricane blasted the city in 1915 and sent a six-foot storm surge racing through the three canals, easily topping their banks, drenching the city, and killing nearly three hundred people. After that, ignoring Bell's warning became routine; instead, raising the levees became the solution after every storm, and indeed there were several that pushed a storm surge that slopped over into the city. In 1947, the city's canal levees were destroyed again, and the state congressional delegation asked the federal government to take over the chore of protecting the city from storm surges, or at least assist. In 1955, Congress authorized the initial planning for what would eventually be called the Lake Pontchartrain and Vicinity Hurricane Protection Project, a project that continues to this day.

Instead of closing the canals or belatedly taking Bell's advice, the Sewerage & Water Board built taller floodwalls along the banks of the canals. And in succeeding years, when storms overwhelmed the system and flooded the town, this became the only solution: Leave the canals open to the lake and build the floodwalls higher. Thus did the Sewerage & Water Board set New Orleans on a path to eventual catastrophe.

In the 1940s, the federal government, through the Corps of Engineers, began taking a role in storm protection in New Orleans, and over the years its engineers would repeatedly point out the city's folly. From the mid-1960s through the early 1990s, the Army Corps would suggest that the three canals be outfitted with swinging floodgates that could be shut in the face of a hurricane threat. But in the end, through a combination of sheer stubbornness and sly politics, the Sewerage & Water Board prevailed with its policy of building ever more expensive and elaborate floodwalls to keep the canals at bay. Ultimately, this policy would prove catastrophic.

The work of the Sewerage & Water Board complements that of the Orleans Levee District, which was created by the state of Louisiana in 1890 to bring rigor to the haphazard construction of levees along the Mississippi River and to handle flood issues citywide. The district, governed by the Orleans Levee Board of Commissioners, was charged with building a coherent flood control system to complement the outfall canals' pump structures and keep the various bodies of water at bay.

The Levee District's early revetments were crude affairs that could be counted on to head off standard spring surges from upriver thaws but provided little protection from unusual weather events. Sometimes the levees held the river out of the city, and sometimes they didn't. These early levees were constructed with shovel and pickax, usually in haste and often with reluctant labor. Even so, in its first six years of existence, the Levee District managed to heap up an estimated one million cubic yards of earth between the river and the city. The advent of steam shovels in the early 1900s sped up the work considerably; by about 1910, the Levee District had managed to line the city outskirts with some 15 million cubic yards of fill to keep the streets dry and the houses safe.

It was the Levee Board more than any other agency that encouraged people to build on some of the lowest and most vulnerable land in the city. In the 1920s, the New Orleans city government turned its attention to the back marshes that extended toward Lake Pontchartrain and began eyeing them for development. In the beginning, these areas were essentially watery sewer pits, filled with muck and pestilence and huge clouds of mosquitoes. Over time, they would become some of the city's priciest real estate. But they had to be drained and cleared before that would occur.

Governor Huey Long saw this fallow land as opportunity. A farm boy from the piney woods who took the populist philosophy of governing to its very extreme, Long saw a way to build levees without raising taxes much, by turning the city's flood protection agency into a general development concern. The lakefront was already home to an amusement park, a string of crude roadhouses and seafood joints, and a yacht club, all of which were accessible from the city by a small railroad line. In 1928, shortly after his election, Long pushed an act through the state legislature, which he controlled, giving the Levee District expropriation rights and overriding control over the city's lakefront development. Unlike other levee districts in the state, which depended mostly on modest property and business taxes to bankroll their activities, the Orleans Levee District was given a way to raise huge sums of cash by actually creating land and flipping it to developers. The Levee District was allowed to use whatever land it needed to build levees; whatever it didn't need, the agency was free to liquidate. So from the 1930s to the present, the Orleans Levee District has had a dual role. It builds not only flood structures but also parks, roads, marinas, airports, "places of amusement," and anything else that might help it raise money. Overseeing all of this is the Orleans Levee Board, six of whose eight members serve at the pleasure of the governor.

As a way to bankroll huge projects without raising taxes, Long's populist plan worked brilliantly. In a notoriously poor state, the Orleans Levee Board was able to raise millions for flood control, and it quickly grew fat with surpluses.

What the Levee Board did to the city's lakefront was nothing short of startling. In a few short decades, a rough district of rude camps and tawdry roadhouses was transformed into a planned community of gently curving roads and scenic parks. Employing a battalion of dredges, the Levee Board reclaimed a stretch of lake bottom some five and a half miles long and nearly a mile deep—some two thousand acres in total. On one side, the Levee Board built an eight-foot-high breakwater of stepped concrete along the new shoreline of the lake—a structure that even seventy years later serves as the city's first-line defense against storm surges.

On the rest of the reclaimed land, the Levee Board built parks and other amenities and it platted out a series of neighborhoods, which were then sold off to developers. From 1939 to 1960, the Levee Board readied enough land to create six subdivisions, which soon appreciated in value. And in addition to the money it received from developers, the Levee Board has always collected a citywide flood protection millage, which helped it fund increasingly elaborate projects. In 1931, the Levee Board began work on what is now called the Lakefront Airport, the first of the district's so-called enterprise projects, which were designed to throw off cash to finance additional flood protection endeavors. The airport was originally named after Abraham Lazar Shushan, the Levee Board's president and a political crony of Governor Long. Shushan eventually was convicted of corruption. Though profitable in its early days, the airport is now an albatross, routinely costing $1 million more annually to operate than it takes in.

The airport was just the first of a string of increasingly outrageous moneymaking schemes mounted by the Levee Board, nearly all of which ended up costing, rather than making, money. In 1982, the board developed a $64 million yacht basin, which like the airport cost more to operate than it grossed in boat slip fees. In 1992, desperate to conquer the groaning debt the boat harbor had fostered, the Levee Board hatched a controversial plan to berth a floating casino there. Though the casino throws off about $4 million a year in rents, the venture is at best break-even, given the tremendous amount of money it cost to develop the boat harbor—and the $6 million road the casino demanded to handle the expected hordes of gamblers who never actually materialized. Throughout the 1990s, the casino was consistently the lowest-grossing gambling hall in the state.

When the federal government assumed a larger role in the city's hurricane protection system in the 1960s, the Levee District found itself with less to do. Though its payroll was large, the Levee District was basically reduced to a landscaping operation, responsible for mowing the grass on the levees and reporting any problems to the Army Corps of Engineers. Consequently, the Levee Board began to spend more time on the development side of its operation, hatching elaborate plans for all manner of commercial and residential development. By the 1980s, the Levee Board was the de facto landlord of a variety of commercial and civic property, owning apartments, shopping centers, restaurant complexes, and vast recreational areas. The district's staff, which hovered at around three hundred, included a fire brigade and a fifty-man police department that worked only in the nearly all-white neighborhoods along Lake Pontchartrain. Residents of the majority-black city wondered why the white-dominated enclaves near the lake were entitled to a separate police force and a chain of parklands that were in better shape than those in their own neighborhoods—and bankrolled in part with their tax dollars, thanks to the citywide millage.

Unaccountable to voters and flush with cash, the Levee Board was known more as an outlet for political patronage and questionable developments than it was for aggressive flood control. Indeed, in 1982, the Levee District even asked the corps to relax its floodwall standards to "provide more realistic hurricane protection," arguing that the federal design standard was too expensive. In the minds of many New Orleanians, the Levee Board was no longer about flood control, it was about cops and commercial real estate, and an ever-expanding agenda of vaguely wacky, often fanciful development schemes.

"Wild ideas. Grandstanding. Political back scratching," the Levee Board wrote about itself in a 1995 "annual report" that touted its various non–flood development projects, both existing and in the works, while dismissing the accusations of excess that others routinely leveled against it. "[People] wonder aloud why the Orleans Levee Board gets involved in building anything except levees," it said, dismissively. The answer, according to the board, was that state law required it to do so.

State politicians have lately made much of the Levee Board's cavalier attitude toward the job of maintaining the city's flood protection structures. They reacted with shock to accounts of the annual "inspection" tours that the Levee Board staged with corps officials— jaunts that included a short bus tour and a long seafood lunch to cap off the day. But in truth, anyone who cared to know more about the Levee Board's contribution to flood protection knew exactly what the Levee Board and its district had been doing for a generation. In a 1996 document spelling out its role in maintaining the 17th Street Canal, the Levee Board itemized its responsibilities for that particular body of water—mowing grass on the levee, pulling weeds, removing graffiti along the concrete floodwall, and painting the floodgates every year.

In January 2005, the Levee Board resurrected a scheme to build a four-mile-long artificial island in Lake Pontchartrain and fill it with homes, parks, restaurants, and hotels. "Everyone agrees it's a wonderful project," said James Huey, the Levee Board's president, who was soon to be cashiered for secretly paying himself an extra $100,000. And as that year's hurricane season kicked off, the Levee Board concerned itself not with improving flood protection but leasing property and maintaining its airport and boat harbors. In the spring of 2005, the Levee Board had a single flood-control project in train—a bridge project that technically sat outside of its district. Pressing flood issues, such as repairing a floodgate that had been destroyed by a freight train, didn't get completed.

Left mostly undiscussed in the months leading to the 2005 hurricane season were the various well-known weaknesses in the city's storm-defense system. At the board's March meeting, Huey urged his fellow members to lend $1 million to the Army Corps so it could finish a project to floodproof a small bridge over the London Avenue Canal. "It would be a terrible shame for this project not to be completed," Huey told the board, "especially if we get hit with a storm."

*   *   *

Despite thirty years of work and $650 million in contracts, the city's hurricane protection system was still not complete in 2005, and it had been ten years since engineers had done any serious work on the network of canals. But the situation was less desperate than it had been in 1982, when a portion of the floodwall bounding the London Avenue Canal had simply given way. Thankfully, the weather was clear and the water level in the canal was low; no serious flooding occurred.

In the early 1980s, the city's patchwork protection system was clearly ailing, even as the Sewerage & Water Board continued to add pumping capacity all over the city, which increased the strain on the system. More pumps meant more water and more stress on the canal walls, which were thirty years old and in dire need of replacement.

All told, upgrading these canals from their 1980s condition would cost around $100 million—a chunk of change well beyond the means of the Levee District and the Sewerage & Water Board. And the corps, which at the time was agnostic about projects exclusively devoted to drainage, simply balked at putting up 70 percent of the money. Instead, it proposed sealing off the three outfall canals with floodgates. Though the Levee Board wasn't strictly involved in drainage issues either, it sided with the Sewerage & Water Board, opposing the corps' canal-capping proposal. And instead of upgrades, the city's canal system rusted while the three organizations settled in for a years-long standoff.

What the corps proposed to do seemed sensible enough. It wanted to close off the three outflow canals with what it called butterfly valves, a sort of hinged gate that would automatically swing open when the city's pump stations cranked up and then fall shut when a hurricane approached. Corps engineers hadn't actually put these gates to a real-life test but had subjected them to modeling exercises, and they seemed to work well. Moreover, the corps predicted the gates would cost one-third that of "parallel protection"—armoring the entire length of the canal banks against a Category 3 hurricane.

Unfortunately, at one modeling exercise, attended by officials from the Sewerage & Water Board, the butterfly valves failed to work.

If that were to happen in real life, during a storm, the canals would back up and the city would likely flood. The Sewerage & Water Board pronounced itself opposed to the butterfly valves. But it had other reasons to resist the idea. As an agency, the Sewerage & Water Board had a singular interest in sucking the maximum amount of runoff from the streets and sending it out into the lake through the three outfall canals. To handle more runoff, the Sewerage & Water Board needed to install more pumps; to stuff more runoff into the canals, it would have to upgrade the floodwalls along the three canals. So instead of floodgates, the two local agencies stood firm: To protect the city from a hurricane, they wanted parallel protection, in the form of high, expensive floodwalls that would bound both sides of all three canals.

Since the federal government had agreed to shoulder the load for hurricane protection, this was a neat trick: With parallel protection, the canals would stay in their beds during a hurricane. And with up-graded floodwalls along the canals, the Sewerage & Water Board could add far more pumping capacity. "It gives them a higher capac-ity for pumping stormwater at no cost to them," said Al Naomi, proj-ect manager for the corps' New Orleans District. "They got two things out of it—the perceived ability to pump during a hurricane and the capacity to pump more. But it caused problems—the pri-mary one at the time was the expense."

Parallel protection cost much more than butterfly valves. And the corps, which operated on a strict "least cost" system when it chose designs, refused to put up the estimated $100 million for par-allel protection. For years, the two city agencies stood at loggerheads with the corps over this issue. But in the late 1980s, the Sewerage & Water Board could no longer hold out. The steel bulkheads along the London Avenue and Orleans canals were so rotten, corps engineers said, that a man could put his fist through them in some places. The 17th Street Canal leaked like a sieve, and it was a common for home owners along the waterway to complain that seep from the oversized ditch was pooling on their patios.

With all three canals failing and the locals in a standoff with Washington over upgrades, the Sewerage & Water Board, in partnership with the Orleans Levee District, decided to design its own upgrade for the 17th Street Canal.

In civil engineering circles, there are three kinds of floodwalls. There are dirt levees, such as those along the Mississippi River—huge sloping structures that are very strong but eat up acres and acres of land and are often unfeasible to construct in established neighborhoods. Almost as rugged are flood control structures involving the so-called T-wall design. These structures, which also take up a fair amount of land, employ a floodwall that looks like an inverted "T," with wide footers on the bottom and diagonal legs coming out the side, which add tremendous stability to a floodwall and make it much harder to topple, even in shifting soil.

The third design, the most common along the New Orleans outfall canals, is called I-wall. This is a sheet of corrugated steel that is pounded into the ground and topped with a layer of dirt and sometimes capped with a concrete wall. Though this design works fine in stable soil, it can be tricky to use in the alluvial soils around New Orleans, which are filled with all manner of organic material, slippery clay, and prehistoric beaches. If the ground around an I-wall shifts, the whole wall can topple over. And this can happen no matter how deep the I-wall might be buried: If the ground surrounding the structure is unstable, the entire structure is at peril of failure. New Orleans has about thirty-five miles of I-wall in its flood control system. The 17th Street Canal is bordered by I-wall.

There are two advantages to an I-wall: First, it has the smallest footprint of the three designs. And second, at about $1,600 per running foot, it is less than half the cost of a T-wall. For its side of the 17th Street Canal, the Orleans Levee District originally selected T-wall, but it balked when it saw the $44 million estimated cost. The same job constructed with I-wall would cost about $21 million. In engineering tests, the I-wall design met a safety factor that came in at the very low end of what the Army Corps allowed. The Army Corps approved the project. Years later, corps officials would say that the agency provided only cursory oversight on the job.

Because it was a Sewerage & Water Board–led project, the endeavor started with the installation of new drainage pumps. Then the Water Board dredged the Orleans Parish side of the canal so it could hold more storm runoff. Then the Levee District tackled the floodwall and levee construction, using I-wall.

In the end, the corps, which exercised very little control over the project, agreed to finish the job along the 17th Street Canal, topping the Levee District's I-walls with a concrete cap, which set the structure high above the adjacent neighborhood and made it look immensely strong and durable. But local engineers knew even during construction that the canal upgrade was a bit of a jackleg job. "They were trying to cut every corner," said Fred Young, a corps supervising engineer, of the local agencies' work. Indeed, it was apparent the two local agencies struggled to keep costs down—the first design they commissioned would have cost $10 million more than the second design did. The second design was the one that got built.

In 1990, the standoff over the butterfly valves came to an end when the Louisiana congressional delegation, at the behest of the local agencies, got Congress to pass a resolution ordering the corps to scrap the butterfly valve proposal and proceed with parallel protection for all three of the city's outfall canals. "They beat us," Young said. "So that was that."

Installing parallel protection on the canals in New Orleans was the Army Corps' "least cost" method at its finest. Having been outmaneuvered politically and tricked into essentially paying double for a job that would benefit the city's pumping stations as much as it provided hurricane protection, the Army Corps paid scrupulous attention to the cost of the three projects. In 1993, the corps began designing floodwalls for about ten miles of bank along the London Avenue and Orleans canals. For London Avenue, it rejected T-wall out of hand; instead, it incorporated the Levee District's I-wall design from the 17th Street Canal. And for the Orleans Canal, which sits higher than the other two canals for much of its length and is more challenging from an engineering standpoint, the corps attempted to design I-wall for its length but couldn't quite reach the minimum standard of safety. "They tried," Fred Young said of his fellow corps engineers. "But there was no way you could get an I-wall to work there." They went with T-wall.

The contract to plan the Orleans Canal floodwall and oversee its construction went to a local firm called Design Engineering, which is headed by a New Orleans native named Walter Baudier. Baudier grew up on the New Orleans lakefront and spent his childhood messing around in pirogues and flatboats and tying little strips of bacon to sticks to coax crawfish out of their little mud chimneys and into a plastic bucket.

Taming the Orleans Outfall Canal took about three years and cost about $42 million. And as he drove by the structure recently in his king cab pickup, Baudier slowed to get the full effect of the imposing structure with its creamy white walls and decorative urns that rises some twenty feet in the air and towers over the neighborhood that surrounds it. "That's a man of a levee," he said.

But for all of their muscularity, the floodwalls have a deep flaw. For the last two hundred feet or so, near where the canal terminates at Pump Station No. 7, the floodwall simply stops. At that point, a low earthen berm is all that keeps the canal from overflowing into the neighborhood. A similar, though smaller, gap exists at the end of the London Avenue Canal. Baudier was willing to finish the job, but the corps had other priorities. "I was dismissed," he said primly.

For more than ten years after Baudier completed his work on the Orleans Canal, this chink in the protective system remained. And when the corps got around to tackling the problem, the tide of Washington money had simply dried up. "We had plans ready to go," Fred Young said. "We just needed the money."

In the succeeding decade, the corps made little headway on its hurricane plan for the metropolitan area. It built a handful of floodproof bridges across the upgraded canals in New Orleans and got some work done in surrounding parishes. By the late 1990s, the Clinton administration had begun cutting back on money it was willing to put toward the project; in 2001 and forward, the Bush administration essentially brought construction on the project to a halt. In 2005, exactly forty years after it had been authorized to proceed, the corps was only about 75 percent done with its work to protect New Orleans from the storm surge of a killer hurricane.

3

A MOUNTAIN OF FAILURE

Virginia Route 601 runs just outside of Leesburg, and if there has been a recent snowstorm, it will be the only cleared road around. The blacktop highway winds up through the Shenandoah Mountains and on to Bluemont and Mount Weather, home of the nation's premier doomsday bunker. The subject of popular spy novels and endless conspiracy theories, the Mount Weather bunker complex is an underground city, complete with dormitories and three-story office buildings, streets and sidewalks, a crematorium, cafeterias, and a hospital. It was designed to survive an all-out nuclear war and is where the post-apocalypse government will go if the situation ever comes to that. Mount Weather is the "undisclosed location" where congressional leaders fled following the twin terrorist attacks on New York and Washington in September 2001.

Mount Weather is no military installation but a civilian one. Though developed in the 1950s by the Army Corps of Engineers, oversight of the bunker complex fell to the Federal Emergency Management Agency upon its creation in 1979. The facility has lost whatever hush-hush status it had during the Cold War, and its presence is

well marked by big highway signs. For decades no one in government was allowed to admit that Mount Weather even existed, though
by the 1970s it wasn't much of a secret to those who study the clandestine operations of the federal government.

The installation sits adjacent to a well-traveled highway and is in
plain sight of several popular hiking trails. A 1962 thriller, *Seven
Days in May*, offered a thinly camouflaged description of the place
and its role in the nation's emergency response network. People in
the area knew all about the mountain and still tell stories of delivery
drivers who pulled their trucks off the road and fled from their rigs
because they were frightened by the reticent "men in suits" who were
required to ride shotgun with them up to the compound gates.

As a bunker for America's post-apocalypse government, Mount
Weather may have outlived its usefulness. The idea that societies and
governments would outlast an all-out nuclear assault is an antiquated
if not preposterous proposition. And hardened bunkers do little to
foil the enemy of this millennium—shadowy Islamists who target office buildings and transportation depots and seek to kill civilians, not
soldiers.

But Mount Weather still serves as an apt metaphor for the historic misplacement of national emergency response priorities. To
understand the nation's balky emergency response system is to understand the two-headed agency known as FEMA and the unusual
role it plays in disasters. On the one hand, FEMA is the federal government's own "Red Cross" agency—Washington's cavalry of relief
workers that brings money and equipment to help local governments overwhelmed by rogue rivers and cyclones and earthquakes.
On the other hand, FEMA is a top-secret spy shop charged with
keeping the federal government functioning on the day after doomsday and is a guardian against threats both probable and fanciful, be
they from homegrown militants, foreign governments, or international terrorists. Striking a balance between these dual roles has tor-
mented the agency through its entire existence.

Though FEMA was not formally established until 1979, its programs have existed in one form or another for more than two hundred

years. Since the time that a catastrophic fire raced through Portsmouth, New Hampshire, on December 26, 1802, and became the first recognized major disaster in the history of the United States, Washington has taken an active role in relief efforts. In 1803, national sympathy for the Portsmouth victims prompted Congress to pass a relief package—a waiver on port tariffs—to help local merchants recover. This minor act of Congress became the template for federal disaster response that exists to this day.

Over the next century and a half, Congress would pass dozens of acts providing federal support for all manner of calamities. The federal government waived tariffs for New York City merchants after the Great Fire of 1835 destroyed much of Manhattan's commercial district. After President Abraham Lincoln was assassinated at Ford's Theater in Washington in 1865, the federal government paid the hospital bills for everyone who was injured in the resulting melee. In 1932, during the Great Depression, President Herbert Hoover commissioned the Reconstuction Finance Corporation to lend money to banks and institutions to stimulate economic activity. The RFC made loans to disaster victims as well, making it the first organized federal disaster response agency.

But it was not until the Disaster Relief Act of 1950 that Congress established a permanent pot of federal money to deal with emergencies. Even so, by the lights of most officials, disaster relief was a local operation, if not a private, charitable one. So in the early days, direct federal rebuilding money was used only to replace government buildings. But after Hurricane Camille raked the Mississippi coastline in 1969, virtually wiping out whole communities and killing 143 people, federal disaster recovery money was extended to cover individuals and private businesses.

In the years leading up to FEMA's creation, the main complaint of local governments was that there was no central agency where they could seek disaster assistance. Piecemeal congressional action over the years, often linked to specific calamities, had left federal disaster aid programs scattered over dozens of Washington agencies; piercing the vast bureaucracy to get at this assistance tied the states in knots. For instance, the Bureau of Roads (later the Department of Transportation) rebuilt highways destroyed by floods, while the U.S. Army Corps of Engineers was in charge of the rebuilding of other infrastructure. The National Fire Prevention and Control Administration enforced fire safety, and it was inexplicably located in the Department of Commerce. The Department of Housing and Urban Development operated the national flood insurance program, while the Pentagon ran the nation's emergency management system. In total, scores of agencies managed more than a hundred different disaster relief programs, leading to all manner of confusion and inefficiency.

Then there was the nation's Civil Defense network, Washington's public face for attack preparedness. It was a web of paramilitary agencies that put air raid sirens in every mill town, established nuclear bunkers, and taught "duck and cover" drills to legions of schoolchildren. For these agencies, disaster management was a sideline to the greater effort of nuclear preparedness. But while World War III never materialized, natural disasters kept coming. And in the early 1960s, when disasters struck, response was left generally to the locals. This friction over disaster priorities—Washington's preoccupation with foreign threats versus the states' emphasis on real-world natural disasters such as fire and flood—would come to define the uneasy relationship between federal disaster responders and their local counterparts.

In the end, this diffuse federal approach to disaster response didn't make for good politics. But when it came to voter fallout it was the local politicians who suffered most. The canniest of these politicians learned this lesson early. In 1965, for instance, when Hurricane Betsy slammed into New Orleans, killing eighty-one people, causing $1 billion in damage, and leaving thousands homeless, Russell Long, Louisiana's powerful senator, put the political implications of the disaster in the strongest terms in a telephone call to President Lyndon Johnson. "You lost that state last year," Long told the president a few days after the storm hit. "If I do say it, you could elect Hale Boggs and every guy you'd want to elect in the path of this hurricane just by handling yourself right." Long urged Johnson to come to Louisiana himself, to see the damage firsthand and to assure the victims there that a strong federal response would come swiftly.

When Johnson demurred, promising to send his "best man" instead, Long pressed his case. "We are not the least bit interested in your best man," he said. "I'm just a Johnson man."

Johnson got the point. That afternoon, he boarded Air Force One and headed to New Orleans.

The president was shocked by what he saw in New Orleans, and a few months later, he signed the Flood Control Act of 1965, a massive civil works program that would provide the area with its first modern protection against hurricane strikes. But this was still something short of a comprehensive program. Succeeding years brought a succession of disasters—Hurricane Camille in 1969, the 1971 San Fernando earthquake, and Hurricane Agnes in 1972. After each disaster, the federal government created another program until 1974, when Congress refined the system of presidential disaster declarations—a designation that automatically triggers a Washington response.

Still, the states weren't satisfied, since seeking relief involved full immersion into Washington's thicket of bureaucracy. So the nation's governors began lobbying to bring a measure of rigor to the federal system of disaster relief. What they proposed was the creation of a single coordinating agency that could draw on all of Washington's resources during a calamity to provide them with one place where they could find buses, bulldozers, and cash with equal aplomb.

On March 31, 1979, the governors got their wish. In an action that received scant attention outside of government halls, President Jimmy Carter signed Executive Order 12127, creating the Federal Emergency Management Agency. With the stroke of a pen, all of Washington's disaster relief programs were collapsed into a single agency. Carter made no grand statement when he signed the order; he simply promised that the agency "would be independent, apolitical and adequately funded." The governors got their one-stop disaster shop.

But that would hardly be the end of the problems. Unlike other federal agencies, FEMA wasn't cut from whole cloth. Indeed, the agency's official history of its birth is little more than an alphabet-soup recitation of the stub ends of Washington's bureaucratic apparatus that were collected under its auspices. FEMA was an amoeba-like collection of disparate agencies, from the Federal Insurance Administration and the Federal Preparedness Agency to the Federal Disaster Assistance Administration and the National Weather Service Community Preparedness Program. FEMA got control of federal housing programs and hazardous substance mitigation initiatives and a degree of oversight of nuclear power plants. It also inherited civil defense responsibilities from the Pentagon, including Mount Weather and its spooky cadre of doomsday planners.

From the very start, FEMA's bureaucratic brass had trouble integrating all of these subdepartments, with their starkly different cultures, into one cohesive federal agency. President Carter did his best to work out the problem by appointing John Macy as FEMA's first director. A career bureaucrat with a knack for organization, Macy attempted to unite the various fiefs behind a common philosophy that all disasters—be they unseen or expected, extraordinary or run-of-the-mill—demanded the same response from Washington. He developed what he called the "Integrated Emergency Management System," which people now refer to as the "all-hazards approach" to disaster preparedness. It is a simple concept, rooted in the assumption that many response tools such as warnings, evacuations, and damage assessments are equally applicable across the universe of disasters. It was an approach that showed fair promise. The first emergencies FEMA tangled with had a certain sameness: the aftermath of the nuclear accident at Three Mile Island, Hurricane Frederic, the toxic contamination of Love Canal, the Cuban refugee crisis, the eruption of Mount St. Helens. All were the result of manmade and natural hazards and involved lots of civilians who needed help and homes.

As it faced these disasters, the new agency responded swiftly with cash and quick thinking. Soon after the 1979 incident at the Three Mile Island nuclear plant near Middletown, Pennsylvania, FEMA recognized sweeping changes would be needed in emergency response planning for protecting the health and safety of the communities living nearby and started drawing up new plans. In the case of Love Canal, the agency not only relocated 950 families but also paid out millions of dollars to the state of New York. The successes drew plaudits from local politicians and validated Macy's belief that a combination of civil defense techniques and natural disaster response skills—along with a healthy wad of cash—ably served as a template for the agency's activities.

Alas, the plaudits wouldn't last. Macy wasn't running the agency long enough to make a real difference: He was turned out with the rest of the Carter administration after a scant seventeen months in office. And with Ronald Reagan's landslide victory in 1980 came a new direction at FEMA, one that elevated foreign threats and Cold War fears over the more mundane calamities of nature.

Ronald Reagan made nuclear competition with the Soviet Union the centerpiece of his administration. Appointments followed suit. To run FEMA, Reagan chose his former security adviser from California, Louis O. Giuffrida, to remake the agency. Giuffrida had run the California Specialized Training Institute, an emergency management–counterterrorism training center that taught some 28,000 police how to put down urban riots and respond to earthquakes and floods.

Giuffrida's philosophy about civil defense and disaster was forged by the social unrest of the Vietnam era. In 1970, while studying at the U.S. Army War College in Carlisle, Pennsylvania, Giuffrida wrote a paper called "National Survival—Racial Imperative." The treatise laid out a strategy for containing what Giuffrida believed to be an inevitable race war in America, starting with the imprisonment of 21 million "American Negroes" and the imposition of federal martial law.

Blunt-spoken and sharp-featured, with a full head of thick, dark hair, Giuffrida, a retired Army colonel and a brigadier general in California's state militia, cultivated an exaggerated military bearing and demanded martial discipline at FEMA. His obsession with all things military pervaded the agency. He insisted on always being addressed as "General." One of his first official actions was to query FEMA's legal department to see if the agency's name could be changed to the Office of Civil Defense. The answer was no: FEMA's name was embedded in statute. Rebuffed on the name change, Giuffrida came up with a motto for the agency, "Service in Peace and War," which he emblazoned in Latin on the FEMA seal.

Though Giuffrida denied he was changing the agency into a paranoid harbinger of World War III, it became clear early on that the general in fact had exactly this in mind as he set about turning FEMA into a black-budget agency in the style of the CIA, relegating the agency's disaster response duties to subordinate status. FEMA expanded its nuclear survivability programs, drawing up "crisis evacuation" plans to herd residents of some four hundred American cities into remote rural areas, where they would wait out a missile attack from Moscow. This came as a surprise to officials in some of these rural areas who complained that they had never been consulted on the sketchy, secret plans. The agency likewise investigated whether factory workers could save themselves in a nuclear attack by jumping into large pools of water. (The ultimate conclusion was that they could not.) Even the agency's public information section got into the game, producing a coloring book to help children identify what they should bring to a bomb shelter (water and crackers were in, fresh fish and cheese were out). Long after mainstream scientists had concluded that all-out nuclear war was not survivable, Giuffrida's disaster agency posited the theory that in fact it was.

Though Giuffrida was hardly the only Reagan appointee who believed a nuclear war was winnable, he offered perhaps the most detailed predictions of its outcome. In a 1982 interview with the *New York Times*, he suggested that some 30 percent of New York City's population could weather a missile attack. "Sure, it'll be a hell of a mess," he said. "It'll be terrible. It boggles the mind. But do we just throw up our hands and say, 'Forget it, the job's too big?' Do we give up?"

Certainly Giuffrida was taking no chances. Under his guidance, Mount Weather received a facelift—an array of fancy new communications equipment, teleconferencing capabilities, and the most sophisticated computers of the day. He built regional bunkers for military leaders and embarked on a variety of schemes to ensure the government would survive nuclear assault, at least long enough to strike back.

One of Giuffrida's most elaborate schemes involved the creation of the Mobile Emergency Response Support, or MERS, a top-secret fleet of three hundred trucks mounted with state-of-the-art electronics that could fan out during a disaster from hidden locations to pick up senior government officials and drive around in a sort of elaborate shell game during a Soviet nuclear strike. These MERS vehicles, camouflaged with company logos to make them look like ordinary delivery trucks, are still on the road, though their existence has been declassified. The Academy of Public Administration, a nonpartisan group created by Congress, estimates that this doomsday fleet costs taxpayers upward of $130 million a year to maintain.

Emboldened by its top-secret missions and exempt from any vigorous scrutiny, FEMA's doomsday planners conjured up ever more schemes, both creative and bizarre. Some involved teams of faceless agents permanently assigned to pace around America's airports, grasping briefcases containing $50,000 in cash, ready with handoff plans in case of civil uprisings or foreign attack. The cash would be used to bankroll other classified activities designed to keep the government running and the chain of political succession intact.

But some of FEMA's black-budget activities were truly troubling. Between 1982 and 1984, Giuffrida and his top aides developed a secret contingency plan in the form of a draft executive order that called for a declaration of martial law and suspension of the Constitution, turning control of the United States over to FEMA during a national crisis. The plan did not define what would constitute a "national crisis," but it was understood to refer to nuclear war or a similarly paralyzing event, including violent and widespread political unrest.

Though the takeover scheme was dismissed as a canard by FEMA officials and by others in the Reagan administration, there is a fair amount of evidence to indicate such a plan indeed existed. In the 1987 Iran-contra hearings, Representative Jack Brooks of Texas attempted to question Lieutenant Colonel Oliver North about the successor government plan but was gaveled to silence by the joint congressional committee's chairman, Senator Daniel Inouye of Hawaii. "May I most respectfully request that that matter not be touched upon at this stage," Inouye said as he closed off the discussion. "If we wish to get into this, I'm certain arrangements can be made for an executive session."

And at least one Reagan administration official was convinced the plan existed. In an August 1984 letter to National Security Adviser Robert McFarlane, Attorney General William French Smith wrote, "I believe that the role assigned to the Federal Emergency Management Agency in the revised Executive Order exceeds its proper function as a coordinating agency for emergency preparedness. . . . This department and others have repeatedly raised serious policy and legal objections to the creation of an 'emergency czar' role for FEMA."

As far as is known, President Reagan never approved the successor government plans. Giuffrida, however, continued in his attempts to expand FEMA's authority. Citing the 1972 attacks at the Munich Olympics as an example, Giuffrida asserted that Los Angeles faced the risk of terrorism when it hosted the games in 1984. He argued that FEMA should be at the forefront of preparing for such a contingency.

Whether he went too far or not, Giuffrida's ride came to a swift end. Though Congress had limited control over FEMA's secret programs, it did oversee the other parts of the agency's budget. And from what its investigators could determine, the general had used his influence to steer federal contracts to cronies and to use $170,000 in taxpayer money to build a private residence for himself (including a $29,000 gourmet kitchen) at a firefighter training center in Emmitsburg, Maryland. In the face of the mushrooming financial scandal, Giuffrida resigned in September 1985. Today, the historical narrative posted on FEMA's Web site makes no mention of the director who carried a sidearm to work and demanded to be called "General."

By the time Giuffrida left, nearly half of the agency's 2,400 employees were working exclusively on black-budget programs and assorted doomsday scenarios, and the agency's spending on such programs outstripped its disaster response spending by twelve to one. In four short years, the natural disaster shop that had been so integral to FEMA's original mission was a withered appendage. The natural disaster staff was segregated from the doomsday workers, who worked on the fifth floor of FEMA headquarters in downtown Washington, behind a wall of tight security. There were armed guards at the elevators and the stairwells. The natural hazards experts lived a far more relaxed existence. They came and went as they pleased. FEMA truly was a two-headed agency.

"The national security folks thought the disaster folks were just a bunch of weenies who went out and chased storms. So there was a real rift between the two parts of the agency and there was no sharing of resources," said Bruce Baughman, a career disaster worker who joined the agency in 1979 after graduating college and serving four and a half years in the Marine Corps. Baughman and others in the agency said that FEMA's disaster-response side did good work dealing with the mostly small disasters that visited the country during the Reagan years. But it was, Baughman said, a begging-bowl operation.

There would be a price to pay. On September 22, 1989, Hurricane Hugo, a massive Category 4 storm, blasted ashore near Charleston, South Carolina, having trashed the U.S. Virgin Islands five days earlier. Now, 1,500 miles later, the storm struck again with punishing 135-mile-per-hour winds and a powerful, twenty-foot storm surge. The hurricane caused damage as far away—and as far inland—as Charlotte, North Carolina, which sits 175 miles from the coast.

FEMA was caught flat-footed. Having sent response teams to assist local authorities on the Caribbean islands of Guadeloupe and Montserrat, the agency was undermanned on America's own shores. FEMA reacted with a maddening bureaucratic slowness, demanding that local officials follow rigid procedures and apply through their governor for every type of federal support they might need. One longstanding FEMA employee sent to help respond to the storm recalls that the agency was so unprepared that he and his team had nowhere to sleep and not even the most basic supplies. "We didn't know where we were going to be from one day to the next," he said. "How can you help others when you couldn't even take care of yourself?"

In the city of Charleston, Hugo damaged 4,000 buildings and left 100,000 people homeless. The cleanup fell largely to the city's mayor, Joseph P. Riley, Jr. Riley recalled that during a lull in the storm, when Hugo's eye was passing over City Hall, he turned to the FEMA official weathering the storm with him and asked for advice. "You need to make sure you're accounting for all your expenses," the FEMA man said.

This was the FEMA that was prepared for nuclear winter and little else: lumbering and lethargic, unimaginative, practically a caricature of Washington bureaucracy. "A bunch of bureaucratic jackasses" is how Senator Ernest F. Hollings of South Carolina characterized the agency at the time.

Even as it fumbled with the aftereffects of Hugo, FEMA got walloped again a month later, when the magnitude 6.9 Loma Prieta earthquake rocked the San Francisco and Monterey Bay regions of California on October 17, 1989, collapsing a freeway in Oakland and a deck on the Bay Bridge, and interrupting Game 3 of the World Series at Candlestick Park.

Having been blasted by public opinion just weeks before for its obsession with red tape, FEMA didn't wait for the locals to request help this time. It swung into action before being called, operating on the assumption that the earthquake would formally be ruled a disaster at some point. FEMA also benefited greatly from a much better trained and financed state emergency operation. California had been training for years to respond to earthquakes, and unlike the Carolinas during Hugo, it was ready for disaster. Within hours of the quake, the state called up 32,000 National Guardsmen, the largest deployment of the Guard in the history of the country. FEMA's new streamlined approach won rare praise.

But that triumph would prove an anomaly, and the old problems would return soon enough. The following year, President George H. W. Bush appointed a new director of FEMA—Wallace Stickney, a former New Hampshire transportation commissioner and regional official for the Environmental Protection Agency. Since Giuffrida's departure, the agency had been led mostly by Julius W. Becton, Jr., a retired Army lieutenant general, who served from 1985 to 1989. A combination of bad press and bad pay had made it hard to find a permanent replacement.

Initially Stickney—a former neighbor and an old friend of Bush's chief of staff, John Sununu—did not want the job either. But he changed his mind after realizing that a few extra years of service on the federal payroll would entitle him to a juicy government pension. "I already have 17 years with the federal government," he told the Associated Press at the time. "If I go back to work for them for three years it would give me enough time to put a nice retirement package together."

Many in Washington viewed the appointment as a crony hire. Stickney had no disaster experience and brought little to the table to address the agency's vast shortcomings. He was essentially ignored by the black-budget operators, and he complained that the agency's "security cult" cut him out of meetings and refused to share secrets. By 1992, the agency had become a dumping ground for friends of friends, groaning under the weight of political appointees and liberally seeded with hacks.

And then disaster struck. In an eerie replay of Hugo, Hurricane Andrew came ashore just south of Miami, at Homestead, Florida, on August 24, 1992. Packing wind gusts of up to 180 miles per hour, the rare Category 5 storm reduced much of Dade County to toothpicks, causing some $25 billion in damage. In Homestead, more than a quarter of the community's 26,000 homes were destroyed. And again, FEMA proved unable to cope. For days, national television news aired footage of survivors living in the streets, searching rubble piles for food and water, pleading on television for Washington's help. Three days after the storm, Kate Hale, the emergency director for Dade County, Florida, appeared on national television and began to cry. "Enough is enough," she said, looking directly into the camera. "Quit playing like a bunch of kids. Where the hell is the cavalry on this one? For God's sake, where are they?"

This time there were political repercussions of the sort that Russell

Long had alluded to nearly thirty years before. Andrew had hit in stride with the presidential election season, and when President Bush visited the stricken area a few days after the storm, he found little had been done to help the victims. And he also found that a once-reliable bloc of voters had turned into a wasp's nest of recrimination.

Stickney was scapegoated, summarily dismissed from overseeing the disaster, and replaced with Transportation Secretary Andrew Card, who conceded that "a significant amount of red tape" had hobbled federal relief efforts. "We have a horrendous situation here," Card said. "We're working together to address individual lives and make sure people are back on their feet."

The response eventually righted itself, but the political landscape was in shambles. The Bush administration blamed Florida's governor, Lawton Chiles, a Democrat, for the bungled response, saying that he was ill prepared for the disaster, had no plan, and could not articulate what help the state needed from the federal government. Chiles shot back that he didn't see a need to ask, when the national news networks were broadcasting wall-to-wall coverage and there were 160,000 hungry and homeless storm survivors wandering the streets of their wrecked communities. In truth, there was plenty of blame to go around.

Though the administration quickly dispatched some 20,000 troops to Florida, it was too late in the minds of many voters. Bush failed to win reelection that November.

Congress demanded an immediate investigation and over the next year held dramatic hearings, launched a variety of inquests, and produced several pounds of reports that condemned FEMA. One report damned the agency as a dumping ground for political appointees and a "turkey farm" for washed-out bureaucrats. Some in Congress called for the Pentagon to assume first-responder responsibilities for the nation; others said FEMA should simply be dismantled.

By this point, FEMA was near extinction whether Congress abolished it or not. The agency had become synonymous with ineptitude, and only the IRS had a worse reputation. After Hurricane Andrew, the *Wall Street Journal* published an article in which several disaster specialists said the nation was better off with FEMA dissolved rather than reformed. And some in Congress agreed. "The view on the Hill at the time was that nothing short of a messiah could save the agency," recalled Bruce Baughman, then a senior manager in FEMA's federal response division.

The man President Bill Clinton chose to fill that role was James Lee Witt, the forty-nine-year-old son of a sharecropper from Dardanelle, Arkansas. A high school dropout who had learned to drive a tractor by the age of six, Witt had served with Clinton in Arkansas as the director of the state's office of emergency services, overseeing fifty-one employees. Small though it was, it was enough to make Witt the first candidate for the FEMA director job to have any disaster experience at all.

The two men had first met in the summer of 1974. Witt, who ran a successful construction firm and was something of a big wheel in his rural community, was approached by Clinton, a charismatic twenty-eight-year-old candidate for Congress who was looking for some financial backing. The men hit it off immediately. Witt recognized a kindred spirit in Clinton, who himself had come from poor, rural roots. Clinton lost the race, but within a few years was elected governor, and Witt had won the job as the chief elected official of Yell County, a rural county in northern Arkansas.

It was Witt's experience as the Yell County administrator that gave him insight into FEMA's bureaucratic soul, as he dealt with small floods and modest disasters. Witt is fond of recounting his experience with FEMA in 1983, after a flood had washed out some old wooden bridges. Witt proposed replacing the lost bridges with something more solid, something that wouldn't wash out, something made of concrete. But no matter how hard he argued, FEMA refused, saying he had to cost out exact replicas because that was all the agency would pay for. "FEMA made me count every nail," he said with a laugh.

In the end, the agency cut Yell County a check for $15,000. But Witt also sought state money and some private donations. And he built his concrete bridges, using local labor. But he never forgave FEMA for making it so hard.

When Clinton won the presidency in 1992, he brought Witt to Washington, seeking to install his old friend at FEMA's helm. At first, the capital elite were deeply concerned about Witt's lack of a formal education, but he eventually won over the U.S. senators who would have to confirm him through his contempt for the buttoned-down bean counters at FEMA and his views for a reinvigorated federal relief agency. "I'm delighted to see President Clinton has selected someone with practical experience in emergency preparedness," said Senator Thad Cochran, a Mississippi Republican.

In his written statement to the confirmation committee, Witt said that FEMA needed to quit focusing on doomsday scenarios and start working in the real world. He added that the agency needed to repair its relations with local disaster responders and to pursue mutual aid pacts between states. It also needed to loosen its procedural rules and figure out ways to harness the giant resources of the Pentagon. And then Witt made an argument that demonstrated his grasp of what FEMA could be. Disasters, he said, were political events, and there was no reason FEMA couldn't be harnessed by Congress for political gain. Witt promised to make FEMA an agency that could deliver on political promises. "I asked them for a year," Witt said. "I said that if I couldn't turn FEMA around in that time, then I'd support legislation to do away with it."

The Senate was impressed. "I haven't spent a lot of time complimenting the President on his appointments, but I sure did on this one," said Senator James Inhofe, an Oklahoma Republican. Witt got his year.

At 6:30 A.M. on April 7, 1993, the morning after he had been confirmed and sworn in, Witt stood at the front door of FEMA headquarters and greeted every employee who arrived. "Many of them had never even seen the FEMA director before up close," Witt recalled. And then he went on a tour of the building, making a stop on the fifth floor, the one that housed all the black-budget programs— the satellite communications, the doomsday trucks, the Mount Weather program, and the rest.

The first thing that struck him were all the guards. He asked what the security detail cost the agency and was told it worked out to about $300,000 a year. "So I told them it's gone," Witt recalled. "I want these doors opened up." There were plenty of protests, but they fell on deaf ears.

As the weeks passed, Witt kept up his war against the black-budget programs, pushing back hard when told they couldn't be used to support disaster relief programs. The "continuity of government" plans were summarily cut back, and whole programs were transformed or killed outright, longtime employees said. Witt even talked briefly about selling the Mount Weather doomsday bunker; but instead he turned it into a disaster training facility and converted many of its secret assets like the MERS into communication and command platforms to help out in disasters.

Witt labored to refocus the agency on its disaster role. He called on a team of senior FEMA managers to remake and reorganize FEMA from the top down. Soon enough, FEMA was taking a lead role in disaster response. Money that once went to nuclear survivability now went to hurricane preparedness. Witt reassigned virtually every senior manager in the agency.

The first true test of Witt's reforms came with the Mississippi River floods that began in June 1993. President Clinton immediately dispatched senior administration officials to the area, while Witt sent survey teams to staff the emergency operations centers in the nine midwestern states battling the cresting river. The aim, a White House press release said, was to lay the groundwork necessary for federal disaster assistance and "insure disaster victims receive the help they need as rapidly as possible."

Witt was on the phone with his people every day. He used the Mount Weather classified emergency communications center to scramble response teams, and he sent the newly declassified MERS doomsday vehicles into the disaster area to provide communications and logistics support. Witt then got on the phone to the congressmen from all nine states to ensure that they were getting the supplies they needed. And when he traveled to the affected states, he stood humbly at the press conferences, a few steps back from the governors. "I wasn't there to showboat," Witt said.

But he got plenty of attention nonetheless. FEMA's most dogged critics in Congress fell silent. The praise was truly bipartisan. Witt talked like a marketing man, emphasizing "customer service." As a result, Congress withdrew its bill to abolish FEMA, and Witt was commended for his revamping of the agency that was nearly euthanized.

But Witt's real genius lay in his ability to redefine FEMA's role. FEMA traditionally arrived after a disaster to provide emergency relief and financial assistance, but Witt urged the agency's officials to focus more on preventing the damage from disasters, through an intergovernmental and public-private effort. FEMA developed a "life-cycle" model of disaster management. Disasters—and their costs—were the product of planning and mitigation that needed to begin far in advance of disasters and continue long after to prevent their recurrence.

Instead of waiting for a hurricane to hit and dealing with the aftermath, Witt worked with local officials to pre-position supplies and personnel in a state ahead of emergencies. He also strengthened regional offices to work with the states on improving evacuation rates and routes. And he junked the old way of waiting for states to formally request help—a bureaucratic rule that had slowed FEMA's response countless times. "I went back and read the reports on what went wrong with Andrew and I said we're not going to have another Andrew," Witt said. "I said we're not going to let any state or any city fail."

Amazingly, the emergency operations center in FEMA's Washington office had been mothballed years before; Witt installed one. "I went down to the room that was supposed to have been the operations center and all I saw were some coffee tables and folding chairs in a room where wires were hanging out of the ceiling," Witt said. By the time he was finished, the room looked like the bridge of a starship, draped with banks of television monitors, linked computers, overhead projectors, and phones that connected directly to Mount Weather—FEMA's new all-hazards communications center.

The changes were paying off. Disaster struck again before dawn on January 17, 1994, when a 6.9 magnitude earthquake struck Northridge, California, about twenty miles northwest of Los Angeles. The quake shook the area for almost ten full seconds, producing the worst earthquake in the Los Angeles Basin in nearly a quarter century. When it was over, fifty-seven people were dead and 9,000 were injured. Initial cost estimates of total damages were $25 billion. If the quake had happened a few hours later, the death toll would have been far worse.

FEMA and the state of California sprung into action. Within fifteen minutes, FEMA regional teams were in contact with state and local responders and calling on various federal agencies for help. Within ninety minutes, special emergency response teams that help coordinate federal response had arrived on the scene. By the next day, a special telephone registration center had opened to help victims of the quake process federal assistance claims. Witt flew in to work with the governor and to keep President Clinton informed, while his operations team did what they had to do.

Newspaper articles began to run stories about the new FEMA that could. State disaster officials were pleased. In opinion surveys, more than 80 percent of respondents rated the agency's service as good to excellent. Witt had kept his promise to create an agency that would help politicians, restructuring FEMA's check-writing shop and its damage-claim section and upgrading the agency's computer system to make sure it processed forms as efficiently as possible. Even Republicans were impressed.

Clinton and Witt clearly subscribed to Russell Long's philosophy, viewing disasters as golden opportunities to help regular folks, to connect with local politicians, and maybe pick up a few votes along the way. Clinton demonstrated the importance he attached to FEMA when he elevated the agency to cabinet-level status in 1993.

In his first year in office, Clinton set a new record for disaster declarations, logging fifty-eight of them. And the bar for a disaster declaration was low. One winter, Clinton even declared disasters after snowstorms, something that had never been done by the federal government before.

Witt had managed to convert FEMA from a spooky, inept, bureaucratic backwater into a brand name. His secret weapon was simple: At any time, the president of the United States was a mere phone call away and always ready to help. And with the president behind him, everyone took Witt's calls. It was an important link that helped produce results.

When Hurricane Marilyn hit the U.S. Virgin Islands as a Category 3 storm in 1995, FEMA had plastic sheeting, cots, and generators staged stateside but needed aircraft to get them to the disaster area. Witt requested that the Pentagon send as many C-141 and C-17 transport carriers as it could, but there were not enough in the area. Witt waited on the tarmac in St. Thomas for the planes, but when they failed to show up after a few hours, he signaled for a satellite phone from the young Pentagon liaison who had been assigned to him for the storm. He dialed the secretary of the Air Force.

"Mr. Secretary," Witt drawled. "James Lee Witt here. To get right to the point, those damn planes haven't landed yet and I want to know where in the shit they are. They better be getting here pretty quick because the next call I'm gonna make you're not gonna like." The secretary knew exactly what Witt meant. Within the hour the planes were stacked up in the sky over the Virgin Islands. "It was a sight to behold," Witt said.

But it wasn't just the stepped-up response that delighted Congress; it was FEMA's ability to deliver loads of pork as well. During his eight years as director, Witt oversaw some 370 presidentially declared disasters. Often, communities hit by a disaster used federal cash to bankroll pet projects that had previously been shot down by Congress. So while money did go to people in need, some of it was spent expressly for political gain. And this fired up some critics of the president, who fumed that disaster relief was being used as a political tool.

It's not something either Clinton or Witt ever attempted to deny. "Disasters are very political events," Witt told Congress in 1996.

But politics turned on Witt after the bombing of the Alfred P. Murrah Federal Building in Oklahoma City in April 1995. The attack had awakened national security experts to new forms of terrorism that simply couldn't be ignored. Clinton and Congress would eventually convene the Hart-Rudman Commission to examine terrorist threats and national security needs. The commission would support FEMA's all-hazards approach as a way to maximize federal support for disasters and minimize bureaucracy, but it also would advocate a new role for FEMA: antiterror shop.

A 1995 FBI report on terrorism noted that "large-scale attacks designed to inflict mass casualties appear to be a new terrorist method in the United States." Congress began paying attention, and in 1996 the Defense Against Weapons of Mass Destruction Act was passed to address the lack of domestic preparedness against the threat of a nuclear, biological, or chemical attack inside the United States. This law assigned initial responsibility for domestic prepared-ness to the Department of Defense, but envisioned FEMA eventually taking over the program. In the wake of Witt's deft handling of the response to the Oklahoma City attack, policy makers urged him to play a role in terrorism response. But Witt refused.

His reluctance stemmed from a concern that if FEMA picked up terrorism as a new responsibility, it could well drag the agency back to the days of Louis Giuffrida; time, energy, and resources would once again be sucked away from the certainty of natural disasters to prepare for a new bogeyman. FEMA risked being plunged back into clandestine preparation strategies at the expense of Witt's all-hazards approach. Besides, by 1997 Witt had embarked on a new program known as Project Impact which aimed at getting local communities to make themselves more resilient to storms, earthquakes, and ulti-mately man-made events. Taking on terrorism directly, he feared, might destroy this important program.

Bruce Baughman, now the head of FEMA operations and one of Witt's top lieutenants, and Ellen Gordon, the head of Iowa's division of emergency management and a leading light in the field, urged Witt to reconsider. "Terrorism was a hazard with its own special de-mands, and if FEMA didn't do it someone else would," said Baugh-man. Gordon also pushed Witt in this direction. "It was going to be about money and grants and it was better to have the agency already thinking about response issues to figure out how to integrate these new monies," she said.

Witt now says he always wanted to incorporate terrorism training programs into FEMA but that the Justice Department under Attorney General Janet Reno beat him to the punch, creating the Office of Domestic Preparedness (ODP), which took over the Pentagon's program that helped local police departments train for potential terrorist attacks involving weapons of mass destruction. Perhaps realizing he had made a mistake, Witt in his final days in office pressed Reno to move the ODP to FEMA. She refused. Before leaving office in January 2001, he made several public speeches warning that trouble over the issue was brewing. At a luncheon with reporters that marked his final days in the job, Witt said he was worried that if federal law enforcement agencies stayed in the preparedness game, they were doomed to repeat the mistakes that FEMA had made in its twenty-year history. The problem, he said, is "they are trying to reinvent everything." He had no idea how right he was.

4

HOMELAND INSECURITY

On Wednesday, February 28, 2001, just before 11:00 A.M., a strong earthquake measuring 6.8 on the Richter scale jolted Seattle. The shaking lasted for almost a full minute, and tremors were felt as far away as Salt Lake City. It was so powerful that Seattle actually slid about five millimeters to the northeast. According to geologists, a temblor of that magnitude lasting for more than thirty seconds should have devastated the city. But remarkably it didn't claim any lives, and it caused only relatively minor damage. Power was knocked out for hours, trapping people in elevators including at the Space Needle, the city's landmark observation tower. A few bricks fell from buildings, some roofs collapsed, and a scattering of small fires broke out. In all, just 270 people were injured. Compared to what could have happened, it was a nothing short of a miracle.

When asked why he thought his city had fared so well, Seattle mayor Paul Schell, had two words: "Project Impact." The Project Impact disaster preparedness campaign was the FEMA grant program that James Lee Witt had started in 1997 that encouraged local communities to take steps to reduce the risk of disasters in their cities and towns. Though the national program never received more than $25 million per year from Congress, the money was said to have worked wonders. With its $1 million share, Seattle secured matching funds from local businesses and put volunteer groups to work anchoring bookcases to walls at libraries and schools and bolting television sets to shelves at local nursing homes. City officials used some of the money to improve building codes and to retrofit public buildings, schools, and critical facilities with earthquake-resistant technologies.

But on the very day the earthquake struck and Mayor Schell was singling out the program as a national treasure, the Bush administration, in its first published budget proposal, killed Project Impact. The administration offered a blunt assessment of the program in its budget statement: "Project Impact: $25 million in savings are achieved by canceling the program, which has not proved effective."

That night, Vice President Dick Cheney appeared on CNN to defend generally the proposed cuts to FEMA. "Well, I'm not aware of that particular program," Cheney said of Project Impact. "But I would venture to guess that perhaps it has not been effective in the past, and lots of programs that make lots of sense or that have nice titles to them nonetheless don't work."

It was a minor embarrassment, unlikely to derail an agenda that had been set in motion months before. President George W. Bush came into office determined to roll back taxes—it had been the signal initiative of his 2000 presidential campaign. And in vowing to cut taxes, he also promised to slash federal spending to balance everything out. FEMA, which had grown like a weed under the Clinton administration, was an easy target. In addition to cutting Project Impact, the administration proposed eliminating FEMA's popular and successful $100 million annual Fire Grant program, which subsidized firehouses around the country as well as fire prevention programs. In all, the Bush administration proposed lopping $500 million from FEMA's $2.5 billion annual budget. (Congress eventually gave in to the administration on Project Impact but rebuffed it on the fire grants.)

In the eyes of the new administration, FEMA was a spendthrift agency, a symbol of the Clinton populism it had come to Washington determined to expunge. "Too much of what the White House saw in FEMA was identified with James Lee Witt, and by extension, Bill Clinton," said Bruce Baughman.

The precedent established by Bill Clinton of putting someone with emergency management experience in charge of FEMA was also rejected by George W. Bush, who revived the practice of treating the FEMA director's job as a patronage post. He nominated his long-time political adviser Joe Allbaugh as FEMA's director, a choice that struck some political observers as surprising.

A son of an Oklahoma wheat farmer, Allbaugh had studied political science at Oklahoma State University, and had toyed with the idea of going to law school before ending up in Republican Party politics. In 1994, he moved to Texas to help George W. Bush pull off an upset in the race for governor against the popular incumbent, Anne Richards.

Bush was well known for keeping his team of top advisers tight, and Allbaugh had earned a place at the top of a very short stack. He was the third leg of Bush's "Iron Triangle," which included longtime confidants Karl Rove and Karen Hughes. When Bush decided to run for the White House, Allbaugh was his choice for campaign director. If Karl Rove was the brain behind Bush's political machine, then Allbaugh was its brawn. In many ways he was less a strategist than a political enforcer, and he certainly looked the part. At six-foot-four and 270 pounds, with a military-style crew cut and cowboy boots, Allbaugh was well suited to his nickname among the staff, "Sgt. Rock." Bush preferred to call him "Big Country," and his closeness to Allbaugh made the Oklahoman a force. His personality and position instilled a strong sense of discipline in the 2000 Bush campaign.

So when Bush arrived in Washington, it was a bit of a surprise to many that Andrew Card got the nod to be the president's chief of staff over Allbaugh. Some said it was because Allbaugh's sandpaper demeanor grated on the capital's delicate sensibilities. Allbaugh thought it was because Bush wanted a Washington insider and that he and the president had grown perhaps too close over the years.

"Hell, it got to the point that we were finishing each other's sentences and that's not necessarily a good thing," he said. "That's when mistakes happen."

When Allbaugh was presented with a list of positions open to him—including the secretary of agriculture, an appeal to his farmer roots—what caught his eye was the directorship of FEMA. James Lee Witt had turned the agency into a household name and a personal platform, and Allbaugh viewed the job as a chance to do some good while grabbing a few headlines. "One of the things about FEMA is that you're not always in the limelight," he said, "but when you are in the limelight, it's for all the marbles."

Allbaugh would have big shoes to fill. As the *National Journal* put it, Witt's turnaround of FEMA had imbued him with "enduring hero status in Washington." As many in Congress well knew, FEMA either impressed voters or enraged them but rarely sparked ambivalence when it was called to duty. At this point, FEMA was at the top of its game, and Democrats and Republicans alike believed the agency was finally working as it should. (In fact, during the 2000 presidential debates, both Al Gore and George W. Bush had bent over backward to heap praise on FEMA and Witt.) And at Allbaugh's confirmation hearing, senators were effusive in their praise of the outgoing director. "No one needs to remind you that you'll be following [the] footsteps of a big man," said Senator Daniel Akaka of Hawaii. Allbaugh agreed. Witt "did an outstanding job," he said, "and I think the country owes him a debt of gratitude for his service over the last eight years."

It was clear in the confirmation hearing that the U.S. Senate believed that Washington had finally hit on a winning formula for FEMA and believed that attention from the White House was what it needed most. Allbaugh was plugged in to the administration; he was confirmed 91–0.

Though they were both country boys, Witt and Allbaugh couldn't have been more different. Witt was a natural politician—easygoing, engaging, and agreeable. Allbaugh was brusque and brittle, even insensitive, some would say. And though Allbaugh may have indeed respected what Witt had done for FEMA, in his first months in office he began shutting down those programs he viewed as being too closely identified with the Clinton administration. Witt's FEMA, Allbaugh argued, had become a purveyor of federal patronage—a source of easy cash that had spun out of control. In truth, there were few disasters under the Clinton administration that weren't eligible for some level of federal funding, and the states used the cash to widen roads, purchase generators, or underwrite some major project outside of formal budget oversight. "I was concerned that federal disaster assistance had evolved into both an oversized entitlement program and a disincentive to effective state and local risk management," Allbaugh later explained.

He was determined to eliminate programs he thought were wasteful. Apart from Project Impact, which Allbaugh had dismissed as "more propaganda than substance," his main targets were FEMA's "post-disaster mitigation" programs. Often state emergency managers found the best time to reduce the risks of a future calamity was after one had already hit. It was almost always easier to get a home or business owner, and sometimes even a whole town, to move out of a one-hundred-year floodplain if it had recently been underwater. Under FEMA's disaster rules, the federal government reimbursed 75 percent of state emergency expenditures to reduce future risks after a disaster. This gave governors and mayors the financial muscle to buy back property from disaster victims, raise housing elevations, build floodwalls—expensive endeavors all.

Allbaugh thought the whole approach was upside down. Surely, he reasoned, it was more cost-effective to give states money up front for projects to reduce risks than to wait for trouble to happen before acting. He proposed creating a pre-disaster mitigation fund while turning the post-disaster mitigation support formula on its ear: States should only get a 25 percent reimbursement for post-disaster mitigation as a disincentive to go all-out on urban renewal in the wake of a disaster.

Emergency managers and many longtime FEMA officials who had prospered under Witt began to complain that while pre-disaster mitigation was a great idea, cutting the money available to states after a disaster actually would fuel more risk. But Allbaugh was nothing if not resolved.

Nature provided the new FEMA director with a real-life example. In April, just a month after Allbaugh's Senate confirmation, the Mississippi River overflowed its banks and flooded the town of Davenport, Iowa, for the third time in eight years. With a population of almost 100,000 people, Davenport is the largest city on the Mississippi without flood protection. Having decided it didn't care for the aesthetics of levees, the city instead compounded its exposure to disaster by turning the riverfront into a tourist attraction and developing property all the way to the river's edge. Then the flood came. Even as water slopped into city streets, Allbaugh was on television excoriating Davenport for not building levees. "How many times will the American taxpayer have to step in and take care of this flooding, which could be easily prevented by building levees and dikes?" he asked. "There is a point of no return. I don't know whether it's two strikes, you're out—three strikes, you're out. But obviously these homes and properties that are continually flooding, it is not fair to the American taxpayer to ask them time in and time out to pay for rebuilding."

Davenport's mayor, Phil Yerington, hit back, calling Allbaugh's remarks an insult to families fighting to save their homes. "Don't insult what we tried to do, and the people who we are, because we're in the Midwest and we live along a major river," Yerington said. The dispute was covered for days by television news networks. The public consensus was that Allbaugh's remarks were insensitive and that he should have waited at least until Davenport had shoveled the silt out of its streets. Even the White House, which was rarely inclined to admit mistakes, said Allbaugh was out of line. Allbaugh should have "chosen his words differently," Chief of Staff Card would later say. "The right priority is to care for the victims of the flood and try to address the immediate concern."

Allbaugh apologized, though it was clear he was hardly contrite. In future meetings, he began referring to local emergency managers as "goobers." From that day forward, Bruce Baughman said, "they were all goobers."

As the veteran FEMA staff grumbled, Allbaugh began to take aim at people who he felt were Witt loyalists. "It was like de-Stalinizing Russia," said Leo Bosner, a FEMA medical emergency response specialist and the head of the agency's union. "If anything or anybody was deemed too close to Witt, they were viewed with a certain suspicion." Indeed, by the end of 2002, twenty-two senior staffers would quit in frustration or be fired. Not everyone left, of course. Bruce Baughman, who had risen to become Witt's director of operations, and Lacy Suiter, an associate director and FEMA's de facto second-in-command, remained in senior positions largely out of a sense of duty to the agency and because their experience and seniority protected them.

But the impact of Allbaugh's management on morale was huge. Applications for FEMA jobs began tailing off. "People felt that the old days were returning," Bosner said. Adding to this sense were Allbaugh's efforts to refocus FEMA's efforts on counterterrorism. Allbaugh convinced Vice President Cheney that because many of FEMA's activities were related to terrorism response (like its role in "continuity of government" operations and its role assisting the Department of Energy in responding to accidents at nuclear power plants), the agency should be in charge of all terrorism preparedness issues, to help coordinate a common policy across the country. Cheney agreed, and in May 2001 the White House said FEMA was getting into the counterterrorism business.

In fact, under the administration's plan, terrorism prevention would be a major plank for the agency. And firemen, the likely first responders in any terrorist event, would now become the focus of FEMA's attention and financial support. Allbaugh planned to announce his vision of the future to emergency officials at the annual meeting of the National Emergency Management Association, which was being held at Big Sky, Montana, from September 8 through September 12, 2001.

On the morning of Tuesday, September 11, the day Allbaugh was slated to speak, Craig Fugate, the acting director of Florida's Division of Emergency Services, wandered down to breakfast in the lobby of the Big Sky Resort lodge where the conference was being held, taking his place directly behind the FEMA chief in the buffet line. Fugate nodded at Allbaugh but concentrated on a conversation he was having by cell phone with his deputy in Florida's emergency operations center about a storm brewing off the coast. In the middle of the conversation, while Fugate was sitting down and eating, the deputy said that something strange had just happened in New York—a plane had crashed into the north tower of the World Trade Center. "I thought it had to have been a small plane but my guy told me it was a jet," Fugate recalled. As the two men discussed the event and the pending storm, a second jet plowed into the south tower of the World Trade Center.

Allbaugh, who didn't have a cell phone, knew nothing of this. As the FEMA director walked through the lobby after breakfast, Fugate stopped him to ask if he knew what was going on in New York. Allbaugh shrugged. Fugate then told his deputy at the other end of the phone, "I'm handing you over to the director of FEMA—brief him." He then pressed the receiver into Allbaugh's hand.

Allbaugh listened, asked a few questions, and then sped to his room to call the White House. He then found his deputy, Lacy Suiter, who was at the conference with him, and told him to pack his bags because they were heading back to Washington.

By the time Allbaugh reached the airport in Big Sky, all air traffic was grounded. The FEMA director had to wait now for military transport. The first available plane was an F-16 fighter jet—too small for him and Suiter. Finally, the two hitched a ride on a KC-135 tanker plane for the four-and-a-half-hour flight back to Washington. On the way Allbaugh reached his wife, Diane, on her cell phone. She was stuck in traffic trying to pick up their daughter, Taylor, from school in Virginia. The traffic jam would last over four hours. "Our conversations were sporadic, hit and miss," Allbaugh said. In the car, Diane Allbaugh heard on the radio that their friend, the lawyer Barbara Olson, the wife of Solicitor General Theodore Olson, was believed to have been on the plane that had crashed into the Pentagon.

With Allbaugh and Suiter out of pocket, Bruce Baughman took charge at FEMA headquarters, activating the emergency operations center, dispatching disaster medical personnel, and establishing emergency communications for New York. Once the towers collapsed, Baughman called up the first of FEMA's Urban Search and Rescue teams, which specialize in making rescues from collapsed structures. Baughman knew the drill. It wasn't so different from what he had done in leading the response to the 1995 Oklahoma City bombing. Over the next days and weeks, FEMA would work with state and city officials to recover bodies, remove the debris from the fallen towers, and support operations at Ground Zero.

On October 4, Allbaugh told CNN that he believed FEMA had performed admirably following the attacks. "James Lee Witt left the agency in good shape," he said. "Unfortunately, it's now time to go the next step into the twenty-first century for all federal agencies, quite frankly, and they need to be thinking about the unthinkable."

What Allbaugh had in mind was making FEMA the nation's main counterterrorism agency. But this was not to be. Even as the ashes were still being sifted in Manhattan, a cry was going up in Washington for the creation of some sort of superagency—an umbrella department that would collect all the tools needed to fight the scourge of terrorism, including preparedness and response, and house them under a single, cabinet-level official who would report directly to the president. The Bush administration opposed the idea of expanding the federal bureaucracy and resisted it at first on philosophical grounds. But the White House soon realized that resistance was futile: Congress was determined to act. Senator Joseph Lieberman, a Democrat from Connecticut, was already crafting legislation to create a new Department of Homeland Security that was catching on in both houses of Congress. The White House realized the only way to take control of the situation was to embrace the concept.

President Bush brought in Pennsylvania governor Tom Ridge to head the Office of Homeland Security inside the White House and asked him to start thinking about how he would assemble and organize a Department of Homeland Security if he had to. In some ways Ridge was an inspired choice. As a decorated former infantry staff sergeant in Vietnam, he understood and had the respect of the military. As a former governor he had firsthand knowledge of how states worked, which was vital because any new department would have to work closely with local governments to be successful. He had also served as a congressman and had played a pivotal role in creating the Stafford Act, which governs FEMA and the federal response to disasters. He also knew the ropes in Washington and understood that government bureaucracies hated and resisted change. So the efforts to figure out how to form the department had to be conducted in secret.

Ridge worked with Chief of Staff Card to assemble a team of Bush staffers who became known as the "Gang of Five," or as they liked to call themselves, the "G-5," to address this question. Two of the G-5 worked for Ridge—Army major General Bruce Lawlor and Richard A. Falkenrath, a security expert from Harvard. The others were Card's deputy, Joel D. Kaplan, associate White House counsel Brad Berenson, and deputy budget director Mark W. Everson.

Several times a week, the five men met with top administration officials, including National Security Adviser Condoleezza Rice and Vice President Cheney's chief of staff, Lewis "Scooter" Libby. They drew diagrams and sifted through a number of alphabet soup agencies that could form the nucleus of the new department—the Federal Aviation Administration, the Drug Enforcement Administration, FEMA. They even considered throwing the National Guard into the mix. The group's boldest idea—seizing the FBI from the Department of Justice, for instance—was vetoed by the White House as being too politically explosive. But gradually, a consensus emerged: Immigration was in, as was Customs, the Coast Guard, and the Secret Service. And FEMA, they all decided, would certainly be subsumed into the new department. "If you didn't have a FEMA at Homeland Security, you'd have to create one," Ridge said. "Its mission of response and recovery is at the very core of what we do."

In June 2002, Allbaugh got a whiff of what was going on and immediately called Card. "I told him it was a big mistake," Allbaugh recalled. He told Card that FEMA's strength lay in having a clear line to the White House. "The fact that FEMA could report directly to the president, any president—Democrat or Republican or independent—was what made the agency effective," he said.

But the train had left the station. "This thing has a head of steam on it and I don't think it can be stopped," Card told Allbaugh.

"I realized then that there was no sense in resisting," Allbaugh said later. "But I kept telling them, they would regret their decision sooner rather than later."

When the G-5 had hacked out a list of agencies it planned to deposit into Homeland Security, it brought in a team of technical experts under a senior aide named Clay Johnson to sort through the details. The technical team included some people from the affected agencies. Allbaugh nominated a trusted friend, a deputy director at FEMA and a fellow Oklahoman, as his representative. His name was Michael D. Brown.

Brown, the son of a printer and a homemaker-cum-Avon saleslady, was a lawyer by training who started out his political career as an assistant to the city manager of Edmond, Oklahoma. His work, he said, often had him dealing with problems in the local police and emergency services. His coworkers and supervisors remember him being loyal, punctual, and well dressed. "He always had on a suit and a starched white shirt," said one.

Before coming to Washington to take up his post at FEMA, Brown was the commissioner of the International Arabian Horse Association, a subsidiary of the sport's governing organization, which was part of the U.S. Olympic Committee. It was a place where backstabbing, faint praise, and subterfuge were commonplace, making it, Brown liked to joke, a perfect training ground for political life in Washington.

Despite Brown's attempts to connect his background to first responders and the inner workings of the capital, the truth is that he had little experience either with disasters or with Washington. But many state emergency mangers say that what Brown lacked in know-how, he made up for in enthusiasm. He had an agile mind and was able to pick up the Byzantine workings of FEMA, almost by osmosis, it seemed. Indeed, Brown understood the department better than many people who had spent their whole careers there. He also became a passionate defender of the all-hazards approach to disaster response, which just made logical sense to him. "There is no doubt that Mike caught the disaster management bug," said Craig Fugate, from Florida.

But Brown was a complicated and divisive figure, hardly beloved by all. His fondness for using cornball phrases like "dad-gummit" contrasted with his sometimes sanctimonious nature. He could be personable and warm on a one-to-one basis and yet still come off as smug and uncaring when standing before a large group. In short, Brown could be deeply irritating, even when that wasn't his intention. Once when speaking to a group of first responders and their families in Toledo, Ohio, a woman prefaced a question to Brown by saying that she was "just a housewife." The offhand remark prompted a patronizing and tedious lecture from Brown about the virtues of stay-at-home moms. The room quickly filled with confused and shocked silence.

People either liked Mike Brown or they didn't. James Lee Witt liked him immensely, but Witt liked practically everyone. "I thought he was nice. He was always nice to me," Witt said. Bruce Baughman, who worked with Brown at FEMA, despised Brown. "He was a know-it-all smartass," Baughman said. And Baughman was hardly alone. Brown's dual nature would haunt him as he sought to lead FEMA's transition from an independent cabinet-level agency into the new Department of Homeland Security.

Allbaugh had initially tapped Brown to serve as the agency's general counsel, but as FEMA went through yet another period of downsizing, the Oklahoma lawyer began taking on management responsibility. In December 2001, when Lacy Suiter left for a teaching post at the Naval Postgraduate School in Monterey, California, Brown was selected for the deputy director's position. After a forty-five-minute Senate confirmation hearing marked by soft questions and kind words, Brown became FEMA's deputy director in August 2002.

As a detailed schematic of the Department of Homeland Security began falling into place, Brown's office on the eighth floor of FEMA headquarters became something of a hangout for those officials who were strongly opposed to the concept of a monster security department. These officials met over Diet Cokes and complained about how Tom Ridge was ruining their lives. Among the attendees at the whining sessions were Michael Jackson, the deputy secretary of transportation, and Ralph Basham, the second in charge at the Secret Service. Basham was worried that the Secret Service, one of the few law enforcement agencies to escape taint after 9/11, would be destroyed when it was wrenched from the Treasury Department and dumped into the new behemoth department. Jackson was angry that he was losing both the Coast Guard and the newly created airport screening agency, the Transportation Security Administration. For his part, Brown was wary of what was going on but hoped that as a member of the Transition Planning Office he would be able to influence the process.

The White House officials who designed the department originally envisioned a more robust FEMA leading America's efforts to prepare for and respond to terrorist attacks as well as natural disasters. Under their original plan FEMA would lose its independence but would inherit the FBI's National Domestic Preparedness Office, as well as the National Disaster Medical System, with its teams of physicians around the country ready to respond to any emergency and the national drug stockpile from the Department of Health and Human Services. FEMA was also supposed to assume control of the Justice Department's Office of Domestic Preparedness (ODP), which distributed antiterrorism grants to police agencies. But the ODP and its patrons on Capitol Hill, who had never forgotten that Witt had originally turned down the program in 1997, blocked the Bush administration's effort to meld it into FEMA. At the same time, the FBI stripped most of the National Domestic Preparedness Office staff before sending it over to FEMA, and after an emotional appeal by Tommy G. Thompson, the secretary of health and human services, Ridge agreed to keep the drug stockpile where it was.

So Brown, who had thought he was drawing up plans for an enhanced FEMA as a central hub of the nation's homeland security efforts, suddenly discovered that FEMA would lose programs under the new configuration and drop a rung in stature. In fact, it wouldn't even be called FEMA anymore. Instead Ridge let it be known that the agency would be called the Directorate of Emergency Preparedness and Response. Brown thought that if FEMA lost its "brand," it would lose whatever influence it still had.

Brown insisted that FEMA at least be allowed to retain its name, taking his fight to his friends in the White House, behind Ridge's back. Ridge and his aides, eager to create a unified brand for the new department that would signify the integration, saw Brown's resistance to a name change as part of a larger campaign of resistance against being absorbed into the Department of Homeland Security. "He fought being part of DHS from Day One," another top Homeland Security official recalled. Brown prevailed on the name—even Ridge admitted that "FEMA" sounded better than "EP&R." But this would hardly be the last time the two men butted heads over policy matters both minute and profound.

In November 2002, the Senate, as predicted, passed the Homeland Security Act, amalgamating twenty-two agencies in whole or in part, from the Coast Guard to the Customs Service to the Secret Service to FEMA, creating a 180,000-employee behemoth that represented the largest reorganization of government bureaucracy since the formation of the Department of Defense in the 1940s.

Soon after, President Bush nominated Ridge to run the massive department, and almost simultaneously Allbaugh said he would be leaving as FEMA's director. Allbaugh had never made any bones about his resistance to the creation of Homeland Security in the first place. He said the White House had offered him a job as Ridge's deputy but he had declined it. "I didn't want a role if I wasn't running the things and to be honest it wouldn't have been fair to Tom if the deputy had a closer relationship with the president than he did," Allbaugh said. "I decided it was better if I stepped aside."

When Allbaugh departed, Brown took over as acting director of

FEMA, and under the plans drawn up by Congress automatically became Homeland Security's undersecretary for emergency preparedness and response. Working with Brown wasn't something Ridge relished. "I didn't like him," Ridge said bluntly. "I don't know what his problem was, but I felt that he wanted to be the guy in charge."

Tensions between the two men grew worse when Brown sent a memo to Ridge in early 2003 urging him to defy Congress and move the ODP into FEMA. Brown saw this as key to FEMA's success: The nation's disaster planning should be joined at the hip with its response apparatus. Moreover, Brown thought that if the ODP controlled terrorism grants, which after 9/11 had grown into the billions of dollars (compared to the few hundred million on offer for natural disasters), it risked skewing the way states prepared for all-hazards management. Keeping the ODP separate would also widen a divide between police and other emergency responder disciplines. Already there were struggles in cities like New York between firefighters and police over who would control the money to respond to chemical incidents. Traditionally, firefighters were in charge of responding to hazardous material incidents, but as the issue became more closely linked to terrorism and involved vast sums of cash, the police saw it as something they should control. The tensions even spilled over into fistfights between cops and firemen during terrorism exercises.

The dispute over the ODP represented a wider philosophical battle that was raging at the heart of the new department. On one side were former law enforcement officials who advocated secrecy, tight security, and intelligence as the key to minimizing the trauma of any terrorist attack. On the other side were firefighters, rescue workers, and emergency managers who emphasized collaboration, information sharing, public awareness, and mitigation efforts to reduce the impact of all disasters, whatever their origin.

Ridge rejected Brown's arguments out of hand.

On February 28, 2003, the day before the Department of Homeland Security opened its doors, President Bush ordered it to take all the various plans that existed in the federal government for dealing with terrorist events, nuclear accidents, oil spills, and natural disasters and create a "unified, all-discipline, and all-hazards approach to do-mestic incident management." The country's existing blueprint for coordinating disaster response across the federal government was a document known as the Federal Response Plan. Although it had been used with great success during the days of James Lee Witt, the Bush administration now viewed it as too oriented toward acts of nature. For example, it didn't have a role for the FBI, which would have to be a key player in the next terror attack. What President Bush and Secre-tary Ridge wanted was a bold new approach for a frightening new world, which would put the Department of Homeland Security at the helm but drew on the experience and resources of the entire federal government.

Within days of receiving the president's directive, Ridge com-menced work on a new National Response Plan, or NRP. But instead of assigning the task to FEMA, which had actually started to draw up ideas, he contracted the job to the RAND Corporation. This was an odd choice. Considered one of the foremost think tanks in the coun-try, RAND had more experience in military affairs than emergency management. Tensions soon broke out between the RAND project directors and FEMA's staff, and FEMA essentially dropped out of the project. In May 2003, Homeland Security sent the first draft of the report to governors, emergency managers, fire chiefs, and others for their comments. The reaction was outrage. State officials said not only was the NRP difficult to follow but it turned emergency man-agement on its head by ignoring the role local responders play and putting the federal government in charge of everything. The project was sent back to the drawing board. Again Ridge bypassed FEMA, giving the job of fixing the NRP to his aide Robert Stephan, a retired Air Force colonel.

Some fifteen months and several drafts later, a new version was sent out to the states. The result was similar: Few liked it. It was 426 pages long, consisting of a base plan plus thirty-one annexes describ-ing incident-specific responses. It was complex and bureaucratic and practically unintelligible in spots. It introduced new positions with fancy titles like "principal federal official" whose responsibility and authority were unclear at best. It drew fuzzy distinctions between natural disasters, now called "incidents of national significance," and catastrophes, which everybody took to mean a terrorist nuclear strike. It put the secretary of homeland security in charge during an event but gave much of the day-to-day responsibilities of dealing with response and recovery to FEMA, which had to report back to the secretary through the Homeland Security Operations Center, a high-tech information clearinghouse. Brown never bought into the concept and said it would slow response time and sow confusion with its multiple chains of command and overabundance of decision makers. He was never able to galvanize any support among the states, though, to push back. The states didn't like the revised NRP but saw the latest version of the plan as an acceptable compromise that at least recognized that disasters are best managed at the local level. In January 2005 the department rolled out its new National Response Plan to great fanfare as the centerpiece of its efforts to protect the American people.

In the wake of the frustrating NRP process, local disaster managers complained that the Department of Homeland Security was becoming too obsessed with terrorism, to the exclusion of natural disasters. They complained that applications for grants were being kicked back if they didn't contain an antiterrorism component. In New Orleans, for example, the department rejected a proposal to outfit the police and fire departments with a fleet of aluminum flatboats under the Urban Area Security Initiative, because it didn't include an element to combat chemical or biological threats. And in Shelby County, Alabama, which is often visited by killer tornados, officials received $250,000 for chemical warfare suits but were unable to get funding for an emergency operations center that could link computers, phones, and televisions to better respond to tornadoes. "I really don't think Osama bin Laden wants to attack Shelby County," said Don Greene, the local emergency manager. Meanwhile, incidents of waste under these programs abounded and became a running joke in disaster circles. The city of Newark, New Jersey, bought air-conditioned garbage trucks with a Homeland

Security grant, while in Ohio, firemen used taxpayer money to buy bulletproof vests for their dogs.

Funding was also an issue for FEMA. When Congress created the Department of Homeland Security, it empowered the secretary to move money around the department as he saw fit, without congressional approval or authorization. Congress believed the secretary of homeland security should have maximum flexibility to shift money between agencies inside the department in order to meet an ever-changing terrorist threat. Tom Ridge thus had the power to comb through the budget of each agency, to kill off programs he thought dubious, or to move money from redundant projects. He could then use those funds for any of the department's needs, from unifying dozens of disparate computer and payroll systems, to merging office space around the country, buying new uniforms, or repainting Coast Guard boats.

The semiannual departmental shakedown became known inside the department as "Homeland taxes," and like taxes in real life their assessments sometimes seemed arbitrary and were a perennial cause for complaint. As one of the smallest agencies in Homeland Security, FEMA felt the squeeze more than most, and was dunned for as much as $80 million a year. For an agency with only a $550 million operating budget on average, the loss was huge. "For us it wasn't fat they took off of us, it was muscle. They were cuts to the bone," Brown said. But his complaints were ignored. "They told me everybody feels the pain. Now get on with your job."

The extent to which the department saw FEMA as a piggy bank that could be used to bankroll other endeavors became apparent when the Department of Homeland Security sequestered $10 million in 2003 from FEMA's $20 million annual Flood Mitigation Assistance Fund. Homeland Security poured the money into what it considered vital work, embarking on a branding initiative that Ridge said would mark a "new recognizable and distinct Homeland Security culture." In its first year, some money for this branding initiative went toward the purchase of gift bags, pins, pens, and refrigerator magnets emblazoned with the department's coat of arms. But the flood mitigation money wasn't really Ridge's to take: It was made up of premiums that property owners had paid to maintain federally backed flood insurance, and the proceeds were earmarked to pay for mitigation projects. State officials howled when they applied for grants, only to discover the money wasn't there. Homeland Security promised to pay the money back eventually, but several states like Iowa weren't able to move ahead with their mitigation plans that year.

Homeland Security often didn't consult FEMA when it raided the agency's accounts or formulated new plans. Ellen Gordon, a veteran emergency manager in Iowa, was engaged in a big fight with Homeland Security officials who demanded she employ a new "buffer zone" security plan around some petrochemical plants in her state that could be seen as "soft targets" for terrorists. The problem was some of the plants were built in a flood plain, and Gordon believed Mother Nature was a far more likely threat to the plants than terrorists. But the plan being forced upon her would have made it difficult, if not impossible, for rescuers to reach the plant and shut it down in the event of a flood. Exasperated, Gordon asked FEMA how it could allow Homeland Security to dictate the plan. "But when I gave the security plan to FEMA they had never seen it before," Gordon said. "They wanted to know where I got it. They were not even consulted."

Brown complained to Ridge that such actions undermined the nation's emergency preparedness. Planning, preparedness, and response efforts had to be united, he said. FEMA needed to run the whole show, so states would have a one-stop shop to deal with grants. Therefore, Brown said, FEMA needed to control the ODP.

Brown was backed by the majority of emergency management experts around the country. But the more Brown complained, the angrier Ridge became. Finally, in September 2003 Ridge shot back. Using Brown's own arguments about the need to consolidate preparedness grants, Ridge took FEMA's preparedness grants and put them under the ODP. Brown had his one-stop shop. He just didn't control it. With one blow, virtually all of FEMA's grant programs were taken away, leaving Brown with less influence than ever. During a visit to Ohio soon afterward, Brown felt the sting of his waning influence when state officials spurned the agency director to spend time with Suzanne Mencer, the head of the ODP, who was in the state at the same time. "She has the money," a state spokesman explained.

Though the steady erosion of authority was taking its toll on the agency, FEMA's emasculation wasn't readily apparent. Brown was scrupulously loyal to the Bush administration, and with a presidential election season approaching, he kept his own counsel. The 2004 hurricane season, though very active, spared FEMA a real test. Four major hurricanes made landfall that summer in quick succession, but they hit the one state, Florida, where even FEMA would be hard-pressed to fail.

As disaster experts like to say, FEMA didn't rescue Florida, Florida rescued FEMA. Of all the southern states vulnerable to hurricane strikes, Florida was the best prepared. Thanks in part to the debacle following Hurricane Andrew in 1992, the state had gotten serious about preparedness. It had one of the most professional disaster preparedness regimes in the country, led by the widely respected Craig Fugate, who was promoted to director of the Division of Emergency Services in November 2001. But even more conducive to success was the state's political alignment. Florida's governor, Jeb Bush, was the president's brother. His state, rich with twenty-seven electoral votes, was key to George W. Bush's reelection. And both men were keenly aware of the humiliating reelection loss their father had suffered in the wake of the poor federal response to Hurricane Andrew. As four hurricanes plowed through Florida in advance of the 2004 election, including a Category 4 monster called Charley, Washington pulled out all the stops to ensure that the state—and its voters—got everything they needed. FEMA moved down unprecedented amounts of food, water, and ice. Emergency medical teams were on hand to help out local hospitals. FEMA pushed in trailers at a breakneck speed to provide temporary housing to people who lost their homes.

As the storms hit, Brown used the political urgency to his advantage. He fought for and won the right to deal directly with the White House through Chief of Staff Card, without any interference from Ridge. And by most accounts, FEMA did well. Bush won reelection, taking Florida handily. Brown boasted that he had saved the presidency. And he considered leaving the agency on a high note. "I should have got out then," he would later say.

But despite the success in Florida, Brown's high-handed management style was creating internal problems at FEMA. In September, Brown met with his top disaster operations experts, the federal coordinating officers, or FCOs, who had been moaning for months about their dissatisfaction with the agency's management. The FCOs presented him with a paper drafted by Bill Carwile, a former Army colonel and emergency manager from California, which outlined nineteen problem areas that they felt Brown needed to address. "As you sensed, all is not well in Denmark," the paper began. The FCOs demanded that Brown take a more engaged role in day-to-day matters inside FEMA and pay attention to internal problems like the fact that its National Emergency Response Teams, which were Brown's best tool to handle a catastrophic disaster, were incapable of responding because they were untrained and underfunded. Brown promised to address the problems, but the more he sought resources from Homeland Security the more he ended up back in arguments with his superiors.

By October, Brown had chosen to act as if the larger department didn't even exist. He refused to have anything to do with helping the department plan the upcoming $16 million TOPOFF3 terrorism response exercises, scheduled for April 2005, often ignoring memos from the department begging for his input. Eventually the inspector general had to broker a deal for his participation.

Shortly after President Bush won reelection in November 2004, Tom Ridge resigned. In the ensuing shuffle, Brown was touted as a possible chief deputy to the incoming secretary. But it was not to be. First came the abortive nomination of former New York City police commissioner Bernard Kerik to replace Ridge, which imploded amid indications that Kerik had not been completely forthcoming about his past, and then came the nomination of Michael Chertoff, a federal judge and former Justice Department official. Chertoff thought the department was dysfunctional and identified as his top priority (and biggest challenge) the knitting of its many fiefs into a cohesive whole. The White House installed Michael Jackson, Brown's old friend from the Department of Transportation, as Chertoff 's deputy. Brown got nothing.

FEMA's image took some tarnish when Homeland Security's inspector general issued a review of its activities during the 2004 Florida hurricanes. The report said that FEMA's computer systems couldn't track the personnel, equipment, and commodities it had sent into the disaster zone. FEMA had no way to check whether resources ever arrived on the scene, the inspector general said; in many cases, the supplies never made it to their final destination. Brown disputed the findings, insisting that the agency's systems were "highly performing."

With a new secretary of homeland security in place, Brown made yet another pitch to expand FEMA's role and to take control of the ODP and its grant programs. Chertoff listened but later said he never had any intention of giving Brown more authority in the department. Instead, he reduced Brown's authority even further, stripping away the last small grant programs from FEMA and awarding them to the ODP. He then admonished Brown to concentrate on relief and recovery.

Instead of energizing FEMA, Chertoff pulled it apart. Where James Lee Witt's FEMA had included branches dealing with all aspects of managing disasters, Homeland Security viewed FEMA as if it were a federal firehouse, where employees flipped burgers until the alarm bell rang. But that's never what FEMA was intended to be. It was a coordinating agency, not a fire company.

On July 27, 2005, Dave Liebersbach, the head of the National Emergency Management Association, an organization of state and local emergency managers, warned in a letter to Congress that Chertoff 's disassembly of FEMA was a disaster in the making. "The proposed reorganization increases the separation between prepared-ness, response and recovery functions," Liebersbach said. "Any unnec-essary separation of these functions will result in disjointed response and adversely impact the effectiveness of departmental operations."

Three weeks later, Liebersbach led a delegation from his organi-zation, including Bruce Baughman (who had left FEMA in 2002 to head Alabama's emergency management office), to see Michael Jack-son, the deputy secretary, and his top aides. "We told them straight out that they were weakening emergency management with poten-tially disastrous consequences," said Liebersbach.

Jackson had heard the argument before. After losing his bid to re-vive FEMA, Brown dashed off an angry note to Jackson. "In this new era of heightened security, we have created an ever evolving depart-ment and sometimes emergency preparedness is inadvertently con-sidered the same as other DHS functions such as law enforcement duties at airports, interception of illegal aliens and inspection of cargo at ports of entry," Brown wrote. "Those are true law enforcement du-ties inherent to the DHS mission. For these organizations, their pre-paredness mission is focused on prevention of incidents, not response to disasters. Emergency Preparedness means the capability to respond to a disaster, regardless of what causes that disaster."

Brown went on: "FEMA is a very small part of DHS in terms of budget, personnel and other resources. Merging FEMA's small pre-paredness functions with the prevention mission of the department will destroy the emergency management cycle and lead to failure. I don't want to see us fail this President or the nation because of a de-sire to consolidate that which shouldn't be consolidated."

Brown often said that from a response perspective what caused a building to catch fire was far less important than the fact that it was burning. "If 9/11 was the result of an accident instead of a terrorist attack the firefighters, paramedics and ambulance drivers that ar-rived that day would have responded exactly the same way that they did. But there is now this notion that terrorism is different and more important than other disasters," Brown told the *Wall Street Journal* in 2004.

In the Department of Homeland Security, few agreed with this assessment. Instead, Brown's argument was dismissed as just another attempt to avoid integrating FEMA into the new structure. "Undersecretary Brown didn't think he worked for the department," said Matthew Broderick, who ran the Homeland Security Operations Center.

"Mike was often his own worst enemy," said Bill Carwile, a former FEMA employee who worked closely with Brown. "He was smart and he was often right but he always undermined himself with this bizarre mix of insecurity and arrogance. He never cultivated any friends in the department or anywhere in Washington for that matter that I could see who were willing to go to bat for him. And the sad truth is FEMA suffered for it. FEMA suffered because people were making stupid decisions and Brown could not stop them."

From where Brown stood, FEMA was like an iceberg drifting inexorably toward the equator. Some days he would awaken to find that entire programs in his agency had summarily disappeared overnight, transferred to his rivals at the ODP or sometimes simply shuttered. This is what happened to a raft of popular emergency response programs that trained local citizens in basic firefighting, search and rescue: They all disappeared and resurfaced in the ODP, given a spot of counterterrorism varnish and renamed Citizen Corps.

Brown had plenty of opportunities to blow the whistle, to alert the nation, to take a public stand. He let these opportunities pass. Brown got a chance to tell all in April 2004, as the keynote speaker for the National Hurricane Conference in Orlando, Florida. As he stood before hundreds of the nation's disaster planners and consulted his White House–approved remarks, Brown said he knew he was about to tell lies. "Should I or shouldn't I?" he said he asked himself as he stood at the podium.

In the end, loyalty trumped honesty. "I'm not going to give you lip service about the merger of FEMA and DHS," Brown told the assembled crowd. "I'm going to give you real life examples . . . why we're stronger."

Brown wound up his speech and paused. "I think I should introduce the next speaker," he said. "And I want you all to listen really carefully to what he has to say, because he can say things that I can't."

The next speaker was James Lee Witt.

Witt laid it on thick. He blasted the Bush administration for merging FEMA with the Department of Homeland Security—and for the other changes that had come to the agency since he had left. "I am extremely concerned that the ability of our nation to prepare for and respond to disasters has been sharply eroded," he said.

Witt drew a standing ovation. As Brown stood and clapped, he leaned over to an aide and spoke through a frozen smile. "I guess I should start looking for a new job," he said. For better or worse, he had become the public face of an agency that was in a steep and obvious death spin.

Brown often pondered resignation, and in March 2005, while planning his departure, he scraped together $500,000 and contracted the Mitre Corporation, a special consulting firm that only works for government agencies, to study FEMA, identify its flaws, and chart a way forward for the troubled agency.

Mitre's report was unflinching, laying bare a broken agency, which it said lacked leadership, a properly sized staff, and a sufficient budget. Mitre concluded that FEMA was incapable of carrying out its core mission, in part because it operated blindly, unable to develop a clear picture of disasters as they unfolded and incapable of moving information from the ground up. The report noted that FEMA had no ability to track supplies once they left government warehouses and no ability to tell whether they were ever distributed. One unnamed employee interviewed for the Mitre report fretted about holes in the antiquated tracking system, noting: "White House is asking, 'Where are the water trucks?' I didn't know. . . . We don't have confidence that the trucks have checked in, arrived at the destination."

Mitre also criticized Brown, saying the agency chief "wasted too much time" fighting his superiors at the Department of Homeland Security, which had cost him influence and crippled the agency. Instead of complaining about the National Response Plan, which was clearly going to be adopted, Brown should have taken control of it. "Senior management has to lead [and] provide guidance, give orders, follow through and hold people accountable," the report said. In short, Brown was part of the problem, and he should either change his management style or move on.

Part Two

CATASTROPHE

5

THE BIG ONE

Hurricane Katrina was born in typical fashion, as a wisp of wind somewhere over the Ethiopian highlands in early August 2005. As the scrap of weather drifted westward, it picked up a bit of steam and a bit of rain until it hit the Atlantic Ocean. It caught Max Mayfield's attention on Thursday, August 11.

As the director of the National Hurricane Center in Miami, Mayfield had seen such weather patterns hundreds of times before. Few amount to anything, and this dot of low pressure wasn't remarkable in the least. But two days later, the little disturbance combined with the remnants of Tropical Depression No. 10, gained some heft, and was named Tropical Depression No. 12. And then it started to move.

Over the ensuing days, the depression chugged northwest and got bigger in the late summer heat. And as it approached the Bahamas from the south at 11:00 A.M. Eastern time on Wednesday, August 24, it got a name: Tropical Storm Katrina, the eleventh named storm of what was shaping up to be an unusually active hurricane season. Six hours later, the National Hurricane Center in Miami issued its first advisory for the east coast of Florida.

Call it a hunch, but two hours after that, Mayfield went home, toted his lawn furniture to the garage, and rolled down the steel shutters on his windows. He packed his shaving gear and some fresh clothes. It looked like he'd be sleeping on his office couch for a while.

The business of predicting hurricanes is as much art as it is science. Better and faster computers, improved simulation programs, high-tech ocean buoys, and a fleet of hurricane-hunting aircraft (capable of flying into storms to measure wind speed, temperature, and humidity) have made it easier to predict where a hurricane is going. But all this advanced technology belies the fact that storms are mysterious, capricious phenomena; they weaken when scientists think they'll strengthen, or veer off to hit Biloxi when forecasters think they'll strike Brownsville. Predicting storm tracks is a mug's game. "We've learned to expect surprises," Mayfield said. "No one can tell you with any certainty where a hurricane will make landfall."

Much of Mayfield's life has revolved around weather; even his wife is the daughter of a National Weather Service forecaster. Growing up in Oklahoma City, tornado warnings were part of his childhood. So was hunkering in a closet with his family waiting for the twisters to pass. Mayfield graduated from the University of Oklahoma in 1970 and joined the U.S. Air Force, where his bad eyesight kept him grounded, so he became a meteorologist. In 1972, he joined the National Hurricane Center. Back then, the center was all grease pencils and chattering teletype machines. Forecasters rode on a sort of feel that was rooted in prior observation and years of experience.

Mayfield had a knack for calling storms. But more important to his bosses was his talent for converting complex forecasts into calm prose. Mayfield could persuade people in a hurricane's path to board up their windows and get in their cars. He just seemed to know what he was talking about, and he seemed really to care. It may have been his folksy manner or his giant grandpa glasses or the calm, direct way he had of looking into the camera. Reporters loved him. Viewers trusted him. In the opinion of many people, he was the Walter Cronkite of weather and one of the best hurricane directors of all time.

And yet Mayfield became a controversial figure when he was

named the National Hurricane Center's seventh director in 2000 and the first one to lack a doctorate degree in meteorology. His lack of formal training caused a stir in forecasting circles, especially among purists, who thought the national hurricane director ought to be a top scholar in the field. Mayfield didn't really care what such people thought; he didn't share their philosophy. The most important thing, he believed, was getting people to move to high ground. Spinning symbols on maps didn't get people moving; persuasive talk did. A perfect forecast was nothing, Mayfield reckoned, if people died in the storm. "The whole point is to change outcomes," he said. He used his position like a pulpit. The gospel was evacuation.

On Thursday, August 25, Tropical Storm Katrina passed the Bahamas packing 50-mile-per-hour winds. Fourteen hours later, its winds hit 75 miles per hour, making Katrina a small Category 1 hurricane, bearing down on South Florida. As the storm churned toward Miami, Mayfield went into high gear, warning people to "sit up and take notice." The local citizenry, conditioned to evacuate, did so. When the small and decisive storm made landfall just before sunset on Thursday, most residents were not there to see it.

For such a small storm, Katrina packed a surprising punch. Making landfall just north of Miami, Katrina knocked down a lot of trees, two of which fell on top of people, killing them outright. On its eight-hour sojourn across South Florida, Katrina killed six people, knocked out power to the entire region, and soaked everything in thirteen inches of driving rain. And when the storm hit the warm waters of the Gulf of Mexico, it started to grow.

The Hurricane Center predicted the storm would stay in the Gulf for a few days and then make landfall somewhere along the Florida Panhandle. That day, Mayfield ordered hurricane-hunting airplane flights into the storm to look at the eyewall and measure the wind speed. They came back with news that Katrina was now a Category 2 storm, with 100-mile-per-hour winds. It was expected to strengthen. On a noon teleconference with FEMA officials and emergency managers from Florida, Alabama, and Georgia, Mayfield warned people not to believe the National Weather Service's projections of storm strength. "Right now, we're forecasting it to be a strong Category 3 hurricane," Mayfield said on the videoconference. "It's going to be stronger than that."

And though it didn't appear in public reports, Mayfield added that he had seen a storm track model from the U.S. Navy, which ran counter to what the National Weather Service was saying about Katrina's likely direction. The National Weather Service was predicting that the storm was most likely to make landfall in Apalachicola, Florida; the Navy forecast model predicted New Orleans, three hundred miles to the west. And just a few minutes later, evidence came in that seemed to support the Navy's model. The National Hurricane Center's Bill Reed broke in on the videoconference to say that the National Weather Service's Global Forecast System was now predicting that Katrina "has definitely shifted well to the west."

"So I just want to make the point here that we've really got to pay attention all the way from Louisiana over into the Florida Gulf Coast," Reed said.

But Louisiana was not on the list of states likely to be affected by Katrina, and its officials weren't even participating in the videoconference. Even so, the state of Louisiana activated its emergency operations center in Baton Rouge, and Governor Kathleen Blanco put the National Guard on alert. Oil rigs offshore began to evacuate.

But by late afternoon on Friday, August 26, Hurricane Center forecasters began predicting that Katrina would hit west of where they had originally thought, perhaps near Gulfport, Mississippi, about one hundred miles from New Orleans. Blanco canceled a trip she had planned for Saturday, even though the Hurricane Center forecast no more than a 17 percent probability that the storm would hit anywhere within the state.

Though the storm didn't appear to be bearing down on New Orleans, Max Mayfield had a feeling about this particular tempest. He called an old friend in Jefferson Parish, just to the west of New Orleans, emergency management director Walter Maestri. "And it was a phone call that, truthfully, changed my life," Maestri said. The call wasn't based on science; it was based on gut. "He told me that he was now convinced that the storm was coming to New Orleans, that it would make landfall, in his opinion as a Category 4 or 5 storm, and that it was, in his words, 'the Big One.' "

On Friday afternoon, FEMA supervisor Leo Bosner was enjoying his day off, shopping with his wife on Dupont Circle in downtown Washington, when his pager sounded, calling him to report to FEMA headquarters for an emergency night shift. A few hours later, Bosner stepped off the elevator onto the second floor of FEMA's National Response Coordination Center and walked straight into Hurricane Katrina.

Gray-haired, bearded, and lanky, with a long, thin face and a warm gaze behind horn-rimmed glasses, Leo Bosner looks more like a college professor than a career first responder, let alone a decorated Vietnam veteran. But Bosner has been with FEMA since the agency began in 1979, starting out in flood-mitigation programs and later working to coordinate emergency medical response issues.

In November 2004, Bosner was promoted to watch officer at FEMA headquarters, where his job was to monitor and analyze potential disasters around the country and collect and coordinate reports from the agency's ten regional offices, as well as information coming out of the state capitals. At the end of his overnight shift, Bosner's staff of six analysts boiled down all the information they had gathered into what is called the National Situation Update, which gets distributed to all employees in the Department of Homeland Security at 5:30 A.M. each day.

Bosner's reports offer a national snapshot of trouble in the making. They cover weather developments, seismic activity, and man-made disasters, such as tanker accidents and train derailments.

When Bosner arrived at FEMA that Friday, he immediately turned to the latest on Katrina. The storm worried him. "Any storm above a Category 2 hurricane heading to New Orleans was something that needed to be treated with extra care," he said. "It's the potential nightmare scenario." Bosner and his staff began compiling as much information as they could about the storm. Was there an evacuation?

What was the worst-case scenario? Bosner looked at FEMA capacity and historical precedents. He didn't like the odds for New Orleans.

Bosner and his team worked through the night. They had done the same just six weeks before, when Hurricane Dennis menaced the Crescent City. Dennis was a Category 4 storm that set on a direct path to New Orleans but then took a sharp turn east. "We all remembered the newspaper reports from just a month before saying how New Orleans had dodged another bullet," Bosner recalled. "We were talking about the possibility of people being stuck on rooftops and the need for body bags just six weeks before."

At 5:30 on Saturday morning, August 27, Bosner's report went out by e-mail to the top officials at Homeland Security and FEMA and by a Web site posting to the rest of the department. Accompanying the report were maps and charts, predictions, historical context, and newspaper clips. The report went to Secretary Chertoff's staff. (Chertoff doesn't like or use e-mail, preferring his staff to hand deliver reports to him.) It went to the Homeland Security Operations Center (HSOC) and its supervisor, Matthew Broderick. It went to Michael Brown. It warned in bold type that Katrina was a Category 3 storm, growing in strength and heading for the northern Gulf Coast. "New Orleans is of particular concern because much of that city lies below sea level," Bosner's report said. "If hurricane winds blow from a certain direction, there are dire predictions of what may happen in the city."

Bosner's report concluded with a historical reminder. "The last time a hurricane of this magnitude hit Mississippi and Louisiana, 143 people died." The hurricane in question was Camille, which only grazed New Orleans in 1969 but absolutely demolished the Mississippi Gulf Coast.

Bosner felt he had done his job. "We put in there pretty clearly that this was an extremely serious situation," he said. "We used big bold black type. We said there's a storm going toward New Orleans that's strong and getting stronger. We said there were resources being mobilized but not enough for that kind of storm. And we sent the report to top officials that this was a very serious situation."

After filing his report, Bosner went home to sleep. Though it was morning, he drank a beer and ate a bagel before turning in. He expected that when he returned, FEMA headquarters would be a madhouse. There aren't many disaster scenarios worse than a major hurricane plowing into a major city that sits on the coast, below sea level, next to a large, shallow lake.

At 9:00 A.M., FEMA senior staff presented a five-page Power-Point briefing to agency and Homeland Security officials that outlined a catastrophic scenario for New Orleans as a result of Hurricane Katrina. The briefing was ripped straight from the Hurricane Pam exercise book. The presentation warned that the storm surge could overtop the city's flood protection barriers, that it could kill 60,000 people, and that it could leave tens of thousands more stranded and needing rescue. Secretary Chertoff would later tell congressional investigators that he didn't attend the briefing and that he couldn't recall whether the presentation had been forwarded to him. Chertoff said he remained at his Maryland home on Saturday, "working on immigration matters, which is obviously another part of my portfolio." His chief of staff, John Wood, would recall that in the run-up to the storm, his boss didn't issue any memos, specific orders, and "things like that" as the killer storm menaced the northern Gulf Coast.

While Chertoff labored over immigration policy and Bosner slept, Michael Brown spent Saturday in his office, working on hurricane preparations. He appeared on the daily videoconference at noon Eastern time, making comments that seemed aimed more at bucking up the low morale of his agency than passing on information to the staff. "I know I'm preaching to the choir on this one but I've learned over the past four and a half, five years to go with my gut on a lot of things," Brown said by way of preamble. "And I've got to tell you, my gut hurts on this one. It hurts. I've got cramps. So we need to take this one very, very seriously."

Brown continued, delivering a long soliloquy that seemed to sum up FEMA's travails in a nutshell. "I want you guys to lean forward as much as possible," he said. "This is our chance to really show what we can do based on the catastrophic planning that we've done, based on the teamwork that we've developed around here. This is our chance to really shine. And I know you can do it and I know it's been stressful the past couple of years with everything else. But there's no question in my mind we can do it." Brown urged his staff to "lean forward and get right to the edge of the envelope" to get things done. "You're not going to catch any flak from me," he said.

And then Brown introduced another participant at the videoconference, Joe Hagin, the White House deputy chief of staff, who was with President Bush during a month-long vacation at his Texas ranch. Andrew Card, Hagin's boss, was in Maine on his own vacation. "Coming to you from Crawford, Texas," Hagin said. "We're here. But it sounds like the planning, as usual, is in good shape."

Neither Brown nor Hagin asked any questions. The call broke up shortly after that. White House counselor Dan Bartlett, who was also with Bush in Crawford, later said Brown was at his most frantic on Saturday afternoon, eaten up with concern that the city of New Orleans wouldn't evacuate in time.

In the afternoon, Brown had an argument on the telephone with Bruce Baughman, the longtime FEMA man who was now the state emergency management director in Alabama, over the lack of ice deliveries to his state. Baughman had faced the same problem weeks earlier during Dennis and wrote it off as just a glitch. But here was a big storm, and again FEMA's logistics were falling down. "Where's my goddam ice?" Baughman demanded of Brown. "What happened? Why can't you ever get me ice?" Brown blamed the problem on the contractors FEMA used to deliver commodities like water and ice before a storm. Baughman, in turn, blamed Brown for refusing to take responsibility, saying he was not waiting for FEMA any longer; he was going out to buy his own ice before the storm struck. Then he abruptly hung up the phone.

That day in Washington, FEMA deputy director Patrick Rhode had served as moderator for the videoconference. He scrambled to scare up a few copies of the Hurricane Pam drill—a plan the agency had paid for but apparently had essentially ignored. All day long,

FEMA officials sent e-mail messages back and forth as they attempted to track down the massive report and its various annexes. By midafternoon, FEMA officials managed to dig up a single copy, which they feverishly duplicated and distributed. The task wouldn't be completed until evening. By then, Katrina was a full-blown Category 3 storm, and the likelihood that it would hit New Orleans was increasing by the hour.

On the ground, advance teams of FEMA coordinators were moving supplies of food and medicine into staging areas in a rough semicircle around the likely impact area. Some of these staging areas, such as Jacksonville, Florida, and Denton, Texas, were a good ten-hour drive from New Orleans. FEMA also moved to cancel employee leave and readied its local contact lists. It pre-staged the usual amount of supplies in Louisiana, but there was a desultory nature to the preparations—if this was the "Big One," as many feared, FEMA seemed to be treating it as a garden-variety hurricane. There was no frantic activity or doubling of pre-positioned assets. When Bosner returned to FEMA headquarters on Saturday evening, he was struck by the ordinary way people were acting, as if Katrina were just another storm. "The sounds of routine" is the way he described the noise level as he stepped off the elevator onto the second-floor emergency operations center in Washington.

Bosner said the lack of activity was disappointing, not only to him but also to others on his staff. "When we all came back in on Saturday night we began to follow these different briefings and the stuff coming in saying what FEMA was doing," he said. "And sometime around midnight in one of the briefings we were having with a section chief we were looking at all the activity going on in the federal government, and all of a sudden there was this silence. Finally one of the senior guys asked, 'Is that all? Is that all there is? Excuse me, why aren't they treating this like a real emergency?' "

Bosner was astonished. A massive hurricane hitting New Orleans had made the list of the fifteen worst disasters that planners could conceive, up there with a nuclear bomb and a coordinated biological scare. "They were doing the 'we'll get ready part,' I'll give them credit for that," Bosner said. "But they weren't doing the decisive actions for the Big One. They weren't ordering buses for evacuations. They weren't throwing government agencies into the fray as FEMA has the power to do. That was never done. When they say we're getting ready, we had people on standby, that's true. But we do that for any hurricane. It's a difference between saying, 'Hey, I think I just saw some guy cut through my yard at night,' versus 'There is an angry mob of a hundred people with torches heading for my house.' There are two different levels of response called for here."

Bosner wanted to see more. He especially wanted to see some attempt to organize a bus evacuation of New Orleans, but that, apparently, was not even being considered. "Under law FEMA has the authority to get agencies like the Department of Transportation moving people out of harm's way," Bosner said.

Alas, there was little the FEMA man could do. Bosner's job was to compile reports. He didn't call the shots. "We didn't have the authority to pick up a phone and scream at people," he said.

In Baton Rouge, Governor Kathleen Blanco looked at the latest forecasts on Saturday and took the unusual step of asking President Bush to preemptively issue a disaster declaration for Louisiana, which he did. He would do the same the following day for the state of Mississippi. Bush's action, which was unprecedented, ensured that the money the state had so far spent on hurricane preparations would be reimbursed by the federal government. Lacking the declaration, the state would not necessarily be paid back if Katrina were suddenly to veer off and leave the state unscathed.

At the time, both states had instituted voluntary evacuations for coastal and low-lying areas. Louisiana, in accordance with its plan, instituted a contraflow scheme, effective in midafternoon, under which the interstate lanes into New Orleans were reversed, giving the area twice as many lanes out of town. But Louisiana's experience with contraflow didn't inspire confidence.

Bound by the Mississippi River, Lake Pontchartrain, Lake Borgne, and the Gulf of Mexico, southeast Louisiana suffers from a notable lack of evacuation routes, and state officials had never been able to demonstrate they could empty a metropolitan area of 1.4 million people with anything approaching efficiency. It was a simple matter of choreography: Because the parishes in the area fell into a rough line and communities on both the east bank and west bank of the Mississippi River used the same routes, it was important to evacuate the smaller, more vulnerable communities along the coastal areas before calling on residents in New Orleans and its suburbs to move out. If everyone moved at once, nobody would move anywhere. And the plan had never really worked.

In September 2004, when Hurricane Ivan menaced Louisiana, state officials implemented the contraflow system, but the evacuation was a stunning flop, primarily because communities involved in the evacuation made no attempt to coordinate their activities. Contraflow meant free-for-all: An eighty-mile trip to Baton Rouge became a fourteen-hour slog when an estimated 600,000 people took off for Texas and points north at roughly the same time. After being hoodwinked by Ivan, which veered off and missed New Orleans, many residents vowed they would never evacuate again.

Shortly thereafter, the state instituted a phased evacuation system, to ease the traffic crush. According to the plan, the coastal parishes would evacuate fifty hours before landfall, while the city of New Orleans would evacuate thirty hours before landfall. The system would have worked fine for Hurricane Dennis in July 2005, state officials said, had Jefferson Parish not jumped the gun. The suburban parish, just slightly smaller than New Orleans with a population of 450,000, ordered its people on the road at the same time the coastal population was urged to evacuate. Again the traffic snarled. And again, many of the residents who evacuated vowed never to try again.

Governor Blanco had seen enough of the gun-jumping. Though she didn't criticize Jefferson Parish's leaders in public, she admonished them privately to stick by the schedule. "A premature decision causes you problems," she told local reporters, without naming names. Her staff was slightly more irreverent. They called Aaron Broussard, Jefferson Parish's president, "the premature evacuator."

Evacuation before a storm hits is a local responsibility (and a local expense), and in Louisiana, parishes have traditionally exercised fierce independence when it comes to evacuations. So while Plaquemines Parish sent sheriff's deputies door to door to roust its citizens, as was the tradition in this vulnerable, easily swamped rural community, the city of New Orleans instituted a "voluntary" evacuation order, using mild terms to urge its residents to flee and assuming thousands would ignore the warning. When the Hurricane Pam scenario predicted that just under half of the city would sit tight in the face of a catastrophic storm, this was an assumption based on experience.

Meanwhile, Katrina was sitting about 380 miles off the mouth of the Mississippi River. It wasn't turning east as had been originally forecast. And the most probable place for landfall was now the New Orleans metropolitan area. At the National Hurricane Center in Miami, one of Max Mayfield's colleagues suggested that he might want to make a round of calls to politicians in Louisiana and Mississippi, to give them a nudge, to inject them with a little urgency.

Mayfield knew all about the region's problems with past evacuations. He also knew what catastrophe looked like, and Katrina had the makings of a classic. His people had participated in the Hurricane Pam exercise the year before, and he could see what the stubborn storm in the Gulf was doing. Katrina was growing like Topsy, dropping in pressure, organizing around a massive eye, packing 115-mile-per-hour winds, and taking a late shift to the west. But in New Orleans, most people still thought the storm was heading for Florida or Alabama. The golf courses were crowded with duffers; the ballfields were filled with fans; it was sunny and hot and a perfect day for a picnic. In Mississippi, the story was much the same: The cities were issuing ordinary, voluntary evacuations, and people were taking their time leaving—if they were making preparations at all. "We all knew what a bad hurricane in New Orleans would mean," Mayfield said. So he took his colleague's advice, picked up the phone, and set about scaring some politicians.

The first to be called were the emergency directors in both

states—Mayfield had no interest in sparking tensions between governors and their disaster chiefs. The second round of calls went to Governor Haley Barbour of Mississippi and Governor Blanco in Louisiana. "Sometimes politicians are isolated," Mayfield said almost apologetically. "I just thought it would be good to let them know."

Mayfield found a receptive audience in Blanco, who was growing increasingly concerned over the evacuation after her staff reported that people in New Orleans were lollygagging. Katrina was relatively close to Louisiana when it began shifting toward the city, and Blanco urged Mayfield to jostle the mayor of New Orleans, C. Ray Nagin. Mayfield was happy to oblige.

Nagin had gone home that evening believing he had fulfilled his duty by calling for a voluntary evacuation and offering up a few sound bites for the local television crews. But as he was sitting down to supper with his wife and six-year-old daughter, the phone rang. It was Mayfield. Do more, Mayfield said.

A mandatory evacuation? Odd as it may seem, New Orleans had never called one. "I told him, 'Max, I've never ordered a mandatory evacuation,'" Nagin said later. "And in truth, I wasn't even sure I had the authority."

His own emergency response plan gave him clear authority, but there were a number of things Nagin still did not know about being mayor. Indeed, his naiveté had played no small role in his election victory in 2002. A political neophyte who was given practically no chance of winning when he shouldered his way into City Hall, Nagin, a former cable company executive, ran an outsider campaign in a race dominated by sophisticated political machines. He won over an electorate weary of the patronage and corruption that accompanied machine politics and professional politicians. Shortly after taking office, Nagin spearheaded corruption probes of the city's Taxicab Bureau and vehicle inspection department and abruptly canceled or renegotiated several massive consulting contracts he characterized as sweetheart giveaways to the politically connected.

Surrounding himself with a cadre of advisers who were as politically unsophisticated as he was, Nagin carved out a reputation as a maverick, honest but rash and often insensitive to convention, a lone wolf, a Democrat in name only, who had given $1,000 to Bush's first presidential campaign. Though Nagin ran as a black candidate in an overwhelmingly black city, he drew his political power from the Uptown white establishment—a fact not lost on the city's black constituency, which relied heavily on City Hall for jobs and contracts. A "white man in black skin," is how the Reverend Paul Morton characterized Nagin during a televised sermon in 2004. When Nagin signaled that he planned to dismantle the city's minority set-aside programs, Morton, the head of a 20,000-member megachurch in eastern New Orleans who was accustomed to deference from the city's politicians, accused the mayor of allowing the city to revert to an "apartheid state."

In the end, Nagin didn't dismantle these programs. Indeed, though Nagin often talked about shaking up the political establishment, he rarely followed through. But in keeping with his reputation as a political outlier, the mayor stunned many in 2003 when he endorsed Bobby Jindal, a Republican candidate for governor, over Kathleen Blanco, then the lieutenant governor and the Democratic front-runner for the state's top office. In retrospect, it shouldn't have been a tremendous surprise—Nagin was a corporate executive, bankrolled and swept into office by other corporate executives. But New Orleans is a deeply Democratic city, and though Nagin acknowledged that many of his supporters wanted him to stay with the party "come heck or high water," the freshman mayor praised Jindal, a former member of an administration in Baton Rouge viewed by many in the city as an enemy of New Orleans.

Blanco did win the governorship, and though there was never evidence that she threatened Nagin with retaliation for his endorsement, the relationship was clearly chilly. In fact, she would later joke that Nagin, no favorite of black New Orleans, had "energized my base" by backing her rival. And though the two politicians had made their peace by the time Katrina aimed at New Orleans, there was a tension between the two camps.

But on the Saturday night before the storm, Nagin was about to embark on the challenge of his political life, one that would tax his inexperienced staff to the limit and challenge his eccentric governing style. Nagin didn't realize this at the time, but Mayfield did. "This is going to be a defining moment for a lot of people," Mayfield said on the phone.

In his own understated way, Mayfield had achieved his objective. Nagin returned to the dinner table resolved to call a mandatory evacuation the following morning. And if he had failed to understand the gravity of the situation before, he understood it after the call. "Max scared the crap out of me," Nagin said. "At that point, I was so shook up I couldn't finish my dinner."

Meanwhile, at the governor's mansion in Baton Rouge, Blanco was in a near panic, her concern about the slow pace of evacuation heightened by what she had heard that evening from a New Orleans legislator named Cedric Richmond.

Richmond, who represented the vulnerable, eastern section of town, had joined a conference call with statewide officials, ringing in on his cell phone while he took in a peewee football game in a park near his home. As he watched the two teams grind it out and listened to the dull drone of state storm preparations with half an ear, it suddenly struck him that there was a problem.

The problem was this: Richmond wasn't watching the ball game by himself. He was sitting with hundreds of other New Orleanians in the bleachers, in the early evening sun. As state officials rattled on during the conference call about shelters they had opened and supplies they had on hand in parishes far inland, Richmond broke in. "All these preparations are great," he said. "But let me tell you, if this storm is the 'Big One' as you say, the seven hundred people at this playground with me don't know it."

As Richmond had passed through the crowd that Saturday evening, some thirty-six hours before Katrina's projected landfall, game spectators seemed more interested in beer and hotdogs than in making their exit from low ground. "It just hit me that I was standing at this game and I was the only one hearing about this hurricane," Richmond said. "I know I got the governor alarmed."

Later that night, Richmond got a call from Blanco's deputy chief of staff, Johnny Anderson. "He told me he was calling ministers, telling them to get the word out to evacuate," Richmond said. Richmond told Anderson he was concentrating on the sinners. "Right now, I'm going from barroom to barroom and club to club telling people the same thing."

Meanwhile, contraflow, such a problem in the past, didn't seem to be causing snarls this time around. But that wasn't necessarily a good thing: With only about thirty hours to go before Katrina's landfall, state police reported that traffic was light on the roads heading north and west.

In Washington before dawn on Sunday, August 28, Leo Bosner and his team at FEMA headquarters decided to go the tabloid route, with screaming headlines and overheated prose. They put a tall, bold headline on their daily report to the top brass at the Department of Homeland Security—"Dangerous Category Four Hurricane Katrina Continues West-Northwestward but Expected to Turn Northward." It followed with a breathless report that the storm's top winds had hit 145 miles per hour and that New Orleans would soon be underwater. "Making matters worse, at least 100,000 people in the city lack the transportation to get out of town," the report warned.

A few hours later, Bosner watched his boss, Michael Brown, hold forth on CNN. The voluble agency chief, in Washington but preparing to fly to Baton Rouge later in the day, displayed typical bravado as he faced the oncoming storm. If Brown had doubts about his staff or the pace of evacuations in Louisiana, he didn't betray it. "We're going to do whatever it takes to help victims," Brown said. "That's why we've already declared an emergency. We're going to lean forward as far as possible and do everything we can to help those folks in Louisiana or Alabama or Mississippi."

Bosner felt himself flush with anger as he watched Brown spout optimism on the morning news show. The man had seen his report, and yet he betrayed no sense of impending doom. "You assume that if there's a fire, you're going to pull that lever and when you do, trucks and sirens will come roaring up to your building and people will jump out and they'll have hoses and fire extinguishers and rescue gear and things will be taken care of," Bosner said later. "Well, now imagine that your building's on fire and you pull that lever and nothing happens—the lever just comes off in your hand. That's how I felt."

Early on Sunday in New Orleans, FEMA's pre-storm cavalry arrived in a rental car at the city's emergency operations center in City Hall. FEMA spokesman Marty Bahamonde had flown into New Orleans the night before with a few changes of clothes, some notepads, and a BlackBerry cell phone. He showed up at the operations center across the street from the Superdome to serve as Michael Brown's eyes and ears in New Orleans. He had been staying at a hotel near the airport, but local staff, happy to have FEMA nearby, invited him to ride the storm out with them at City Hall. And Bahamonde settled in for what he expected would be a short overnight stay.

At City Hall, Governor Blanco was just approaching the podium where Mayor Nagin planned to order a mandatory evacuation on live television. As she walked to her assigned place next to the mayor, her cell phone chirped. It was President Bush, calling from his ranch in Crawford, Texas.

Bush got to the point. Blanco needed to ensure that New Orleans ordered a mandatory evacuation. Blanco told him that this was about to happen. It was a brief conversation. And a few minutes later, the job was done.

Bush had also spoken to Michael Brown that morning. An hour after the press conference in New Orleans, the president would get another earful from Max Mayfield on the daily videoconference staged with state and federal officials.

Videoconferences are often convened in times of emergency and have been a staple of the Bush administration. President Bush relies heavily on the device while on his vacations in Crawford, and he also uses the technology in Washington to keep abreast of the wars in Iraq and Afghanistan. Though the videophone conferences are generally used by FEMA's midlevel disaster coordinators to work out the nuts and bolts of disaster response with their counterparts in the affected states, they are sometimes commandeered by top officials to pass out accolades and generally buck up the men in the trenches.

When a hurricane threatens, the videoconferences occur daily at noon Washington time—11:00 A.M. in New Orleans. They generally begin with a weather report from the National Hurricane Center and a round-robin of briefings from the states that might be affected by the storm. Usually moderated by a senior FEMA official in Washington, the videoconferences conclude with individual reports from FEMA regional offices involved in the disaster efforts. The top officials at FEMA and Homeland Security rarely participate in the calls as a general rule. But on the Sunday before Katrina hit, Michael Brown served as moderator and President Bush joined in. With Bush on the line, this wasn't a videoconference that Secretary Chertoff would miss. He logged in as well.

Sitting in a narrow, plain room with burgundy carpet and pecan wainscoting, Bush appeared on the videoconference, scrunched at the end of a massive conference table, seated next to Joe Hagin, the deputy chief of staff. Bush, wearing reading glasses and a blue blazer, studied a colorful map of Katrina's projected path as Max Mayfield spoke. Mayfield, in Miami, went over the order of disaster. Katrina was growing, located 225 miles off the coast of Louisiana and heading on a steady northwest track toward New Orleans. "I don't have any good news here at all today," Mayfield told the videoconference participants. "This is, as everybody knows by now, a very dangerous hurricane." Mayfield talked for a while about weather conditions and showed a few slides. "I think the wisest thing to do here is to plan on a Category 5 hurricane," he said.

Mayfield laid it on thick and straight. He said Katrina was one of the worst he had ever seen and drew comparisons to Hurricane Andrew, which had absolutely demolished South Florida in 1992. "Right now, this is a Category 5 hurricane, very similar to Hurricane Andrew in the maximum intensity," Mayfield said. "But there's a big, big difference. This hurricane is much larger than Andrew ever was."

Oddly, though, Mayfield seemed to downplay the effect that Katrina might have on New Orleans. Though the state was forecasting a storm surge of up to twenty-two feet for the metropolitan area, Mayfield said that Mississippi likely would take the brunt of the surge, with New Orleans hit by a wave half that size. "Will that top some of the levees?" Mayfield asked rhetorically, adding that he suspected the city proper would sustain only "minimal flooding." He checked himself, however, by noting that the National Weather Service was almost always wrong when predicting the height of a storm surge. "I don't think any model can tell you with any confidence right now whether the levees will be topped or not, but that's obviously a very, very grave concern," Mayfield said.

Even so, Mayfield never mentioned the possibility that the hurricane would breach the city's floodwalls and levees, a far more catastrophic event than just topping them would be. Mayfield seemed more focused on the damage to Mississippi, invoking a comparison to Camille, which had devastated that state in 1969. "We're talking about a Camille-type storm surge here," Mayfield said.

After Mayfield was finished, Michael Brown appeared on the screen from a crowded, cluttered conference room in Washington. "At this time, I'd like to go to Crawford, Texas," Brown said grandly. "Ladies and gentlemen, I'd like to introduce the president of the United States."

Bush looked small in the video picture, with Hagin slumped on one side of him and a staff photographer crouched in the corner. Bush passed a few pleasantries, thanking the bureaucrats and "the good folks of Louisiana and Mississippi and Alabama" for indulging the call. Then he offered some reassurance. "I want to assure the folks at the state level that we are fully prepared to not only help you during the storm, but we will move in whatever resources and assets we have at our disposal after the storm to help you deal with the loss of property. And we pray for no loss of life, of course," Bush added hastily.

Bush then harked back to the four storms that had hit Florida the previous summer, saying they had prepared FEMA well. "Unfortunately, we've had experience at this in recent years and I—the FEMA folks have done great work in the past," he said. "And I'm confident, Mike," Bush said to Brown, "that you and the team will do all you can to help the good folks in these affected states."

The president then went back through a litany of thanks, urged people to work hard, and admonished Brown not to rest "until we've done everything in our power to help—to help the folks in the affected areas."

Brown beamed. "Mr. President, thank you," he gushed. "We appreciate your support of FEMA and those kind words very much. Thank you, sir," he said.

Bush went silent. He asked no questions that day.

With the formalities out of the way, the bureaucrats got down to business. The states gave their view of things and it went quickly, since there was little they could do at this point besides hope the evacuations went well. William Doriant, a Louisiana disaster official, called Katrina "catastrophic," and said catastrophic was what the state had planned for. "So we're way ahead of the game there." Jeff Smith, the director of the state's Department of Emergency Preparedness, said the state was happy enough with the supplies FEMA had en route to the region, calling it "a good first shot." He urged FEMA to roll with the circumstances—"I think flexibility is going to be the key," Smith said.

Then it was Brown's turn again to whip his troops. He talked about the preparations, the supplies in place and the soldiers already on the ground. "We've got everything that we need from the federal government," Brown said. He also poked at the soft spots of preparedness, admonishing his staff to get the water and tarps and food moving. "I want to see that supply chain jammed up just as much as possible," Brown said. "I mean, I want stuff [more] than we need. Just keep jamming those lines full as much as you can with commodities."

And then Brown talked about his fears. In a monologue that

would prove prescient, Brown said he worried about the city's evacuation center, the Louisiana Superdome, being in danger of flooding. He worried about the building's roof and whether it was up to a Category 5 blow. He worried about the city's own efforts. "They're not taking patients out of hospitals, taking prisoners out of prisons and they're leaving hotels open in downtown New Orleans," Brown said. "So I'm very concerned about that." He concluded with a rallying cry, saying, "This is really all hands on deck. And I really do expect to be able to call everyone—everyone within FEMA is actually on call. And we may need you to deploy and go somewhere."

Secretary Chertoff, who had remained silent during the call, spoke up from his home in Maryland. "Yes, hi, this is Secretary Chertoff. And again, as it relates to the entire department, if there's anything that you need from Coast Guard or any other components that you're not getting, please let us know," he said.

Chertoff asked Brown if he was getting the cooperation he needed from the Pentagon. "They are fully engaged," Brown said.

"Good job," Chertoff replied.

At around the same time as the videoconference, the Department of Homeland Security's infrastructure section put out a report on Katrina, warning that if the city's levee system was indeed breached by the storm surge, it might take up to six months to pump the city dry again.

In New Orleans, after a slow start, the local officials were coming around to the possibility of catastrophe. Mayor Nagin offered a layman's prediction of what was in store for the city and stepped far beyond what the federal officials had so far said. "We are facing a storm that most of us have long feared," Nagin said. "The storm surge will most likely topple our levee system."

In a practical sense, many were excluded from the mandatory evacuation. Many of the city's indigent residents, a vast number of whom were said not to have cars, lived in some of the most vulnerable and low-lying districts in the city. City and state officials had a hard time figuring out a way to move an estimated 100,000 city residents who were believed to be without cars of their own. The city's own emergency plan essentially threw in the towel. Evacuating the have-nots, the city's 2004 plan said, was "an ongoing project" that had yet to be addressed. During the Hurricane Pam exercises, disaster planners had made fumbling efforts to solve the problem, but the barriers were huge, especially for a sprawling, crumbling southern city in one of the poorest states in the nation. The city's own municipal bus fleet—about five hundred vehicles—was no match for such a huge operation.

The federal government had long refused to take part in evacuations or even to bankroll modest efforts to set up rescue brigades, deeming it a local issue. Indeed, just that summer, the Department of Homeland Security had refused a request from the city of New Orleans to purchase a fleet of aluminum flatboats that could be used to transport flood victims, since the proposal did nothing to prepare New Orleans against the threat of a terrorist attack.

So though Brown and others worried about the city's indigent class, they didn't actually offer help. On its own, the city had opened negotiations that summer with Amtrak about setting up a rail-based system of resident evacuations, but talks were still in their infancy as Katrina loomed. Amtrak officials would later say they tried to offer evacuees seats on the last train out of town but were rebuffed. The Nagin administration would deny that had been the case.

That's not to say the city had done nothing at all. The Hurricane Pam exercises the year before had emphasized devising reasonable solutions to disasters, and it was during these sessions that the city and adjacent Jefferson Parish had come up with a modest stopgap solution. The plan called on City Hall to enlist the help of area preachers to gather their parishioners into community carpools in times of disaster.

Though the plan was hardly finalized, that Saturday night and Sunday, state workers, along with employees in Jefferson Parish, called scores of churches and put it into effect. And on Sunday morning,

Mayor Nagin issued a letter to three hundred churches in the city, urging clergymen to make arrangements to evacuate their parishioners. As a result of "Operation Brother's Keeper," officials said, thousands of people were evacuated who otherwise would have been left behind.

Nagin made an additional stab at clearing the streets: On Sunday afternoon, he set up a dozen collection areas around the city where people could go to catch a free bus ride to the Superdome. The city managed to put twenty-five municipal buses on the circuit, and hundreds of people took advantage of the service.

Though it would seem unusual to outsiders that the city would have only one evacuation center, New Orleans, at the urging of the American Red Cross and the federal government, had long ago scrapped its plans of opening neighborhood shelters in schools and public buildings, having concluded that no place in southern Louisiana was safe in a killer storm. Maintaining a network of well-appointed shelters might therefore cost lives by encouraging people to sit tight in the low-lying city. Instead, the city opened no traditional shelters and maintained only one public building—the Louisiana Superdome—as a solitary "refuge of last resort." By "refuge" the city meant rustic. Beyond a carpeted floor and bathrooms that were certain to fail in a town where even sewers physically had to be coaxed along with electric pumps, there were no comforts in the Superdome. There was no food stockpiled in the building, no cots where people could sleep. Instead, disaster officials made a point to note that it was an uncomfortable, undesirable place offering nothing more than a solid roof and a spot on the floor. The city had just that summer managed to clear a massive storeroom in the building, which it had intended to stock with at least some basic supplies. The city didn't get around to it.

At his Sunday press conference with Blanco, Nagin emphasized just how uncomfortable the Superdome would be. It would be crowded, he said, and probably hot, once the hurricane knocked out power. "Let me emphasize, the first choice for every citizen is to figure out a way to leave the city," he said. For those who insisted on staying at the Dome, Nagin advised taking blankets and a pillow and five days of food. "You're going on a camping trip," he said.

As it happened, a great number of people arrived at the Superdome on Sunday afternoon behind the wheel of their own automobiles, jamming the streets around the massive arena. Another large group of evacuees to the Superdome caught rides from neighbors, and within hours, a line of entrants snaked down the street for a quarter mile. New Orleans is a dangerous city, and nobody was going in the Dome without being swept for weapons. There was a projected five-hour wait.

Nagin wasn't the only one making unprecedented pronouncements on the eve of Katrina's landfall. Katrina had continued to grow, becoming a Category 5 superstorm, generating 165-mile-per-hour winds and pushing a storm surge projected to easily swamp the city. And as the afternoon waxed on, the National Weather Service cast aside its usual taut language in favor of a shriller tone. If Katrina hit at full strength, the agency warned, the New Orleans area would be "uninhabitable for weeks, perhaps longer." Half of the homes in the city "will have roof and wall failure," and many wood-frame apartment houses would fall to splinters. "High-rise office and apartment buildings will sway dangerously—a few to the point of total collapse," the statement said. It added that household appliances and even small vehicles would become airborne, that most trees in the region would snap in half. "Persons, pets and livestock exposed to the winds will face certain death if struck. Water shortages will make human suffering incredible by modern standards."

Within hours of Mayor Nagin's mandatory evacuation order, the city's highways clogged with traffic heading north and west. At the Superdome, the city had police and 260 National Guardsmen on hand to instill order, and the lawmen confiscated fifty weapons from people as they entered the building. Just after nightfall, when the first strong gusts from the massive storm swept through the city's streets, some 9,000 people were camping in the Dome. And there were hints of trouble in the chain of command. Guardsmen interviewed later would say they thought the New Orleans Police Department was in charge by virtue of the Dome's location in the city. But police would later say that because the Dome was technically a state-owned building, the soldiers were in charge.

As Katrina bore down on New Orleans, Terry Ebbert, the city's emergency director, stood at a ninth-floor window at City Hall and watched evacuees file into the Superdome across the street. He saw that the crowds were large and many people hadn't bothered to bring any provisions whatsoever, but he wasn't particularly alarmed. Still, he ordered his staff and the cleaning crew to gather up all of the toilet paper in City Hall and to take it over to the Superdome as a precaution. New Orleans had been through this routine numerous times, most recently for Hurricane Dennis. And in his experience, it always ended the same way: People stayed overnight, the storm veered off, the clouds parted, and everyone walked home. "We're thinking forty-eight hours and this'll all be over," Ebbert said. "Nobody's going to starve by then."

Not everyone shared Ebbert's optimism. On the day's videoconference, the Superdome had been at the top of Michael Brown's worries. He knew the massive arena was undersupplied, that it sat on relatively low ground, and that it had not really been tested by a killer storm since its construction in 1975. "If I could get some sort of insight into what's going on in that Superdome, I think it would be very—very helpful," Brown told his subordinates.

The Louisiana National Guard was worried as well, sensing that a hungry crowd would be harder to control. Through Baton Rouge, they asked FEMA for more food at the arena. But the hour was late, and the winds were already beginning to kick up. There wasn't a lot to be had. FEMA's pre-staged supplies for the state were at Camp Beauregard, in central Louisiana, a three-hour drive away. Worse, Camp Beauregard wasn't stocked for a Hurricane Pam–style disaster. As the storm slouched toward New Orleans, advance teams of FEMA managers had laid in only about a day's worth of food and ice and just slightly more water. In Washington, Michael Lowder, FEMA's deputy director of response, had been sounding the alarm some two days before the storm hit. "If this is the 'New Orleans' scenario, we're already way behind," Lowder wrote in an e-mail message to the agency's logistics chief. "Let's don't hold back. This may be IT!" But his warnings went unheeded: By sunset, FEMA had about the same amount of supplies on hand on the day of the storm as it did at the time Lowder set off the alarm.

Basic commodities were not the only item in short supply. Steve Sansone, a civilian employee of the U.S. Army Corps of Engineers, was at Camp Beauregard on Sunday and wasn't pleased to find that FEMA had stockpiled only fifty generators, or half of what it had promised during the Hurricane Pam exercises. The corps was responsible for installing the generators, which would be needed when Katrina inevitably knocked out the power to the region; Sansone quickly deduced that nobody was preparing for the "New Orleans scenario," as FEMA officials were coming to call Katrina. Despite the huge number of flood pumps in the region and the battery of oil refineries lining the Mississippi River—all of which would have to be fired by massive generators—FEMA had only "their normal rack" of portable power plants in place, Sansone said. "It wasn't enough, given that we had a Category 5 storm in the Gulf. We just knew right then and there we couldn't execute the mission."

In conjunction with FEMA representatives, Hurricane Pam participants had hammered out a template for the amount of goods that needed to be stockpiled in advance of a storm. It calculated that Louisiana would need sixty-nine truckloads of water, sixty-nine truckloads of ice, thirty-four truckloads of food, and twenty-eight truckloads of tarps. But on Sunday, FEMA had just a fraction of this in place: thirty truckloads of water, seventeen truckloads of ice, fifteen truckloads of meals, and six truckloads of tarps. FEMA had one truckload of blankets in the state, despite promising during the Hurricane Pam drill to have 100,000 sets of bedding on hand. It had no cots and no plastic sheeting. Pam also envisioned that at least four hundred buses and eight hundred drivers would be pre-staged alongside rescue workers to ferry people between high ground and a storm shelter. And while Washington and Baton Rouge were jointly responsible under the Pam scenario for providing evacuees with transportation, FEMA had no buses in the state at all.

Near sunset on Sunday, at the state's lavish emergency operations center in Baton Rouge, television crews were camped on the front lawn when a sedan pulled up and a tall, well-dressed man got out, flanked by an assistant, a tall woman of indeterminate age. As the man prepared to stride in front of the television cameras, the woman dusted the man's lapels and gave a last-minute pat to his dark hair.

Mark Smith, the spokesman for the emergency operations center, stood on the porch smoking a Marlboro, watching the scene unfold. He frowned. "Look at that pussy—who the hell is he?" Smith said to nobody in particular. "That's Michael Brown," a woman next to him said.

Eighty miles to the southeast, the city of New Orleans was quiet. Contraflow had ended before the sun went down, and as the rain beat down and the wind picked up, Louisiana looked to be as prepared as it could be for the catastrophe everyone was certain was coming. Besides the troops at the Superdome, the National Guard had 120 soldiers in twenty high-water trucks dispersed through the city's eight police districts. Neighboring Jefferson Parish had nearly as many, while St. Bernard Parish and Plaquemines Parish also had contingents.

The state Department of Wildlife and Fisheries had about two hundred agents, with boats, sitting in a ring around southern Louisiana, awaiting a call from the governor to begin rescue operations. Though Mayor Nagin had exempted hospitals and hotel guests from his mandatory evacuation order—and would come to regret it—some two hundred of the city's sickest residents had been driven from the region by bus. The state's emergency operations center—along with the full wing of offices for FEMA—was lit up and fully staffed. The New Orleans Police Department and Louisiana State Police were put on twelve-hour shifts. New Orleans was battened down, and it was clear that the Hurricane Pam exercise had a profound influence on these activities.

Moreover, despite the hand-wringing from federal officials, the historic balkiness of the state's contraflow scheme, and the intractable problems of getting the city's poor out of harm's way, Louisiana's evacuation was a stunning success. All day Sunday, city streets resounded with sirens and blasts from bullhorns, radio and television stations broadcast scary prognostications, and the word to evacuate rang out from pulpit to podium. Late that afternoon, when Kevin Collins, a New Orleans Sewerage & Water Board employee, headed for his job at Pumping Station No. 5 in the city's Lower Ninth Ward, he was struck by the number of people outside in the city's poorest district, loading up cars for a ride out of town. "I don't know what they said on the TV but the neighborhood was moving," Collins said. "It was like the day after tomorrow."

It would later turn out that an estimated 1.2 million people had fled the greater New Orleans area, leaving only about 200,000 poverty-stricken people and refuseniks behind. It was an evacuation rate that was twice what the area had ever produced and a success by any measure. Though there were delays and traffic slowed at notorious bottlenecks, Andy Kopplin, Governor Blanco's chief of staff, estimated that some 18,000 cars an hour were moving out of metropolitan New Orleans on Sunday afternoon. By 9:30 that evening, the streets were quiet, some 9,000 people were hunkered in the Superdome, and New Orleans informed Baton Rouge that its evacuation was complete.

At about the same time, in a hint of trouble yet to come, the city sent out its first complaint about the federal contribution. "FEMA medical team didn't arrive, which is placing a burden on the New Orleans area," the city said in a report to Baton Rouge.

In Washington, doomsday predictions about the ferocity of Katrina began churning out of the sprawling Department of Homeland Security. Early on Sunday evening, a forty-page "Fast Analysis Report" predicted that the storm would breach the city's levees, kill its entire communications network, and leave "at least 100,000 poverty stricken people" stranded on their rooftops and fending for themselves. The report was actually a forecast based on sophisticated computer modeling by Homeland Security's National Infrastructure Simulation and Analysis Center. The center laid Category 4 storm data over the city's infrastructure grid, including levees, oil refineries, gas pipelines, and telecommunications installations, data that was crunched by superfast computers at federal research labs in Los Alamos, New Mexico, and Livermore, California.

The results were sobering. "The potential for severe storm surge to overwhelm Lake Pontchartrain levees is the greatest concern for New Orleans," the report said. It predicted some 2.6 million people would lose power, many for weeks. It said the city would be submerged "for weeks or months," and that direct economic losses could hit $2.2 billion after the first week, with damaged property adding another $20 billion to the tab. It added that the damage to the refinery-rich area could disrupt the nation's energy markets. The analysis was sent to the Homeland Security Operations Center, the department's conduit for gathering and disseminating disaster information. Six and a half hours after receiving the report, the HSOC distributed it. The White House got its copy at almost 2:00 A.M. on Monday.

But very few of the senior staff were on hand at the White House when Hurricane Katrina made landfall. President Bush was taking his usual month-long August sabbatical at his ranch in Crawford, Texas, a trip that many of his senior advisers struggle mightily to avoid. At the same time, Vice President Dick Cheney was relaxing in Montana, and Andrew Card, the chief of staff, was on holiday in Maine. With more senior staff absent, Katrina coordination fell to the deputy chief of staff, Joe Hagin, who was with Bush in Texas. At the White House itself, Kenneth Rapuano, the deputy homeland security adviser, was handling the storm. Rapuano, who served on the White House Iraq Survey Group, which hunted for banned weapons in Iraq, was considered an expert on nuclear proliferation. Hurricanes were not his specialty.

And at 5:30 A.M. on Monday morning, with Zero Hour at hand, Leo Bosner sent out another dire National Situation Update: "On the forecast track Katrina will move onshore the southeastern Louisiana coast just east of Grand Isle this morning and reach the Louisiana/ Mississippi border area this afternoon. Conditions will continue to steadily deteriorate over central and southeastern Louisiana, southern Mississippi, and southern Alabama throughout the day. . . . Coastal storm surge flooding of 18 to 22 feet above normal tide levels, locally as high as 28 feet, along with large and dangerous battering waves, can be expected near and to the east of where the center makes landfall. Some levees in the greater New Orleans area could be overtopped."

6

THE UNDODGED BULLET

Jackson Barracks, the New Orleans armory of the Louisiana National Guard, sits at the southeastern edge of the city center, in the Lower Ninth Ward, just five miles or so from the French Quarter. Founded in 1832 on an $87,000 grant from President Andrew Jackson, the barracks survived slave uprisings and civil war as well as "distrustful" Creoles who chafed under American rule in the decades following the Louisiana Purchase. Over the years, Jackson Barracks has weathered all manner of floods and hurricanes, including Hurricane Betsy in 1965, which breached a levee only a mile or so from the garrison gates and flooded the Lower Ninth Ward and the Arabi neighborhood in St. Bernard Parish.

There is a common misperception that the city's Lower Ninth Ward neighborhood sits on some of the lowest, most flood-prone ground in New Orleans. In fact, most of this district, Jackson Barracks included, sits above sea level or nearly so. This is not a flood-prone area—except when the levee fails. And even in 1965, the National Guard garrison stayed dry. "Jackson Barracks had never flooded—not as long as anyone can remember," said Colonel Pete

Schneider, a spokesman for the Louisiana National Guard. But the streak was about to end.

As the main southern armory for the Louisiana National Guard, Jackson Barracks was also the front-line command center for the state's response to Hurricane Katrina. At 8:10 A.M. on Monday, August 29, Bennett Landreneau, the commanding general of the Louisiana National Guard, was in the state's emergency operations center in Baton Rouge, fielding a call from an airman in a guard shack at Jackson Barracks. The airman, who was standing near the northern perimeter of the barracks compound alongside Claiborne Avenue, began delivering a standard report on conditions at the garrison: strong winds, little rain—normal conditions, considering that a hurricane was raging outside.

As Landreneau later recounted the conversation, the airman paused in midreport. "Just a minute, sir, let me check something," he said.

And then the airman was back and talking fast, a hint of panic creeping into his voice. "Sir, I don't know why but there must be a foot or two of water coming down Claiborne. No, check that—three feet." The airman paused for breath. "Sir, I don't know what's happened but there are cars floating down Claiborne Avenue—it looks like a river."

Within a few hours, the entire National Guard compound was sitting under eight feet or more of floodwater. Though the Guard had moved its aircraft and most of its engineering equipment in advance of the storm, much of the rest of what it had in the armory—a collection of rifles for a brigade's worth of soldiers and twenty-six high-water troop transport trucks—sank under the murk and were essentially lost. If there had been any doubt that the state of Louisiana would need federal help to cope with Katrina, the point had just been hammered home. Even as the storm raged outside, the state's front-line defense had just lost its command center; even as the winds blew, the state's National Guard was forced to cease all normal activity in a mad rush to reconstitute its command. Katrina had barely made landfall when it put the Guard in retreat—to the Louisiana Superdome, where about 260 soldiers had already been pre-staged in advance of the storm.

As it happened, Katrina wasn't the textbook doomsday storm that had been predicted. Though larger than most hurricanes, the storm lumbered ashore much diminished from its Category 5 strength of just the day before. Katrina made landfall about fifty-five miles south of New Orleans, near Buras, Louisiana, just after dawn on Monday as a large Category 3 storm, with 125-mile-per-hour winds.

Katrina then moved east back into open water and then north, making a second landfall near the Louisiana-Mississippi line. The storm flat devastated the Mississippi coastline to an extent never seen in that state, not even when Hurricane Camille packed a 200-mile-per-hour punch. The surge broke tide gauges up and down the coast, but watermarks suggest that Mississippi may have been hit by a wave twenty-five feet tall, which slammed ashore between Bay St. Louis and Gulfport and drove some twelve miles inland, sweeping everything in its path. Many communities along the Mississippi coastline were literally taken down to slab. The storm knocked out bridges, moved buildings, and sent giant trees crashing to earth.

Louisiana got better treatment. Though the storm drenched the city of New Orleans with as much as twelve and a half inches of rain in some spots, many areas in the metropolitan area received less than half that amount. The storm surge that hit the city's lakefront area was less than twelve feet at its peak, which is in the range of what can be handled by that area's hurricane protection system. Sustained winds in the city itself topped out at just above the minimum for a hurricane—a good blow, certainly, but not on par with the super-storms of yesteryear, such as Hugo and Andrew or the imagined ones, such as Hurricane Pam. And though the wind and rain caused plenty of damage in New Orleans, Katrina didn't leave the city in splinters in a way that Pam's creators had envisioned.

To be sure, Katrina caused plenty of the usual hurricane-related mayhem in New Orleans. Across the city, Katrina's winds killed the electrical grid, cutting power to the Superdome and pretty much everywhere else. The Dome, rated for 160-mile-per-hour winds, was damaged when the wind caught a piece of the white Teflon membrane that covered its roof and shredded it. Two vents at the top of the Superdome were torn off, which allowed rainwater to cascade onto evacuees some nineteen stories below. In streets adjacent to the Superdome, skyscrapers lost windows by the hundreds, and large pieces of public art crashed to the ground.

Closer to Katrina's second landfall, the twin-span interstate bridge over Lake Pontchartrain that connects eastern New Orleans to Slidell was reduced to a series of dashes, with dozens of concrete segments either shoved aside or toppled by Katrina's wind. Aluminum power poles along the interstate collapsed, and in eastern New Orleans water pooled in vast lakes.

Farther west, along the grand boulevards near the city center, three-hundred-year-old oak trees crashed onto the sidewalks and many New Orleans streets were jungles of broken limbs and dangling electrical wires. As the city's venerable oaks came crashing down, they wrenched gas and water lines out of the earth, which caused plenty of localized flooding and sparked a number of fires. Shortly after Katrina hit, the city of New Orleans reported two buildings in the French Quarter had collapsed and seven other structures around the city were engulfed in flames, the Southern Yacht Club among them. Beyond the reach of firefighting crews, the Yacht Club, founded in 1849, was destined to burn to the ground.

Indeed, the city's lakefront was a Matterhorn of cabin cruisers and sailboats that Katrina's wind and water had heaped into huge piles along the shoreline. Several hangars at the city's Lakefront Airport were shredded by Katrina's wind. The lakefront's restaurant district was in splinters, and the Orleans Levee District, which had pulled back its men and equipment to a large maintenance shed in the Seventh Ward, found itself on an urban island, surrounded by floodwaters at least six feet deep.

Two parishes to the east and south of the city—St. Bernard and Plaquemines—received a wallop from Katrina's storm surge that all but wiped them out. In St. Bernard, a storm surge from Lake Borgne flopped over the low back levee of the parish with such force that it flung huge, outrigger shrimp boats into suburban neighborhoods and washed trophy-sized redfish inland to swim along the parish's flooded roadways. The massive surge swept across the parish like a broom, knocking out the electrical grid and most communications, and flipping cars and boats up onto the rooftops of tract homes. The stormwater ran with such force through the Murphy Oil refinery that it moved a half-filled, 65,000-barrel tank of crude oil off its concrete mooring. The tank flexed and then collapsed like an aluminum can, allowing some 1.1 million gallons of crude oil to cascade into the surrounding community of Meraux, tarring about 1,800 homes.

Stem to stern, virtually the entire parish of St. Bernard simply disappeared under the floodwaters, but Nita Hutter, a state representative from St. Bernard who had weathered the storm in the parish's community center, managed to get out an e-mail message to the governor's office. She said that 2,400 of the parish's homes were underwater. Her estimate was limited by her vista; in fact, virtually every structure in this parish of 67,000 residents—an estimated 27,000 homes and businesses—received some flood damage. And according to a rumor making the rounds that day, Plaquemines Parish—the thin jut of land where Katrina initially made landfall—had simply disappeared, replaced by open Gulf.

In the mind of the federal government, the destruction of the Guard's command center was not a measure of the scale of the catastrophe unfolding along the Gulf Coast. Nor was the word that a towering storm surge from the eastern side of Katrina had all but obliterated one hundred miles of Mississippi coastline. Eight feet of water that had sent hundreds of Lower Ninth Ward residents scurrying to their rooftops was no measure of the scale of the calamity in Washington's mind. And the scores of fires that were burning in the city set off no particular alarms.

Instead, there was a single threshold, a defining element that would determine whether Washington treated the storm as an average disaster or as the catastrophic doomsday scenario everyone had long feared. This threshold would determine the speed and scale of the response that the federal government would bring to bear on the ruined city. And it was a test that state and local officials—and even FEMA's senior staff—never fully understood. In this case, the benchmark was a single question: Had the levees been breached by Katrina's storm surge or had they simply been topped?

In the Department of Homeland Security in August 2005, planning was guided by the newly minted National Response Plan (NRP), which had been put into effect just four months earlier, in April. The NRP is an overwrought and complicated document that few people completely comprehended. And as Hurricane Katrina plowed ashore, this cumbersome and contradictory schematic of national disaster response was about to be put to a stern test.

Although advertised as an all-hazards plan, the NRP makes a sharp distinction between, on the one hand, garden-variety natural disasters and man-made accidents (such as fires, floods, train collisions, tornadoes, and the like), and on the other hand, catastrophic events that were larger and more severe. Standard disasters fall within the capability of local governments, backstopped by FEMA. A catastrophic event, by contrast, assumed that the states, perhaps several states, would be immediately overwhelmed—calling for an overwhelming response from the federal government. In such a scenario, FEMA assumes a supporting role to the Department of Homeland Security, and local officials effectively are bystanders.

Clearly, terrorist attacks are what the department had in mind for the catastrophic designation. When defining catastrophes the NRP waxes on about coordinated evidence collection, crime scene preservation, and the apprehension of perpetrators. In the minds of many, though not all, senior Homeland Security officials, certain large-scale natural disasters that affected a broad geographic area and caused a large number of deaths would also fit this rubric.

The NRP offers no clear guidance on what distinguishes a run-of-the-mill disaster from a catastrophic event. But generally, catastrophic events imperil the national leadership, echo through the national economy, and cause national disruptions. The NRP doesn't make it entirely clear who is responsible for deciding when a disaster reaches the threshold of catastrophe. One section says the designation comes automatically with a presidential disaster declaration, while another section suggests the secretary of homeland security must activate the plan himself. But once an event is designated as catastrophic, the secretary is in complete command of all federal assets. This centralization of authority is intended to speed the federal response and to increase the power and scope of relief efforts.

When the secretary activates the plan, he convenes a panel known as the Interagency Incident Management Group, or IIMG, a panel made up of expert officials from Homeland Security and other federal agencies. The IIMG flips the role of the federal government in times of disaster; instead of Washington waiting for state assistance requests and then fulfilling them, the IIMG is supposed to help Homeland Security anticipate the needs of local officials and push supplies to them before they even ask. All of this is supposed to make the federal response quicker.

In the run-up to Hurricane Katrina's landfall, there had been calls within the Department of Homeland Security and the White House to go preemptively to this higher level of response. But senior officials within the department opposed designating Katrina as catastrophic before it hit. Deputy Secretary Michael Jackson said the designation should be reserved exclusively for terrorist events. "It's not necessary," Jackson told those who had pressed him for days to activate the IIMG. "Brown has it all under control." Chertoff also opposed the idea of convening the IIMG. "I did not feel it was imperative to stand up an IIMG on a formal basis until this event took a different dimension," he said.

To others, such as Matthew Broderick, the director of the Homeland Security Operations Center, convening the IIMG didn't make sense before the disaster. ("You just got a lot of talent sitting around waiting for the fire," he later said.) But even after Katrina made landfall, he didn't see a need to convene the IIMG unless he saw proof positive that a catastrophe was indeed unfolding in New Orleans. If the city's system of levees and floodwalls had been seriously breached by

Hurricane Katrina and couldn't be repaired immediately, then Broderick and many of the top officials at Homeland Security would consider it a catastrophe, the implication being that New Orleans would continue to fill with water that couldn't be pumped out. If the levees had simply been overtopped by a storm surge, filling the streets with a finite amount of water that presumably could be removed with city drainage pumps, then the federal government would consider it a standard-issue hurricane, slightly more powerful than most, perhaps, but well within FEMA's capability.

To Broderick, an overtop—even a severe one—was "normal, typical, hurricane background stuff," he would later tell Senate investigators. "You know, we have floods in Pennsylvania all the time. We have floods in New Jersey all the time. Every time there's a hurricane, there's a flood." He would also say he had no idea that a large hurricane hitting New Orleans fit the federal government's very definition of a catastrophic event, as outlined in the fifteen most serious disaster scenarios that Homeland Security had compiled in 2004.

Broderick's view of what constituted a catastrophe was pivotal, because of his position as the commander of the HSOC. The agency played a prime role in advising whether the IIMG should be activated and was to be a key player when the panel was convened. Moreover, Broderick was responsible for giving Chertoff, his top deputies, and the White House virtually every bit of the information they would use to develop a feel for what was happening at the ground level of a disaster. Every day the HSOC delivers a report to Chertoff, which the secretary reads at 6:00 A.M. in his chauffeured car on the way to work. In times of unfolding disaster, the HSOC expands its list of recipients, issuing a series of special reports to the White House and certain other government officials.

As a military man, a retired Marine brigadier general with some thirty years of operational experience, Broderick spoke often of the "fog of war" and the unreliability of first reports, and therefore he was determined that the information he delivered to Chertoff and the White House be completely stripped of innuendo and speculation and boiled down to the coldest, hardest, verified facts. Unverifiable information, or material containing even small errors of fact, was simply not passed on. "One of the jobs of the HSOC is to not overreact, not get hysterical and get the facts because the first information, even the second, is usually woefully wrong," Broderick said. "And so you're trying to clarify it because the secretary or the president could be using what you're passing in news reports once you pass it to them. So you have to be careful that you're getting the details, and sometimes that takes time."

Under this rubric, much of the information Broderick collected in the aftermath of Hurricane Katrina wouldn't pass this rigorous standard and thus wouldn't be passed on. And that included eyewitness information, ground details with multiple corroborating sources, and even facts gathered specifically by people reporting directly to the HSOC. The discarded information involved a number of subjects, but on Monday, Broderick was focused on determining whether the flood protection system surrounding the New Orleans metropolitan area had suffered actual breaches or had just been overtopped by Katrina's storm surge on its pass through the area. "We were trying to get some clarity on that, pushing hard," Broderick would later say.

In the days following Katrina's landfall, Secretary Chertoff, President Bush, and other federal officials would argue that the city's levees and floodwalls didn't breach until a day after the storm had passed, and would refer to the levee breaches as "a second catastrophe" that, in Chertoff's words, "really caught everybody by surprise." Months later, Broderick and Chertoff would continue to maintain this position, in the face of overwhelming evidence to the contrary. But subsequent investigation by the Army Corps of Engineers offers powerful evidence that this simply wasn't true. In fact, in some cases, the opposite happened: The city's levees and floodwalls collapsed even before Katrina made landfall.

A twenty-foot section of the 17th Street Canal floodwall collapsed around 6:30 A.M. and probably began to collapse "catastrophically," the corps later said, at about 9:30 A.M. The corps based its reckoning on several eyewitnesses, including a man with a telescope in a nearby high-rise, as well as data from a nearby pump station that showed a swift drop in the canal's water level, suggesting the waterway was draining into the city. That places the failure of this particular breach while Katrina was still passing over the area. Similarly, stopped-clock data and eyewitness observations suggest the London Avenue Canal floodwall, which suffered two major failures, collapsed at roughly the same time.

Stopped clocks also pegged the collapse of the Industrial Canal levee on the Lower Ninth Ward side at about 7:30 A.M., which correlates with what the Jackson Barracks sentry told General Landreneau about a half hour later. On the other side of the Industrial Canal (which is also known as the Inner Harbor Navigation Canal), a pair of breaches apparently opened up before sunrise, perhaps several hours before the storm struck. This smaller breach, which received almost no notice by the press or the government, would flood a great deal of Gentilly and downtown New Orleans.

It was barely daylight on Monday when the Louisiana emergency operations center in Baton Rouge began receiving reports of levee and floodwall trouble, specifically in the Lower Ninth Ward, where water was already reported to be eight feet deep, and the lakefront area and eastern New Orleans, where a reported tidal surge of twenty feet was said to have crashed through Bayou Bienvenue, near the St. Bernard–Orleans Parish line. And it was barely daylight in Broderick's HSOC office in Washington when he started receiving the same reports.

Indeed, during a 7:30 A.M. phone call with the state, FEMA, the National Weather Service, and other agencies, New Orleans's disaster chief, Terry Ebbert, made clear that the city had not dodged a bullet by any stretch. The surge from Bayou Bienvenue, he said, "came up and breached the levee system in the canal, so we're faced with major flooding both in the east, East New Orleans and then out on the lakefront." Ebbert didn't elaborate on the breach or where it was located. Nobody pressed him for details.

At 8:00 A.M., the Transportation Security Administration made a report directly to the HSOC, saying that the Industrial Canal levee adjacent to the Lower Ninth Ward was breached and that floodwaters in the northeast side of the city, next to Lake Pontchartrain, "have already intruded on the first stories of some houses." At 8:14 A.M., the National Weather Service issued a report headed "flash flood warning," which went on to spell out the source of the flash flood: "A levee breach occurred along the Industrial Canal at Tennessee Street. Three to eight feet of water is expected due to the breach." This report, like all others from the agency, was almost certainly seen by the HSOC because a Weather Service representative sat in Broderick's command center.

In human terms, the Weather Service report would speak volumes to anyone familiar with the city. The Lower Ninth Ward, a neighborhood of 5,000 homes, is one of the city's most poverty-stricken areas, with 25 percent of its residents subsisting on an annual income of less than $10,000 a year. An estimated 32 percent of its households didn't have a car. From an evacuation standpoint, the Lower Ninth Ward was one of the city's most vulnerable.

At 8:36 A.M., not long after the National Weather Service issued its report, Matthew Greene, a FEMA official based at the National Hurricane Center in Miami, sent a heads-up e-mail message to two of his superiors, including Patrick Rhode, Michael Brown's top deputy. "Report that levee in Arabi has failed next to the Industrial Canal," the e-mail message said.

A short time later, at 9:00 A.M., Louis Dabdoub, who worked directly for Homeland Security as a protective security agent in New Orleans, passed an e-mail message directly to the HSOC, warning that there was already ten feet of water in the Lower Ninth Ward—a clear signal that this particular levee was not likely to have been simply topped by "overspill," as Broderick called it. "It is getting bad," Dabdoub wrote. "Major flooding in some parts of the city. People are calling in for rescue saying they are trapped in attics, etc. That means water is 10 feet high there already. Trees are blowing down. Flooding is worsening every minute."

To the locals—and indeed to just about everyone outside of a small circle of officials at Homeland Security and the White House—

the difference between a breach and an overtop was inconsequential; the city was flooded deep and wide, and people attempting to get away from the creeping water ran the risk of death. This sentiment was probably best summed up by the National Weather Service, which advised all citizens in New Orleans's water-filled neighborhoods "to take the necessary tools for survival." The Weather Service elaborated: "Those going into attics should try to take an axe or hatchet with them so they can cut their way onto the roof to avoid drowning should rising flood waters continue to rise into the attic." In the minds of many, the cause of the water—breach or overtop— didn't matter.

Evidence of actual breaches, though, was mounting. At 10:00 A.M., the city's Sewerage & Water Board, which had staff at a pumping station within sight of the Industrial Canal, reported that the structure had a gaping hole in it. Less than an hour later, FEMA's Michael Heath sent out an e-mail message saying that the New Orleans Fire Department was reporting that "a 20-foot wide breach" had opened at the 17th Street Canal. That particular report was widely disseminated among state and federal officials. It was received by Louisiana's office of emergency preparedness, which shared it with top state officials and with FEMA, including Michael Brown. Brown had received similar news about two hours earlier that the Industrial Canal was breached and draining into the Lower Ninth Ward, a report he passed on by e-mail, without comment, to nine other FEMA officials.

Governor Blanco's chief counsel, Terry Ryder, was among those informed about the 17th Street Canal, just a few minutes before the governor was due to participate in the daily videoconference with regional and federal officials, at 11:00 A.M. Central time. He and other state officials were gathered in the overwatch room of the operations center in Baton Rouge when Colonel Henry Whitehorn, superintendent of the Louisiana State Police, delivered the news. Whitehorn said the breach, which immediately went out in the state police's situation report for 11:00 A.M., "was important information."

Ryder immediately grasped the significance. "To me a breach in the wall of that levee would be catastrophic—recognized to be catastrophic," Ryder said. "That would be—the water would be pouring into New Orleans for hours. I would recognize that as being very, very bad news and everybody else would recognize that."

But almost as soon as Whitehorn mentioned it, someone in the crowded room—he wasn't sure who, exactly—said that the Army Corps of Engineers had already discounted the report. "They said it was an overtop," Whitehorn later recalled. Nonetheless, he rushed off to inform Governor Blanco.

Levee breaches were not the focus of the videoconference; indeed, they were barely mentioned. Louisiana officials didn't even bring up the subject, and neither did most of the federal officials on the call. Max Mayfield of the National Hurricane Center made a reference to the possibility of breaches in the city midway through a protracted weather forecast that led off the discussion, but only to mildly shoot the idea down. Mayfield said that judging from the relatively minor storm surge that had hit the city, the "federal levees" protecting New Orleans were unlikely to have been breached. His Weather Service colleagues spent a great deal of time discussing the amount of rain Katrina might drop as the storm headed up through the Ohio Valley.

Terry Ryder wasn't in the briefing, but other top state officials who knew the same information were there. Michael Brown was on the call, as was Superintendent Whitehorn and Jeff Smith, the head of Louisiana's emergency operations center, both of whom had heard the report. Michael Chertoff was on the call, as was Joe Hagin, President Bush's deputy chief of staff. Hagin, a former firefighter upon whom the White House was relying heavily to track the disaster response, had called in from Air Force One—he was accompanying President Bush on a long-planned trip to Arizona to discuss Medicare.

Chertoff asked no questions at the videoconference. Instead, he doled out some mild praise. "I just want to compliment you all on the hard work you have done," he told the assembled. "Obviously, this is the long haul."

Brown told participants that he had spoken to President Bush earlier, once in Crawford and then later when Bush was airborne.

"He's obviously watching television a lot," Brown said, "and he had some questions about the Dome," which had suffered some roof damage in the storm. "He's asking questions about reports of breaches. He's asking about hospitals. He's very engaged and he's asking a lot of really good questions I would expect him to ask."

Brown alone among the federal officials seemed to have a grasp of the scale of the disaster that had visited the Gulf Coast, whether the levees had breached or not. "I get frustrated when the media talks about [how] it's gone from a Category 5 to 4 to 3," Brown said. "What they don't realize is there is a lot of rain, a lot of storm surge, a lot of potential victims out there." He urged his staff to resist the tendency to think they had dodged a bullet. "There's still a lot of work to do, so keep it up and do a good job," he said.

Across the table, Louisiana's Jeff Smith said FEMA's response had been "outstanding" so far. He told the federal officials not to wait for him to request help before pushing resources Louisiana's way. "Push it, we are ready to receive it," Smith said. "We know we are going to need it."

About halfway through the call, Hagin broke in from Air Force One and briskly asked two questions, both of Governor Blanco: "Yeah, what's the current status of the levee system and the roof of the Superdome?" Blanco answered the second question first: "The Superdome structure is still sound, as far as we know." Then she hesitated. "What was your other question?" she asked. She paused again, then caught herself. "The levees."

Blanco said the state had received numerous reports of overtopping and one report of breaching, which she immediately discounted. "We heard a report unconfirmed," she said. "I think we have not breached the levee. We have not breached the levee at this point in time." She went on to say that many New Orleans neighborhoods were submerged. Some city neighborhoods, along with St. Bernard Parish, were sitting in eight to ten feet of water, "and we have people swimming in there."

And that was it. The conversation moved on to Mississippi. The city's levees weren't mentioned again.

At the videoconference, Smith had made no attempt to correct Blanco, though he knew about the eyewitness report regarding the 17th Street Canal breach and the extremely unusual depth of the floodwater in the Lower Ninth Ward, which would be hard to mark off to anything other than a catastrophic collapse of the levee there. Smith later said that Blanco didn't seem to have misspoken, or even to have spoken rashly. "It seemed to me that she conveyed the important information, which was that there was so much water in the neighborhoods that people were swimming in it," Smith said. "That makes it pretty clear what's going on."

A few minutes later in the videoconference, Hagin again broke in. Air Force One was now on the ground in Arizona. "I'm sorry," Hagin said. "We just landed. We are going to sign off your being able to get ahold of us." As far as he (and the president) knew, the situation in New Orleans was well in hand, and there was no need to ratchet up the federal response. The levees had apparently held, and whatever flooding was taking place could be addressed by ordinary means. Governor Blanco's assurance that "we have not breached the levee" meant that the situation was not "catastrophic." President Bush could continue with his trip to Arizona, as planned. A few hours later, he would share cake with Senator John McCain, who was having a birthday. Later in the day, the president would tell a crowd that he had spoken to Secretary Chertoff that morning, but about immigration, not Hurricane Katrina. In most respects, Monday seemed like an average August day for the White House, and Katrina seemed like an average hurricane.

Chertoff would later remark to Congress how significant this particular videoconference had been. "I, and the other participants heard directly from Max Mayfield and Governor Blanco of Louisiana, as the transcript indicates, the levees had *not* been breached," Chertoff said. He added that nobody on the call had asserted that "the flooding was extraordinary or out of the norm for a significant hurricane with substantial rainfall; or whether the more than thirty pumps in the city of New Orleans would be able to channel the excess water appropriately."

Brown and Broderick would later say that the Army Corps of Engineers was declarative on Monday that the city's levees had not collapsed. Broderick, too, would later say he received most of his information about the city's floodwalls and levees from the Army Corps in Washington. As he would later tell Senate investigators, "The Corps of Engineers kept backing us up and saying, 'No, it is not breaches. These are overtopping.'"

But the corps had no idea what was a breach or an overtop; it had no helicopters in the air, no satellite photographs, nothing it could employ to say definitively what was going on in New Orleans with the flood control system it had built. Indeed, it wasn't until midafternoon that the corps even had a representative on the ground in the city.

Actually, before midafternoon, the corps had exactly nine people in New Orleans, but they were in a sealed bunker miles away from the affected levees, waiting out the storm. The corps had evacuated its massive New Orleans District headquarters; left in town to "show the flag" were the newly arrived district commander, Colonel Richard Wagenaar, and eight aides. The small group had no specialized communications and no transportation beyond a standard SUV. The engineers, who represented the corps' entire ground contingent in New Orleans, knew nothing about the levee breaches, at least nothing firsthand.

Throughout the night, Wagenaar had been bombarded with phone calls from residents and city officials, many of whom reported problems with the city's flood control system. Some also begged for rescue, which the corps was unprepared to provide. "We had hundreds of reports of failures and breaches," Wagenaar said.

But much of what the callers reported was Greek to the colonel, who had only been in town for a month and had little independent knowledge of the city's labyrinthine flood control system. He didn't know the system's peculiarities, and he didn't know its weaknesses. He didn't know how vulnerable the city's three drainage outfall canals were to an approaching storm surge. "I didn't even know where the 17th Street Canal was," Wagenaar said.

When he awoke on Monday morning, the local radio station was reporting that a "levee" in the lakefront area of the city had failed. Also that morning, a corps employee called to say that water was pouring over the top of the levee that bounded the city's Industrial Canal, on the edge of the Lower Ninth Ward neighborhood. When afternoon came, Wagenaar took a pair of his aides, piled into the SUV, and headed out toward Lake Pontchartrain, where numerous people had reported that a levee was breached.

But the roads were all but impassable, choked with storm debris and power lines, and many of them were flowing with water. The corps officials soon realized they'd never make it to the city's lakefront. As the truck picked its way across the city, Wagenaar pondered the calls that had come in. Almost all of the people reporting trouble out near Lake Pontchartrain had referred to broken levees, probably not realizing that "floodwall" was the technical term for the barriers along the city's canals. Crossing town took two hours, and as the SUV crept along, Wagenaar gazed out the window, where he saw "hundreds of people on the street" trudging through the floodwaters in search of help and supplies. He thought Katrina had somehow managed to gash the massive earthen levees that ring the south shore of Lake Pontchartrain. It would be several hours before Wagenaar would come to understand what the callers were saying. By that time, the 17th Street Canal breach would be massive and would prove stubbornly resistant to repair.

When Wagenaar's SUV reached the canal, about two miles from the breach, it had reached the end of the line. The water ahead was deep, up to the telephone wires in some spots. "All I could see were the treetops," Wagenaar said. There were no boats and no helicopters, just a few cops and civilians milling around on top of an interstate overpass. "We just stared at the water," Wagenaar said. "And the whole time, I'm thinking, 'This is a levee failure' when in fact it was a floodwall failure," Wagenaar said. "What I did know is that there was a significant problem." And he knew this problem wasn't attributable to rainfall.

Wagenaar got back to the district headquarters in the late afternoon. Based on his observations and other information, his staff filed a situation report under his name a few hours later that was available to Army Corps commanders nationwide, including the headquarters in Washington. If officials were seeking confirmation about levee breaches, the news was buried and cloaked in jargon. On page five of the six-page report on conditions in New Orleans, just after recounting the "positive media" the corps had been receiving ("Fox News reported 'Corps of Engineers did a miraculous [job] with the levees'"), the report devoted five brief sentences to the matter of levee failures. "At this point, the Corps of Engineers has no confirmed reports of levee breaching or levee failure of any kind during Hurricane Katrina," the report said. "We are investigating for the possibility of any breaching, and we are also investigating whether levees have been overtopped at any point."

But the report was unnecessarily pedantic. A few sentences later, it got around to reporting what many already knew and others were struggling to confirm: "We have confirmed a floodwall failure on the Industrial Canal." It added that the failure was on the Lower Ninth Ward side of the Industrial Canal, which would mean that water was gushing into the neighborhood. And the breach was huge: "It is about one block long," the report said.

Then the report turned to the matter of ensuring all district employees would receive their paychecks and engaged in a short discussion of Mississippi River gauges before returning again, briefly, to the subject of the huge slug of lake water that was coursing through the streets of New Orleans. But here again, the startling news was cloaked in understatement and technical talk that would probably escape the notice of the average disaster response official, coming as it did after the declarative statement about no levee breaches. "I-walls: Floodwalls were overtopped on the east side of the 17th Street Canal and the east side of the (Industrial Canal)," it stated. "Sections of wall failed in each area." Here was the confirmation.

With the floodwalls gashed and hemorrhaging billions of gallons of water into the city, it was only a matter of a few hours on Monday before the communications citywide began to fail as the moisture crept into the ground-based junction boxes and electronic switching stations. Even satellite phones became useless as the water shorted out ground-based transponders. Communications was about to become the biggest problem of the catastrophe.

And unbeknownst to Washington and Baton Rouge, the city was on the move. Most of eastern New Orleans, wracked by levee overtoppings, was swimming in up to fourteen feet of water, and people were literally swimming to highway overpasses and tall buildings. In the Lower Ninth Ward, a pair of catastrophic levee breaches sent a wall of water eight feet deep rushing though the city for more than a mile in every direction. In the heart of the city's residential area, Gentilly and the Seventh Ward, the London Avenue Canal, gashed in two places and seriously overtopped in another spot, was letting loose a cascade of water that filled living rooms miles away. And on the city's lakefront, a twenty-foot-long breach grew like a summer weed.

In fact, the twenty-foot levee breach at the 17th Street Canal was expanding all morning and into the afternoon on Monday. Eyewitness testimony gathered months later by the Corps of Engineers suggested that the twenty-foot breach reported at around 11 A.M. to FEMA personnel and the governor's staff was probably a hundred feet long or more by the time the information had filtered to Baton Rouge.

Nobody knew this. At 4:40 P.M. New Orleans time, President Bush stood in Rancho Cucamonga, California, delivering a speech on the new Medicare prescription drug benefit to a group of elderly citizens. He departed from the script briefly to address the spiraling catastrophe unfolding along the Gulf Coast. "We're in constant contact with the local officials down there," Bush said. "The storm is moving through, and we're now able to assess damage, or beginning to assess damage. . . . For those of you who are concerned about whether or not we're prepared to help, don't be. We are. We're in place. We've got equipment in place, supplies in place. And once the—once we're able to assess the damage, we'll be able to move in and help those good folks in the affected areas."

Marty Bahamonde stood at the door of an open Coast Guard helicopter as a blast of hot rotor wash spilled over to him. He yelled to the pilot that he was from FEMA and needed to go up. It was a hard sell. The last thing the Coast Guard pilot wanted was to take some FEMA public affairs official on a sightseeing tour over storm-ravaged New Orleans. It was 5:15 P.M., and Hurricane Katrina's winds had abated just enough to make flying possible. Hundreds of people were already hanging on to crumbling rooftops and balconies trying to escape rising waters and storm damage. Only three Coast Guard rescue helicopters had managed to get into the air, and each was already overwhelmed by dozens of calls for help. This was no time to give a joyride to a FEMA man.

The Coast Guard's own commander on the ground had vowed the only way Bahamonde would see the inside of a chopper that day was if he needed rescuing himself. But Bahamonde was persistent. He pressed. And he told a little white lie. "I started dropping the president's name," he recalled.

"The president expects me to let him know what's going on here," he bellowed to the pilot.

It wasn't a complete fabrication. Bahamonde, a trusted official with twelve years of disaster experience under his belt, had been told by Brown's special assistant Michael Heath a few days before that he was to chase the storm, go "wherever the hurricane was going to hit" and find a good spot to hold a press conference for when Brown made a visit to the disaster zone. Heath also told Bahamonde to keep an eye out for "any and all" information that Brown might want to share with the White House. Bahamonde had been doing this all day Monday, sending along tips about whatever he saw. Sometimes Brown responded to the e-mail messages, and sometimes he didn't. Earlier in the day, Bahamonde had just happened to be passing by the radio room in the city's emergency operations center when a panicked voice came over the airwaves, reporting a breach in the 17th Street Canal floodwall near Lakeshore Boulevard and 17th Street. "It's very bad," the voice said before cutting out completely.

Bahamonde tried repeatedly to get a call through to his bosses in Baton Rouge to tell them the news. He finally gave up and sent an e-mail message, in which he called the floodwall a levee. But Brown seemed to already know the news. "I'm being told here water over not a breach," was Brown's cryptic reply. Brown later said this information came from Louisiana officials.

Though Brown would later tell a congressional committee that Bahamonde was given to hyperbole, the FEMA man's BlackBerry e-mail missives do not come across that way. Indeed, there was nothing shrill about the reports at all: Bahamonde simply stated what he saw and carefully sourced the rest. "Windows and parts of the east side of the Hyatt hotel have been blown out," he said in one dispatch. "Furniture is blowing out of the hotel."

Also, earlier in the day, Bahamonde had managed to get through to Heath to relate the news that the situation at the Superdome was quickly becoming dire. The building was beginning to fill with people. And the sixteen trucks of food and fifteen trucks of water that FEMA promised for the arena had turned out to be two trucks of food and five trucks of water, Bahamonde said. Moreover, the FEMA medical team due to arrive at the Superdome before the storm had in fact never shown at all. As it turned out, Brown had indeed passed this information on to the HSOC and the White House. Bahamonde didn't know that.

Bahamonde was determined to make himself useful. "I need to be on this chopper," he shouted at the pilot. The pilot blinked. "You got ten minutes," he yelled back. "Take it or leave it."

Bahamonde jumped aboard. "Where to?" the pilot asked. Bahamonde didn't hesitate. "The 17th Street Canal levee," he said.

The New Orleans Downtown Heliport is located on top of a parking garage adjacent to the Superdome. As the helicopter lifted off, Bahamonde could see that the white skin of the massive arena's roof had been pulled back like an orange peel, revealing a grubby brown core. It was an amazing and depressing sight. But it was nothing compared to what lay out by Lake Pontchartrain and points east.

If Bahamonde wanted a strict confirmation of catastrophe, he got it: Even on the ten-minute flight, he saw enough to definitively call Katrina a massive, overwhelming disaster. The 17th Street Canal floodwall was in tatters, its concrete caps bent askew like tombstones in a country graveyard. Water was pouring into the city like Niagara. The breach was now a quarter mile wide. All through the neighborhood, Bahamonde could see people huddled forlornly on the roofs of their single-story homes while floodwater lapped at the eaves. As the pilot quickly circled the breach and headed back toward the Superdome, Bahamonde furiously snapped photographs with his palm-sized digital camera. "I knew I was looking at the worst-case scenario that everyone had feared," he said.

The hour was growing late. The city had been filling with water for ten hours, maybe more. The pilot dropped Bahamonde at the heliport and immediately jacked up into the sky. But within a half hour another helicopter had landed. This one was for Bahamonde. He quickly clambered aboard.

On the second flight, the pilot headed east, and Bahamonde got an eyeful of a city in distress. Whole swaths of New Orleans were submerged, and the water was creeping relentlessly toward downtown. At this point, Bahamonde estimated that 75 percent of the city was underwater. The scene from the helicopter was awesome, even for Bahamonde, a veteran disaster worker. Everywhere he looked, he could see survivors clinging to trees and rooftops. The pilot took Bahamonde for a good long ride. He saw the Interstate 10 bridge across Lake Pontchartrain, gap-toothed and totally impassable. He saw eastern New Orleans as it had never been seen: a lake to the horizon, broken only by roof peaks and highway ramps.

By the time Bahamonde returned to the Superdome, it was nearly 7:00 P.M. and approaching sunset. As he hopped off the helicopter, Bahamonde fumbled with his cell phone to call Brown in Baton Rouge. He got through on the first try. Speaking slowly and carefully, Bahamonde related what he had seen.

Brown said little during the briefing. When Bahamonde finished, Brown thanked his advance man. "I'm calling the White House now," Brown said.

Bahamonde then called Heath, who said nothing upon hearing his news. And then he called the FEMA public affairs office in Washington, demanding that they arrange a conference call with all FEMA top officials at 9:00 P.M. so he could make as many people as possible aware of the situation that faced the city of New Orleans.

It was now almost 8:00 P.M., and Bahamonde left to find Mayor Nagin. As he walked the two blocks to City Hall, his phone rang. It was Cindy Taylor, the deputy director of FEMA public affairs. "Marty, I believe you," she said, "but are you really sure what you saw? Are you sure? Because I'm getting some pushback on this conference call; people here are saying they don't need to talk to you. So I just want to know how far to push it. Are you sure?"

Bahamonde was livid. He knew what he'd seen. He took a breath. "Cindy, I am as sure of what I saw as I am that sure my name is Marty," he said in a measured voice.

Taylor promised to do what she could.

Bahamonde then tracked down the mayor at the emergency operations center. He had found a willing audience. Nagin called in his aides and everyone sat down at a conference table. The mayor listened raptly as Bahamonde delivered a thirty-minute description of what he had seen. "Nagin was stunned," Bahamonde said. "He had this vacant expression as he listened to me that said everything."

Though Nagin was convinced, Brown may not have been, or at least not completely. As he settled in that evening in Baton Rouge for a round of televised interviews, Brown alternately described the levees as both topped and breached. On CNN, Brown hedged. "We have some, I'm not going to call them breaches, but we have some areas where the lake and the rivers are continuing to spill over," he said. Nonetheless, he called Katrina a catastrophe, and said that tens of thousands of people might need rescue. On Fox News that evening, Brown managed bravado even as he acknowledged the defining event that would have elevated the disaster to a top national priority. "Now we averted the catastrophic disaster here, but a lot of the things that we anticipated, that we practiced for are coming true," he said. "We now have breaches. We now have water moving into New Orleans."

A few minutes later in New Orleans, Bahamonde broke off the meeting with Nagin to make his conference call. On the call were

FEMA's deputy director Patrick Rhode and a few agency men who were in Baton Rouge. Bahamonde told them that the heart of the city and many of its suburbs were cut off and inaccessible to trucks. He said the interstate routes east and west sank into flood-waters at the outskirts of town. He said he expected the situation to worsen as the city filled up with water from the breaches, which were real.

Bahamonde lingered on the human toll, describing the hundreds of people on rooftops and bodies floating in the city's streets. He said the situation at the Superdome was dire and that food and water were in short supply. Bahamonde didn't hype what he saw—there was no real need. "I believed that I was confirming the worst-case scenario that everyone had always talked about," he later said.

And yet Bahamonde got the sense that the FEMA men weren't listening. Scott Wells, FEMA's Louisiana deputy in Baton Rouge, thanked Bahamonde for confirming "most of what we know already." Wells told Bahamonde to get ready to leave the city; FEMA was already working on sending someone in to relieve him.

Bahamonde hung up the phone feeling terrible. But there was no time to brood. Nagin and his staff were clamoring for his attention, asking if he could tell them again what he had seen, this time using a map. For two hours, Bahamonde would describe what he saw to the city officials. When it was over, he was exhausted. Bahamonde crawled under a desk on City Hall's ninth floor. He used a spare shirt as a pillow. He fell into a restless sleep.

Bahamonde's report didn't die. It was typed up and flashed around FEMA, and it made its way relatively quickly to the Department of Homeland Security. At 9:27 P.M. Eastern time, following Bahamonde's conversations with Brown and Heath at FEMA, John Wood, Michael Chertoff's chief of staff, and five other Homeland Security officials received an e-mail message from Brian Besanceney, the department's assistant secretary for public affairs, saying that a FEMA employee in New Orleans witnessed destruction there that was "far more serious" than what reporters and others were saying. "FYI in case tomorrow's [reports] seem more 'severe,' " the e-mail message said. The information made it to the White House about two and a half hours later, shortly after midnight.

Bahamonde's report made its way to the Homeland Security Operations Center at about the same time. And there, it was added to the breach confirmation reports from the press and the city and the state and the Red Cross and the Coast Guard and the National Weather Service and the Transportation Security Administration and the Army Corps of Engineers and other agencies within the Department of Homeland Security. Bahamonde's report was just another tile in the mosaic at the HSOC, assigned no more and no less importance than any other piece of information on the same subject. Matthew Broderick wouldn't see Bahamonde's report until months later (he had left the office at 9:00 P.M. on Monday). But when he did, he still discounted its value.

"You know, you can see why we go in and try to get clarification," Broderick later said when questioned about Bahamonde's report. "It says . . . 'Downtown, there is less flooding.' Yet, he says, '75 percent of the city is underwater.' You know, that's hyping something that you would go back and check. A quarter-mile breach in a levee: again, is it a breach or is it overspilling?"

By 5:00 P.M. Washington time on Monday, Broderick's shop had received no fewer than nine reports that the city's flood control system had been breached. Moreover, the HSOC had received at least eight other reports that huge swaths of the city were underwater and that hundreds, perhaps thousands, of people were awaiting rescue in the sultry summer heat.

But Broderick's final report of the evening, sent out at 6:13 P.M. Washington time, shot down the idea that the city's levees had been breached. "Preliminary reports indicate the levees have not been breached," the report declared.

At the end of the day, it was clear in some respects who considered the question of breach versus overtop to be important. Broderick certainly did. Hagin, at the White House, homed in on the question at the Monday videoconference, so he may have realized the significance. Bahamonde seemed to recognize instinctively that the information

Washington needed was sitting at the 17th Street Canal. Chertoff certainly understood the importance of the question—he said so on many occasions afterward.

But the people who didn't know how crucial the question was were the very people who were best situated to answer it. They were the local officials. In New Orleans, Mayor Nagin and his emergency manager, Terry Ebbert, spoke of the breaches in their public statements but didn't emphasize them and indeed seemed to speed over the question in their press conferences. And it seems clear that Governor Blanco, who had carefully calibrated practically every move she made during the early days of the crisis, wouldn't have been so dismissive during the videoconference of the reports of levee breaches had she known that the federal response was hanging on it.

When Broderick was asked months later by Senate staffers why he had stated so declaratively late Monday that the city's flood control structures were intact, the former Marine general said, improbably, that he had never received a single report during the day that suggested otherwise. The Senate investigator asking the question, Jeffrey Greene, was so stunned at the response that he initially asked if Broderick had misheard him.

But Broderick hadn't misheard. "If I had heard there was a breach in a levee Monday evening, I would have—had I been aware of it, I would have been all over it," he said.

Instead, Broderick said, all he had heard out of the city on Monday was the sound of a "normal hurricane situation. The Corps of Engineers had to go in and do a debris clean-up. We have to get power restoration," Broderick said. "We may have to go in and help with search and rescue for a certain amount of people but it's the regular hurricane drill."

Broderick would also tell investigators that he rarely looked at his e-mail and had received seven hundred e-mail messages during the disaster that he had never even bothered to open. He admitted that he didn't read the New Orleans newspaper, the *Times-Picayune*, which on the day Katrina hit had treated the collapse of the 17th Street Canal as fact and had written a long story describing the scene after two reporters on bicycles had visited the area. Broderick would later say he hadn't seen Michael Brown on CNN on Monday night referring to Katrina as a catastrophe and saying that as many as 10,000 people might be trapped in the floodwaters. Finally, asked by exasperated Senate investigators what evidence he had collected showing the levees had *not* breached, Broderick said he had relied exclusively on two sources. The first was the Army Corps of Engineers, but the former general suspected even that agency of hyping the situation, since it had reported "extensive" flooding in New Orleans and " 'extensive' is all relative," Broderick said.

The second source, Broderick allowed, was unimpeachable: CNN Headline News. Late Monday afternoon, the network aired a report from New Orleans. The focus of the video snippet was a scene on Bourbon Street, near the highest spot in the city, where people "seemed to be having a party," Broderick said.

"The one data point that I really had, personally, visually, was the celebration in the streets of New Orleans, of people drinking beer and partying because—and they used, they came up with the word—'we dodged the bullet,' " Broderick said. "So that's a pretty good indicator right there."

7

STRANDED IN NEW ORLEANS

Marty Bahamonde could not get comfortable on the patch of floor he had claimed as a bed early Tuesday morning at the cramped New Orleans emergency operations center on the ninth floor of City Hall. He had crawled under an empty desk, but bedlam followed him there. New Orleans officials were clearly overwhelmed by the scale of the disaster, and they were working frantically all around him to get a handle on the situation. It wasn't easy: The city was pitch black, communications were poor, and it was impossible even to prioritize problems when everything seemed to be cause for panic.

Mayor Nagin had left to grab some sleep at the Hyatt hotel across the street, where he had rented a suite, leaving Terry Ebbert, the city's homeland security director, to draw up a list of supplies and services he thought the city might need from the federal government. Bahamonde had recommended the men draft the list and present it to Michael Brown, who was due to arrive later that morning at the Superdome.

Bahamonde was exhausted, but sleep didn't come easy. He tossed for four hours under the desk, moving in and out of wakefulness.

Then he dragged himself up. It was still dark outside. "This is what I signed up for," he thought to himself.

In a way, Bahamonde was an accidental relief worker. He had started his professional life as a sportscaster, working first in Harrisburg, Illinois, and then Port Arthur, Texas. In January 1988, he took a job in Guam as sports anchor for one of the local television stations. It was a small station, and in August 1992 when Typhoon Omar hit the island, Bahamonde found himself covering the storm. There he met Susan Healy, a part-time FEMA employee. And within a matter of months, he quit his television job, followed Healy back to Washington, and began training for a FEMA job himself.

Over the next several years Bahamonde and his wife chased hurricanes together, parachuted into earthquake zones, and helped tornado victims sort through their lives. It was rough, sad work involving constant travel and leaving little time to start a family. In 1998, he moved to Tacoma, Washington, studying to become a physical therapist and working for FEMA over the summers. But after the September 11 attacks, FEMA asked him to return to the agency full-time, dangling a fat salary to entice him. Bahamonde agreed, and by 2003, Michael Brown had picked Bahamonde to be his advance man. In government communications work, this was the top of the food chain. Over the next few years Bahamonde would jet out ahead of Brown from disaster to disaster, gathering intelligence for his boss and making sure the agency's message was pure and informed. Brown came to trust Bahamonde's judgment on matters of message. And he trusted Bahamonde to pick the right backdrop, to figure out which local officials to meet, and most important, which local officials to avoid.

That was why Bahamonde was in New Orleans. He was there to make Brown look good, not to dole out water and blankets. The plan was simple: When the sun rose, Brown and a cadre of state officials would tour the city by helicopter, land at the Superdome for a press conference, enter the building to hug survivors, and essentially convey the message that help was coming and President Bush had it all under control. Brown wanted to do a ground tour of the city after that. It was the script, a standard one, and likely to be repeated in upcoming days in New Orleans and Biloxi and other cities along the Gulf Coast.

Outside, the sun was just coming up. It was Tuesday, August 30. Bahamonde brushed his teeth and gathered his bag and dug out his BlackBerry to see if Brown was on schedule. Touchdown was at 10:00 A.M. Brown would have the governor and the state's U.S. senators in tow. Bahamonde took the elevator, which was operating under full generator power. Then he headed outside to find Mayor Nagin at the Hyatt.

When Bahamonde stepped outside he was met with disaster: Poydras Street, which separated City Hall from the Hyatt and the Superdome, had become a river of tea-colored water three feet deep and rising. The city's shelter of last resort was quickly becoming an island.

Bahamonde immediately called Bill Lokey, FEMA's federal coordinating officer for Louisiana and the agency's top operational official in Baton Rouge, trying several times before getting through. Bahamonde described the river rushing down Poydras Street, but Lokey seemed uninterested. "Okay, thanks," he said briskly. "We have a team coming in this morning that's going to be able to replace you."

Bahamonde was stunned. There were no questions. No requests for more information. Just a patronizing dab of politeness and a reminder that Bahamonde should pack his bags. Disgusted, Bahamonde took off his shoes and rolled up his trousers and waded across the ad hoc river first to see Mayor Nagin and then to peek into the Superdome.

Bahamonde didn't need to do much more than glance inside the building to see that it would be the wrong place for Brown to say that FEMA had things well in hand. The massive arena was chaotic, crammed with people, and already starting to smell. And with Poydras Street running like a river, New Orleans was no place to drive around. At 6:00 A.M., Bahamonde wrote an e-mail message to his boss, FEMA spokeswoman Nicol Andrews, and said just that. "The area around the superdome is filling up with water, now waist deep," he wrote. "[Brown] can land and do a presser but then [will] have to leave, there will be no ground tour, only flyover."

Michael Brown was in Baton Rouge, standing in the state's emergency operations center with Lokey, Governor Blanco, and some members of the governor's staff. His early morning avalanche of e-mail was laced with reports from FEMA depots in Louisiana, Mississippi, and elsewhere in the region that supplies were not showing up in the amounts that had been expected. FEMA's communications experts at Mount Weather couldn't get Brown's computer connected into their emergency grid and were even having trouble patching him through on phone calls. Worse, the Pentagon seemed to be slow-rolling FEMA's request for assistance to fly in eight swiftwater rescue teams and their equipment from Travis and March Air Force bases in California. California was one of the few states that had such specialized rescue squads, which had boats, trucks, and trailers and could work effectively in a flooded city. FEMA's liaisons to the Pentagon had worked on the request all night, only to be told in the morning that Secretary of Defense Donald Rumsfeld was unavailable to approve the request. In fact, Rumsfeld would be spotted later on Tuesday attending a baseball game in San Diego. This wasn't shaping up to be a good day.

Few in Washington had come to understand the gravity of the situation, not least the man in charge of raising the national alarm, Matthew Broderick.

On Tuesday morning, Broderick woke up early, as was his custom, to beat the morning traffic on his commute from suburban Virginia to the Homeland Security Operations Center in northwest Washington. Since leaving the HSOC at 9:00 P.M. the night before, a great deal of news and intelligence had filtered out of the Gulf region. He was anxious to get to his desk and develop a little "ground truth," as he called it, about New Orleans, Mississippi, and Alabama, and the response to what he still believed was the aftermath of a large, powerful, but essentially standard hurricane.

As he drove to his office, the radio groaned with news of Katrina, describing New Orleans as a ghastly Atlantis where people huddled on rooftops and bodies floated in the streets, as neighborhood after neighborhood succumbed to a relentless, creeping flood. Thousands were trapped by rising waters, the reports said. The levees had been breached in several places. Broderick could hardly believe his ears. He had left the night before to television images of celebrations and the absolute certainty that the worst had passed.

Broderick's instinct was to distrust the reports. "You can't always believe the news," he often said. In fact, he saw it as his duty to "counter the news" and its tendency to overhype by presenting the secretary and the president with nothing but hard, sober facts. And in Broderick's world, those hard facts emerged from a rigorous process of checking and double-checking everything said and written, separating truth from exaggeration and speculation. The military has a word for this process: "validation." Validation was something Broderick took to heart after a thirty-year career in the Marine Corps.

A retired brigadier general, Broderick remained in many respects the quintessential Marine. Though out of uniform since 1998, everything about Broderick screamed jarhead, from the flat-top haircut to the stiff posture, to the jargon-filled cadence of his speech. When not commanding intelligence units or amphibious assault forces, Broderick ran operations centers at all levels of the corps—battalion, regiment, brigade, division, and finally the National Command Center in Washington. He would often boast of his experiences running operations at some of the lowest points in U.S. military history such as the evacuation of Saigon and Phnom Penh in 1975, and the hasty retreat of Marines from a botched humanitarian mission in Mogadishu, Somalia, in 1993.

If Broderick had learned anything from his career, it was that battlefield chatter needed a rigorous and thorough vetting. Acting on "unvalidated" information, Broderick believed, led to confusion, perhaps even death.

Broderick carried these lessons with him when he joined the Department of Homeland Security in 2003. He was working for a defense contractor when Tom Ridge invited him to come build and operate a top-notch operations center for the new department. At the time, the HSOC was little more than a few conference tables laid end to end in the basement of the department's headquarters, staffed by a few dozen people who spent much of their day monitoring television newscasts. Ridge saw the HSOC for what it could be with a big budget and proper organization: the nerve center of the department, the central clearinghouse for terrorist-related information, a smart and carefully calibrated eye on the world. It would be here, Ridge thought, that the myriad reports of suspicious activity that flowed daily from police departments, federal agencies, and sharp-eyed citizens around the nation would be processed and sifted and distilled into reports. These reports would then be pushed back out to the states and the localities and all the federal agencies involved in the general "war on terror." This would be the place, Ridge thought, where the government connected the dots. And during catastrophes, the HSOC would provide the sober big picture upon which the president and his advisers would base their decisions. And everyone involved would have the same view of the disaster zone.

But that's not quite the way Broderick had things set up.

By August 2005, the HSOC was without doubt the largest 24/7 operations center in the country, with a $70 million annual budget, a staff of 300 people from forty-five agencies, banks of computers, plasma television screens, and sophisticated communications gear. But rather than fulfilling its destiny as a massive conduit for smart, forward-looking information, the HSOC was gaining a reputation as a stovepipe into which intelligence disappeared and rarely reemerged. Broderick became adept at demanding information from police departments, businesses, and other federal agencies, but he often failed to return the favor. Police, firefighters, and governors' offices around the country were complaining long before Katrina that the information they got from Broderick's shop was outdated and often useless. "You got more information faster and better watching CNN," said William Bratton, the chief of the Los Angeles Police Department. In fact, one month before Katrina, Bratton was leading a drive by fifteen major city police departments to create their own information-sharing system because they had become so disenchanted with the HSOC.

Hurricane Katrina offered Broderick a new chance to show the doubters they were wrong.

Broderick arrived at the HSOC on Tuesday morning in an agitated state, upset that the radio was broadcasting levee breaches as simple fact. An alp of paper had grown on his desk since he had left. There was a Corps of Engineers report from midevening suggesting that the downtown floodwall had been breached, along with Bahamonde's eyewitness account of the 17th Street Canal, which the HSOC had distributed as a spot report the night before. There was a FEMA report that combined remote sensing imagery and census tract data to estimate that some 136,000 of the city's houses—nearly two-thirds of its inventory—had been flooded. There was a Coast Guard briefing issued at 3:15 A.M. Washington time that said metropolitan New Orleans had suffered "catastrophic" damage. And sitting on top was "Situation Report #8," the HSOC's own top-level summary, which had been distributed to the secretary and the president at 6:00 A.M. The report was declarative: "Industrial Canal at Tennessee St. levee has breached, with water to depth of 5ft at Jackson Barracks; 17th Street at Canal Blvd.; levee has been breached—breach extends several hundred meters in length; much of downtown and east New Orleans is underwater, depth unknown at this time. . . . Widespread and significant flooding has occurred throughout the city of New Orleans, extending eastward across the Mississippi gulf coast into Alabama."

Broderick read the report that had been prepared by the HSOC's overnight shift and cast it aside with the others. He wasn't convinced. Clearly there was flooding, he reasoned, maybe even bad flooding. But there were too many details that just didn't sit right with him. It all smacked of hype and observations from untrained eyes. And at 8:13 A.M., his watch supervisor, Insung Lee, sent out a curious report to the White House and several of Chertoff's top lieutenants that seemed to both confirm and deny the 6:00 A.M. report. "200ft breached levee being assessed at 8:15 EDST," the cryptic e-mail said.

"There is no major damages but MAY require significant air asset to lift the stranded personnel down the cannel [*sic*]."

The effect of the message was that the HSOC no longer stood behind its 6:00 A.M. assessment of the New Orleans floodwall system. Broderick was holding out for verifiable facts. "Tuesday is when we were really pushing," Broderick later told Senate investigators. "Are these breaches, or are these overtoppings? Where are they? What's the extent? What's being flooded? I mean, it could have been flooding a swamp as far as we knew."

Broderick instructed his analysts to contact oil companies in the region and other businesses along the Gulf Coast. Through its various infrastructure protection programs, the HSOC had extensive contacts with strategic industries. But Broderick had an even more powerful link to the business community. In the aftermath of the September 11 attacks, the country's top corporations created a communications network called CEO COM LINK, which was capable of making quick contact with the chief executives of every Fortune 100 firm in times of disaster. Many top executives in fact expected a call on Tuesday, but it never came. The program kicks in during times of national catastrophe; Broderick was still unsure whether the threshold had been reached. The Army Corps of Engineers hadn't given the word. "And the Corps of Engineers does the assessment [on the floodwalls], and they were having a hard time getting around the city to make those assessments," Broderick later said.

Such caution might be understandable on a battlefield where the underestimation of an enemy might mean the deaths of hundreds of soldiers. It made far less sense in a disaster zone, where the only question in the balance was whether to send more help than was already being provided. A battlefield priority is not necessarily a rescue priority; in a rescue, every second wasted is a second that a victim remains in peril. Broderick's inability to recognize this fundamental difference would dog the HSOC through the upcoming days.

In Baton Rouge, the scene was equally addled. Nobody there had much of an idea what was going on in New Orleans, and Brown could see this as he went through his morning checks. Bill Lokey, FEMA's coordinating officer for the state, had spent the morning talking to the Louisiana National Guard and the New Orleans district of the Army Corps, which had fled to Vicksburg, Mississippi, in advance of the storm. They knew nothing. Were the city's flood pumps working? Was the lake still spilling into the city? All anyone seemed to know was that the flooding was bad.

Brown conferred with Lokey and with Governor Blanco, and the three of them came to a meeting of the minds. Be it breach or overtop, the city was lurching toward a superdisaster by just about every measure. Louisiana needed more help. At around 8:00 A.M. in Baton Rouge, Brown called the White House and requested an urgent videoconference with President Bush and Secretary Chertoff. Brown knew Chertoff was leaving that morning for Atlanta to attend a conference on pandemic flu at the Centers for Disease Control. Bush was in San Diego. It was important, Brown felt, that both men understand the urgency of the situation in New Orleans and the problems he was facing getting cooperation from the Pentagon.

At about 8:30 A.M., Brown walked into a room at the headquarters of the Louisiana State Police in Baton Rouge and saw the president and his top people staring back at him from the video screens. There was Vice President Dick Cheney on the screen from his vacation home in Wyoming, Chief of Staff Andrew Card coming in from Maine, and Frances Townsend, Bush's homeland security adviser, from Washington. Michael Chertoff was there as well.

As Brown later recalled it, Bush started it off. "What's the situation?" he asked.

"Bad," Brown answered. "This was the 'Big One.' "

And then it started coming out of Brown in a rush. Laying aside the question of the levees, Brown said, "I can tell you, sir, that 90 percent of the people of New Orleans have been displaced by this event."

Bush looked shocked. "Ninety percent? Are you sure?" the president asked.

The other officials seemed stunned as well. Chertoff asked if

Brown was getting what he needed. Brown said he laid it out: This disaster was too big for FEMA and the National Guard alone. The supply lines to the region were already gumming up; Brown suggested the Pentagon be called in to run logistics. Cheney promised someone would talk to Rumsfeld and wondered if a cabinet meeting shouldn't be called.

While Brown clearly alarmed the president and his top men, it was unclear if he fully impressed the gravity of the situation on them—or FEMA's tenuous grasp on the disaster. "He wasn't saying everything's hunky dory," said White House counselor Dan Bartlett. "But I never got the feeling from Brown that there was any problem that wasn't surmountable."

The chat lasted less than thirty minutes. But Brown said he left the videoconference believing that the top men now knew how desperate the situation was. Brown returned to the state emergency operations center a few steps away and awaited the Blackhawk helicopter that was scheduled to take him, Governor Blanco, and U.S. senators Mary Landrieu and David Vitter to the Superdome.

When the Blackhawk touched down, Marty Bahamonde was the first to greet his boss. He shook Brown's hand, pulled him close, and whispered into his ear. "It's critical, sir, especially here at the Superdome," Bahamonde said. Brown thanked his advance man and overruled Lokey: He wanted Bahamonde to stay put and continue aiding the relief effort. Then Brown greeted Mayor Nagin and moved with him toward the heliport office to confer, their aides trailing behind.

Inside the office Nagin sat down, unfolded a sheaf of papers, and pushed it across to Brown. It was a painstaking list of equipment and support the city needed from Washington. Brown was impressed. Bahamonde had prepared them well. Brown had been worried that Nagin wasn't up to the disaster, but this was a good effort. Nagin was asking for generators, food, water, supplies, technical assistance to restore electricity and communications, and medical support. "Mayor, this is the best list I have ever seen after a disaster," Brown said. The mayor beamed.

Outside the heliport office, another Blackhawk was landing. It was the FEMA emergency response team that Lokey said would be replacing Bahamonde as FEMA's team on the ground, but whose ranks the advance man would now join. The team was headed by Philip E. Parr, a former New York City firefighter who had been one of only a few African Americans to rise to the level of chief. Standing six feet tall and weighing 230 pounds, Parr cut a powerful figure in a crowd. He brought his team in from Texas to establish a joint command with city and state officials and to set up a forward base of operations that would coordinate the city's needs and watch over the situation at the Superdome. He was not on the ground five minutes before Brown gave him his first assignment, pressing Nagin's list into the former firefighter's hand. Then Brown went to find Governor Blanco, who was off getting her own ground truth.

Blanco was very disturbed by what she saw. Standing on the raised concrete apron amid thousands of evacuees, Blanco peered north down Poydras Street and saw a scene that could scarcely be imagined. A tangle of exit ramps a half block down the street was filled with ranks of survivors. Below that, hundreds of people moved through the rusty, waist-deep water, pushing their meager possessions in plastic laundry baskets and buckets. A substantial chunk of the city's 100,000 remaining residents were moving toward higher ground, on a beeline for the city's only shelter, the poor and the infirm and the plain stubborn, walking gingerly through the brown water. As Blanco watched the scene, a nearby soldier told her the Dome's population was rapidly on the way to doubling and that supplies, enough to handle 9,000 evacuees for a couple of days, were almost certain to run out within twenty-four hours.

"We have to get these people out of here," Blanco said to Brown, when he walked up. "We need buses."

Brown smiled. "If there's one thing FEMA's got, it's buses," he said. And before the two boarded the Blackhawk, Brown made the first of what would be a series of calls to Washington about buses, saying that the governor of Louisiana needed five hundred of them, pronto. "Catch up with the paperwork later," Brown told his staff in Washington.

At 10:15 A.M. (11:15 in Washington), a copy of a FEMA request to evacuate up to 20,000 people from the Superdome arrived by e-mail at the White House. But it would be hours before anyone acted upon it.

Parr got an update on the situation from Terry Ebbert, the city's disaster chief. The main concern, Ebbert said, was closing the gap in the 17th Street Canal floodwall, which was the source of all the water inundating downtown. But City Hall knew nothing of any plans for patching the broken floodwall. "No problem," said Parr. "Let me call the Army Corps of Engineers."

Parr whipped out his cell phone. No signal. And no signal on the satellite phones he had in his bag. And then more bad news came, in a rush. The agents from the Federal Protective Service (Homeland Security's police force), who were supposed to be on-site, were in fact nowhere to be found. The MERS communications trucks FEMA had promised were instead sitting grounded in Baton Rouge. The man who operated one of these trucks had actually driven to the Dome to tell Parr that the city was too flooded for the command van to make the trip. It was a sad situation for FEMA—Parr was supposed to set up a ground operation in the ruined city, but in fact he was standing on a flooded island, unable to even make a simple phone call. He was no better off than most of the thousands of evacuees who surrounded him on the concrete apron outside the Superdome. And now he was completely dependent on the National Guard for everything from communications to security.

In New Orleans, Broderick was about to get the ground truth he craved, thanks to Colonel Richard Wagenaar of the Army Corps' New Orleans District, who had managed to get aboard a helicopter and get aloft. Flying low across the sky to the city's Ninth Ward, Wagenaar counted four breaches in the Industrial Canal levee and saw a five-hundred-foot covered barge floating aimlessly among what remained of the homes in the neighborhood. Many of the houses had been flattened by water, not wind. Wagenaar gazed out at the Lower Ninth Ward neighborhood, where scores of people stood on rooftops and hung from tree branches, waving shirts and towels. Then he signaled the pilot to head northwest, toward Lake Pontchartrain and the 17th Street Canal.

Here, the damage was even worse. As Wagenaar circled the canal, he could see it was a breach all right, a massive one. On the ground were two corps employees who had managed to beat him to the scene after commandeering a fishing boat about a mile away. Here, too, racing water had pushed houses off their slabs and into nearby streets. The two corps men eventually realized they had stumbled onto a tableau of amazing futility: a small crew of state workers were tossing twenty-five-pound sandbags into the gaping maw of a breach that was several hundred feet long. As the sandbags went in the gap, they were swept away by the cascade of lake water that was rushing into the city.

The corps men asked the locals if they needed help and were curtly informed that the situation was in hand. "They wanted to take charge of the whole site," Wagenaar said. "They were killing the city."

But in keeping with long-standing protocol, similar to FEMA's, under which federal officials do not interfere unless invited, the corps men withdrew. Wagenaar flew back to headquarters and filed a report. "At that point, I felt like it was their responsibility," he said. The corps wouldn't become involved in the levee repair for two days.

At around noon in Washington, when Wagenaar's report came through the pipe, Broderick was finally satisfied. He called Chertoff in Atlanta and confirmed the breaches. A few minutes later, Kirstjen Nielsen, the president's senior director for preparedness and response, sent an e-mail message to a Red Cross official named Carol Hall. "If you have a few minutes I would like to pick your brain about 'things' that may not be working optimally," Nielsen wrote. She asked Hall whether, in the absence of a catastrophic designation, some "strategic policy issues might be going unaddressed. Some Federal partners have mentioned that they are lacking situational awareness and are having problems getting logistics issues addressed—are you seeing same?"

An HSOC report on the levees arrived at the White House about two hours after Chertoff had been told of the breaches. It was now approximately thirty hours since Katrina had made landfall. "Army Corps reports 300 foot levee breach," the report said. It noted that water from Lake Pontchartrain was pouring through the breach. It added that "multiple" breaches had occurred in the Ninth Ward.

At about the same time, officials in Washington and the Gulf Coast convened the daily videoconference. Bill Lokey, FEMA's operations man in Louisiana, was apparently unaware of his own agency's assessment that the area was too flooded for the MERS communications trucks to get to the Superdome. He reported they were on their way. "That should help some of the coordination there, plus give us some eyes-on visibility of some of the issues down there," Lokey said. They weren't, of course.

In contrast to the Sunday and Monday videoconferences, this call included few senior officials; the White House had not called in. Brown and Blanco were still in New Orleans. Chertoff was not on the line. Patrick Rhode, Brown's deputy in Washington, directed the conversation.

Jeff Smith, Louisiana's state coordinating officer for the disaster, laid out a sketch of the troubles in New Orleans, focusing primarily on search and rescue. He noted that while the rescue operation was proceeding with fair efficiency, disaster workers had failed to establish formal collection points, meaning that evacuees were beginning to build up on highway overpasses and other ad hoc sites. "So that part of the operation, while it's going smoothly, is not going as smoothly as we would like it," Smith said.

In a measured voice, he then went through a litany of other problems: The city's jail was flooded and the state was just beginning an evacuation operation for 4,000 prisoners. Hospitals were flooding as well, and patients were being moved to the Superdome, but Smith admitted the state hadn't yet formulated a plan to handle this problem. Smith mentioned that the state was considering using helicopters to evacuate the Superdome, but with everything else going on, dealing with the crowd there had slipped as a priority. He made no request for buses.

Smith did plead for more resources from FEMA and noted that the agency was having a hard time predicting when supplies would arrive and where they were in transit. "Communications are always tough and we do understand that," Smith said, "but anything that we could [do to] help improve the communications on inbound assets, whether it be medical assets, whether it be commodities, whatever, it would certainly be a tremendous benefit."

Overall, however, Smith's criticisms were mild. "All I would ask is that you realize what's going on and the sense of urgency here needs to be ratcheted up," he said. Lokey assured Smith that help was on the way.

Sporting a shaved head and a droopy mustache, Bill Lokey looked a lot more fierce than he was. In fact, he wasn't a bad man to have in the hot seat: He had a gentle nature and an even way of talking that made him seem unflappable. Moreover, he was a disaster responder with a great deal of experience, having worked in the state of Washington and with FEMA's celebrated Urban Search and Rescue squads.

Lokey had joined FEMA in 1999 as a federal coordinating officer, an FCO, a position that once packed more punch than it did six years later. Appointed by the president and armed with a letter bearing the seal of the Oval Office, an FCO has the power under the law to task the entire Washington bureacracy to help respond to a disaster. But the trappings of the position are far more grand than the reality. Now buried under layers of bureaucracy and new complicated relief plans, the FCO has become just another civil servant. Lokey didn't fuss about the prestige so much as long as the job got done.

His practicality was one of the things Brown liked about him. So when Lokey approached him on Tuesday afternoon and said the disaster was too big for FEMA, a little jolt of fear went up Brown's spine. Lokey wanted to turn the operation over to the Pentagon. And Brown could tell that Lokey was scared. "I remember the discussion clearly," Brown later recalled. "I remember seeing panic in his eyes. I could just see it in his eyes. Something that said, 'This is beyond us.'"

Brown said he told Lokey he would make some calls and mention

Lokey's recommendation to the governor. A short time later, Blanco called Lokey into her office and demanded to know why he was trying to take the disaster away from her. Why, she asked, was Washington horning in on Louisiana's sovereignty? Lokey said that wasn't the case at all. The disaster was big and needed a big response, he said. Someone else in the room chimed in, "The State of Louisiana is still sovereign."

Lokey got Brown, and both men tried to reassure the governor. "Ma'am, we would never do this without coordinating with you," Brown said. "It is similar to what we did with 9/11. We were doing the what-ifs." General Landreneau, the head of the Louisiana National Guard, who had sat quietly listening, now spoke up. The Guard could handle it, he said. And that was the end of the conversation.

But whether anyone could handle the disaster remained an open question. In New Orleans, the hours were slipping by, and the situation was becoming increasingly desperate. More than twenty-four hours had passed since the levee breaches were first reported, and thousands of people had been driven from their homes or were trapped in their attics without food and water. Broderick, Brown, and Lokey had now concluded that the disaster in New Orleans fit the description of a catastrophe. But what Jeff Smith had said mildly in Tuesday's videoconference—that FEMA wasn't getting enough food and water to the city—was becoming a real problem on the ground. The Superdome, ground zero of the disaster effort, received only 35,000 meal packets the entire day—hardly enough to feed a population that was rapidly pushing 20,000. Desperation was setting in. Looters began bashing in storefronts on Canal Street, the city's main shopping corridor, making off with armloads of liquor and expensive running shoes. The big-box stores farther into the city became scenes of merchandise free-for-alls. On street corners in virtually every section of town, people broke into drug stores and bodegas, making off with diapers, canned goods, and cigarettes. What Washington seemed unable to provide, people just took. Some of the pilfering took on a sinister tone. A large pawnshop in Central City was stripped of its firearms stock. Some two hundred vehicles were taken off the lot of a downtown Cadillac dealership, many by cops but some by civilians. The Winn-Dixie grocery store on Basin Street was overrun by residents from two sprawling public housing developments nearby. The looting was open and brazen and went on during the day in plain view of reporters.

On Tuesday afternoon, the Louisiana State Police reported two occurrences that set imaginations wild: the near-fatal shooting of a New Orleans police officer by a suspected looter and the stripping of a New Orleans gun store, which was cleared of its inventory. Suddenly, the city was said to be filled with armed gangs. Uptowners who had remained in the city broke out their duck guns to protect themselves.

The state police superintendent, Colonel Henry Whitehorn, was so jumpy he wrote an urgent letter to FBI director Robert Mueller requesting "any assistance you can provide," noting that New Orleans had "suffered massive damage" and that the state police were "utilizing all state assets to stabilize the situation," but "looting continues to be a significant problem." The White House, too, was becoming concerned about the crime situation in New Orleans; senior officials began preliminary talks with the U.S. Northern Command on the merits of federalizing the disaster and bringing in regular army soldiers. "The problem was law and order," White House counselor Dan Bartlett said. "Large chunks of the New Orleans Police Department had completely disappeared."

Politicians from Baton Rouge to Washington implored Mayor Nagin and Governor Blanco to declare martial law. And in fact, the HSOC reported that such a declaration had indeed been made. But martial law doesn't exist under Louisiana statutes, and the HSOC quietly corrected its assertion later in the day, saying instead that a "law enforcement emergency" had been declared.

But while many stores in New Orleans were looted, many were pilfered only for food, and a surprising number of the city's shops, including grocery and liquor stores, were left untouched. But that didn't stop the calls—and the rumors—from flying, often with generous help from local and even national officials. The state police reported dozens, if not hundreds, of calls on Tuesday about various violent acts in New Orleans. "When responded to, most of these calls are proved unfounded," the state police said.

Meanwhile, three breaches at the London Avenue Canal, which swamped more of the city than any other, continued to flow undetected. Hundreds of people sat on their rooftops in the neighborhoods near the canal, but rescuers were concentrating their efforts on the areas near the known breaches. By then, Nestor James, a pump operator along the London Avenue Canal, had been rescuing people for hours. Trapped in the pumphouse, he and a colleague had walked single-file down the undamaged part of the floodwall until they spied a twenty-foot ski boat they could commandeer. Using fenceboards as paddles, they began plucking stranded citizens off rooftops and taking them to a high-rise building on the University of New Orleans campus, about a half mile away. James said he and his buddy rescued about thirty people on Tuesday. He said they didn't see a single helicopter or rescue boat all day.

Back in Washington, Broderick was trying to assemble his own situation awareness from the top-secret satellite pictures he had ordered from the National Geospatial-Intelligence Agency and matching them with information flowing into the HSOC. Every once in a while, someone stranded in New Orleans would manage to get a phone call through to the center to pass on information or beg for help because they were stranded somewhere. In a few cases Broderick was able to use the department's communications equipment to latch onto the cell phone signals and direct Coast Guard boats to make rescues. But what Broderick needed now wasn't technology but eyes and ears on the ground that he could trust.

By 4:00 P.M. Eastern time, the White House was receiving reports that New Orleans had lost its 911 emergency telephone system, that all of the city but the French Quarter and the business district had flooded, that the Superdome had suffered damage in the storm, and that people in Jefferson Parish were combing the streets looking for food. The White House began to press Chertoff. And Chertoff began pressing Brown.

But Brown was off in the disaster zone. Nobody on his staff seemed to know exactly where he was. And the last time anyone saw him was on television during a press conference with Governor Blanco in Baton Rouge after the trip to New Orleans. Chertoff called the HSOC and demanded they track Brown down. Broderick later recounted the conversation: "Most of the discussion was, where's Brown? Is Brown going to call? Does anybody know where Brown is? Has anybody seen Brown, except on television? It was very, very frustrating. We would see Brown on television, but he wasn't calling us. And we were trying to call him, and we weren't getting calls back."

While he said he would have spoken to Chertoff, Brown later said that whenever he saw the HSOC appear on the caller ID on his cell phone, he simply ignored it. "There was no reason for me to talk to them," he maintained. "I had a disaster to run."

But Chertoff was persistent. At 5:00 P.M. Eastern time, Chertoff called Brooks Altshuler, Brown's chief of staff, and flew into a rage, as he would later admit, screaming that someone had better find Brown or heads were going to roll.

As it turned out, Brown was in Mississippi with Governor Haley Barbour and Bill Carwile, the federal coordinating officer in the state. The Mississippi coast had been absolutely ripped by Katrina's storm surge, and though it was a more conventional disaster than what was unfolding in New Orleans, it was a catastrophe on a scale rarely matched in disaster annals. Entire towns had simply disappeared. If it weren't for the floods in Louisiana, the television crews would have flocked to Biloxi, and Mississippi was facing many of the same supply and communications problems that Louisiana was experiencing.

Altshuler sent an e-mail message to his boss: If Washington called again, he had better pick up the phone. It was early evening. Brown was on a military plane headed back to Baton Rouge when the call came. It was Chertoff, and he was livid. "I could hear his teeth gritting," Brown said. The secretary got to the point. "I can't get hold of you. I don't want you running around, flying around all over the place, I want you to go to Baton Rouge and not leave Baton Rouge," he said. Brown told Chertoff he had set up a meeting with

Governor Barbour two days hence, but Chertoff cut him short. "I don't give a shit about that," he growled. And then he slammed down the phone. Brown went back to Baton Rouge with a queasy feeling in his stomach.

"I knew right then I was screwed," Brown later recalled. "If I couldn't move around and see what was going on, then how could I do my job?" Brown wasn't an operations man. He was a public whip, a political animal, best employed in shirtsleeves, in the thick of a disaster zone, on camera, either urging calm or demanding action. "Flash back to Florida," Brown said, referring to the four hurricanes that hit the state in 2004. "That's what I did. That's how we got things moving. If I was allowed to move around I would have seen the Superdome and the fact that they had no communications and would have blown a fuse. But I was being bolted down in Baton Rouge."

At the state's emergency operations center, Brown was a third wheel. He didn't want to bigfoot his underlings or micromanage them, the way he believed Chertoff did. So he began spending most of his time in "Red October"—FEMA's grounded MERS communications command vehicle, which was parked outside the operations center. Brown fell into a funk of sorts and became even more uncommunicative with Washington, even as Chertoff made the first moves that unplugged the FEMA director from the operation.

It was beginning to dawn on the Bush administration that disaster management along the Gulf Coast wasn't going as well as it should. If Florida in 2004 had been the acme of federal disaster response, Katrina was quickly becoming the nadir. In the White House itself, the operations center was complaining that it wasn't getting the information it needed from Broderick and his HSOC staff. Information that did arrive was coming in late. It was clear by that afternoon that FEMA and Homeland Security were letting the disaster get away from them. It was all over television, scenes of an escalating watery nightmare and a feeble federal response.

President Bush was in San Diego on Tuesday, delivering a speech commemorating World War II veterans and sticking to his set itinerary. He deviated from his prepared remarks to offer a few reassuring words on Katrina. "Our teams and equipment are in place and we're beginning to move in the help that people need," he said.

But beyond view of the cameras, the White House was moving toward panic, as aides scrambled to square live television coverage of the disaster with the reports they were receiving from the HSOC and FEMA. "We were constantly getting paper reports saying one thing and seeing something quite the contrary on TV," White House counselor Bartlett said. And Bush, according to Bartlett, was starting to get angry.

That morning in San Diego, in an unusual move, White House press secretary Scott McClellan put the reporters accompanying the president on notice that Bush had decided to cut his five-week vacation short. Bush would head back to Crawford that afternoon, and he would leave the following morning for Washington. He planned to convene his cabinet and get the federal response on an even keel.

In Baton Rouge late Tuesday afternoon, Louisiana's Jeff Smith, who had earlier been told that 500 buses were coming, received the paperwork from Lokey that would formalize the request. As he looked over the documents, he saw that the number of requested buses had dropped to 455. "I was told that someone at FEMA headquarters had 'done the math' and it was determined that we didn't need 500 buses," Smith said. "It was a little irritating."

It was irritating to Governor Blanco as well. As Tuesday drew to a close, Louisiana and the city of New Orleans had three major needs, all of which had been conveyed to FEMA hours or even days before: Survivors needed food and water, the city needed reliable communications, and the state needed buses to evacuate the Superdome. FEMA had not delivered on any of them.

Blanco had been to the Superdome and knew full well that 500 buses wouldn't be nearly enough to evacuate the arena. She had already directed her staff earlier in the day to begin collecting school buses, church buses—anything with four wheels and a lot of seats—and send it to the Louisiana Superdome. This represented the first direct attempt by the state to work around FEMA. Late Tuesday afternoon, Blanco also called Governor Rick Perry of Texas to see if he could open the Houston Astrodome for her state's evacuees. Louisiana's 113 state shelters were already bursting. Perry said he was happy to oblige.

The state wasn't receiving such cooperation from the federal government. On Tuesday afternoon, Andy Kopplin, Blanco's chief of staff, found himself in a protracted battle with the Pentagon over the use of four helicopters that had been idling on the tarmac at the Fort Polk air base in central Louisiana. Kopplin had been tipped off to the idle craft by a private ambulance service operator who had just happened to see them while driving by. Kopplin called the base on Tuesday morning and spoke to the officer in charge of the flight crews. "They told me the governor needs to direct the Department of Defense to make a request," Kopplin said later. For hours on Tuesday he worked the phones, traveling up the chain of command at the Pentagon in an effort to get the helicopters released. At around five in the afternoon, he got the last permission he needed and hurriedly called Fort Polk to get the choppers in the air. But Kopplin's victory was Pyrrhic: As he related it, a major at the base told him that the helicopters couldn't leave until the next morning. It seemed that by sitting on the tarmac all day waiting for orders, the pilots had exceeded their allowed flight time. "I'm not sure what you call it but this is absolutely not 'leaning forward,'" Kopplin said. "And of course by that point, I'm a little befuddled by the whole thing."

At 8:22 P.M. in Washington, Chertoff declared the Hurricane Katrina disaster an "incident of national significance" and designated Brown as his principal federal official, or PFO, on the ground. The announcement triggered the controversial National Response Plan for the first time. White House spokesman Scott McClellan said the move allowed the Department of Homeland Security to better coordinate the agencies involved in the relief effort. It would prove to be a largely empty gesture, coming as late as it did. But to Chertoff, the action formalized Washington's chain of command: It put him in charge and it put Brown on a short leash since the principal federal officer reported directly to the secretary.

Chertoff's chief of staff, John Wood, would later tell congressional investigators that few people understood Homeland Security's responsibilities under the NRP. But Chertoff would recount that naming Brown as the PFO was meant to strengthen his own hand "so that during our upcoming Cabinet meeting, colleagues would have no doubt that Mr. Brown was my personal representative, with all the authority necessary to address the incident."

Brown was furious; he had always held that the PFO was the punk of the game, an unnecessary bureaucratic layer that added nothing to the response effort and whose only function was to make sure the secretary knew what he was talking about when briefing the president. As Brown viewed things, it was just another way for Chertoff to micromanage the disaster. Moreover, it essentially scrapped the organization that had been managing the disaster in midstride, halfway through the catastrophe. A confused Washington response would only get more confused, Brown felt, with a whole new set of cooks in the kitchen.

Brown's staff tried to console him. In an e-mail message to Brown, FEMA press secretary Sharon Worthy expressed disbelief. "Demote the Under Sec to PFO? . . . What about the precedent being set?" she wrote. "Why would anyone want to be an FCO when at any moment the Under Sec could be sent to the field?"

Down in New Orleans, one federal agency had been able to get in where FEMA feared to tread. The Federal Protective Service (FPS) had managed to drive into the city, set up a beachhead, and begin casing a wider swath of town than Bahamonde and Parr had been able to see from the Superdome. This service, which guards many federal buildings throughout the country, was in town to secure the city's federal buildings, but also to perform other tasks. During disasters, the FPS rides shotgun for FEMA, protecting its personnel and equipment. The service was one of the smallest of the twenty-two agencies that had been folded into the Department of Homeland Security, and one of the few that seemed to have prospered under its new overseers, enjoying access to more equipment and money than ever before.

The FPS had come prepared when it arrived in Louisiana, with two fully outfitted communications trucks, a raft of other vehicles, six rubber Zodiac boats, and about thirty well-armed men. Some agents set up an operations base in Baton Rouge while twenty made it into the city of New Orleans, led by Chief Dwayne Andrews from Fort Worth, Texas, and Inspector David Tyndell, a former firefighter who had driven one of the agency's communications trucks down from Denver. Though Tyndell had left the truck in Lafayette, about three hours west of New Orleans, he and his colleagues meandered into the city on Tuesday with the help of some aerial photographs and directions from the Army Corps of Engineers, making their way to the Hale Boggs Federal Building about seven blocks from the Superdome. The director of the FPS, Wendell Shingler, was driving down from Washington at the time. Shingler had given his agents three orders: Secure the federal buildings, patrol the city, and report up the chain of command, ultimately to the HSOC, whatever they saw on those patrols.

When Tyndell and his colleagues arrived, they discovered the power outage had knocked out the Boggs Building's electronic locking system, and the place was standing wide open. Apparently a few of the building's janitors had kept potential looters at bay. Floor by floor, the FPS agents swept through the building and then used handcuffs and chains to secure the exterior doors. The agents quickly discovered their radios were useless; the tower on the roof of the federal building had been knocked out by the storm. But their walkie-talkie-style cell phones offered sporadic service.

No sooner had the FPS arrived downtown than Andrews's phone began to beep with a litany of information requests from the HSOC and from the White House. Were buildings on fire? Had there been a prison break? How bad was the looting? "We were like a recon unit relaying information to Washington about everything," Andrews recalled. Andrews divided his men into two teams, one to secure the Boggs Building and the other to gather information. They worked well into the night. At midnight, seven agents stayed downtown to do some limited patrolling, while the rest went back to Lafayette to get some sleep.

So the FPS men patrolled, cautiously, not straying too far from the federal complex. And on a street near the river, just a few blocks away, they discovered an unusual scene unfolding in the gloom. Outside a very long, very narrow building called the Ernest N. Morial Convention Center, a crowd had begun to form in the shadow of the building's main entranceway, spilling out onto the adjacent street, which was dry. The agents couldn't quite fathom what had drawn the big crowd, but the people were settling wearily onto blankets on the sidewalks and the grass outside. The agents estimated the crowd at about a thousand people.

The FPS agents didn't venture too close, but they followed the standing orders Shingler had given them. They reported the gathering crowd to their superiors in Baton Rouge, calling it a "spontaneous gathering" and identifying the Convention Center by name. The report was dutifully passed on to Washington and the HSOC a short time later.

8

PROMISES, PROMISES

As Wednesday, August 31, dawned on the ruined city of New Orleans, this much was clear: Washington was receiving rafts of accurate information about what was happening on the streets of the city, but the information wasn't getting to the people who needed it. The White House and Chertoff were flying blind. Most of FEMA's staff was sequestered in Baton Rouge, eighty-five miles away. They may as well have been in Bangkok. Though three of the agency's eighteen Urban Search and Rescue teams were in the city, the crews rarely made contact with Michael Brown and his deputies at the emergency operations center in Baton Rouge. FEMA's window on the city was essentially limited to an agency spokesman and a few midlevel coordinators, all of whom were marooned on the raised concrete apron outside the Louisiana Superdome downtown. This crew, outfitted with little more than a change of clothes, had no reliable way to call or e-mail Brown. They had little to report anyhow: With no transportation, their view of the city was limited to about a half-block of streetscape. Though FEMA had several high-tech MERS communications trucks in Baton Rouge sitting tantalizingly close to New Orleans, the agency seemed not to grasp that certain roads into downtown were dry and passable. It didn't appear to dawn on anyone that supply trucks with sufficient clearance were making regular runs to the Louisiana Superdome and that newspaper reporters and television news crews were moving around New Orleans. The agency's communications fleet included eighteen-wheeled trucks and smaller vans that could easily have made the trip and set up satellite communications for an army, offering videoconferences and wireless Internet access for scores of relief workers. Instead, the gear sat virtually unused in a Baton Rouge parking lot.

From a ground truth standpoint, the state wasn't in much better shape, though its contingent of National Guard troops had a reliable communications suite they could use to contact Baton Rouge. Even so, the Guard had its hands full: The Superdome was packed with demoralized and hungry citizens, its population having almost tripled over the past two days, to about 25,000. The troops were grossly outgunned by the disaster—according to state figures, there were only 1,432 Guard soldiers in New Orleans on Wednesday morning, and more than half of them were either rescuing people or working to close levee breaches. Only 649 soldiers managed the crowd at the Superdome, and they struggled to maintain order, a task made harder by the fact that FEMA's food deliveries had slowed to a trickle. The soldiers were forced to ration food, a decision that didn't improve the mood of the crowd. Strained far beyond its intended capacity, unairconditioned, and lacking running water or toilets (the portable bathrooms requested of FEMA had never arrived), the arena, simply put, was beginning to stink. On Wednesday, apparently unbeknownst to anyone in the state or federal government, City Hall closed the Superdome to new arrivals. Instead, as the *Times-Picayune* noted in a small item on its Web site, rescuers were dumping large numbers of evacuees outside the Convention Center, about ten blocks to the south. That building may have been an even worse shelter than the Superdome, if such was possible. It was locked, unsupervised by police, and had no stocks of food or water. But it was unmistakably dry, and at one point FEMA had identified the half-mile-long building as a possible forward operating base. But the desperate evacuees, dumped in the area by rescuers, beat the agency to it; they immediately set about breaking into nearby shops and restaurants and looting mattresses and blankets from area hotels. By midafternoon on Wednesday, the population outside the Convention Center would number in the thousands. Many thousands more idled on the few dry streets and overpasses in the dry downtown area. Citywide, New Orleans officials put the number of homeless at 50,000.

In Washington, Matthew Broderick continued to receive accurate information from a variety of sources, but he seemed to have no more visibility on the situation than he had the day before, at least judging from the reports his staff was filing. Beyond delivering a few maps of the levee breaches to the White House about thirty hours after the breaks had opened, the HSOC had provided almost no useful insight into what was occurring on the ground in New Orleans.

At 2:00 A.M. Washington time on Wednesday, the HSOC reported that about 12,000 to 15,000 people were at the Superdome, understating the building's population by roughly half. In its daily 5:45 A.M. situation report, the HSOC recycled Marty Bahamonde's news from two days earlier that there was a massive breach at the 17th Street Canal levee. It also claimed that floodwaters were still rising in the city, but by this hour, there was a falling tide on the lake and the Industrial Canal breach had already reversed, allowing water to start flowing out of the drowned Lower Ninth Ward. Johnny Bradberry, the state's transportation secretary, who was supervising breach repairs, would say later that morning that the water level citywide had actually begun falling at a slow creep of about an inch per hour, as the tide in Lake Pontchartrain receded. Nevertheless, the HSOC would doggedly insist throughout the day that the water was still rising, at one point quoting a federal official who predicted that all of New Orleans would be underwater by day's end.

If Broderick's reports were often remarkable in what they stated as unvarnished fact, they were also remarkable in what they left out, offering little insight into the big picture. Though the city was plagued by huge, mysterious fires that broke out along its wharfs and elsewhere, the HSOC's reports made no mention of them. The HSOC gave no context for one significant fact, that hundreds of city bus employees escaped a maintenance building on rubber rafts to take refuge at the Convention Center. Though the HSOC mentioned that Louisiana had requested federal help in evacuating the Superdome (an item nearly twenty-four hours old), it made no attempt to analyze the strength of the city's vastly depleted police force or to determine whether the reports of looting, which had captivated the press and city rescue workers, were in fact overblown.

With the debate over breaches finally settled, Broderick turned his attention to search and rescue and brought the same rigor to that operation as he had to the technical aspects of levee failures. There was no denying the unfolding rescue operation was massive and in a way tremendously effective: By Wednesday, tens of thousands of people had been plucked off rooftops or fished out of the flood-swollen streets. The rescue efforts involved state and federal agencies from around the nation, the U.S. Coast Guard, and hundreds of volunteers from nearby parishes and from around the country. The sky above the city was crammed with helicopters, which aviation officials would later say bordered on a dangerous saturation of the available airspace. Though a handful of the craft were trying to fix the levees, most were dedicated to rescue, dangling baskets and men onto rooftops and hauling out as many people as they could.

And yet the massive rescue effort suffered from the same lack of command and control that plagued other government efforts in the disaster zone. In the chaos, people just improvised. All over town, gangs of rescuers, both official and volunteer, would simply drive down a street to the edge of a flood zone, drop boats, and fan out into a neighborhood. After a while, the boat gangs would return to where they had left their vehicles, dump the evacuees on the nearest patch of high ground, trailer the boats, and leave. Many of these rescue teams had no food or water to give these evacuees, who were tremendously dehydrated from having sat for hours on their roofs in the fierce summer sun. There was often no coordinated system of collecting evacuees in a single place so they could be cared for more easily.

As a result, huge, disparate groups of evacuees, bound together only by their common quest for food and water, roamed the dry slivers of New Orleans in great clumps, seeking whatever necessities they could find. They looted stores and fought among themselves for basic necessities. Some died.

Across all of the government, it was all improvisation, with virtually every federal, state, and local agency conducting an independent operation. City police, who operated a crude command center from the driveway of a local casino, complained that the state agencies and the Coast Guard didn't even attempt to coordinate anything with them. But the police were generally consumed with rescuing their own cops, many of whom had fallen victim to the creeping flood. The state's Department of Wildlife and Fisheries, which was directed from the parking lot of a shopping mall in Baton Rouge, complained about the National Guard, which had its own command at the Superdome.

It would be days before these agencies would get together under a unified command and devise a map and grid system to systematically comb the city for survivors and bring rigor to their efforts. Meanwhile, stories abounded of rescue groups double-teaming neighborhoods while ignoring others, of streets where some people were taken out while neighbors were left pleading for help. In many parts of town, whole neighborhoods were simply overlooked, some for several days. St. Bernard Parish, which was swamped to the eaves and had about 6,000 residents standing on the rooftops, was largely ignored by rescuers until Wednesday, when a forty-seven-man contingent of Canadian Mounties arrived.

Even as thousands of people were being removed from the floodwaters, serious problems pervaded the rescue efforts. But instead of examining these problems, Broderick, obsessed with details, himself became a rescuer in a way, directing search operations by remote control from his office in Washington, using whatever tools he had at hand. Leo Bosner, FEMA's night watch officer in Washington, and Bill Lokey, the top FEMA response coordinator in Louisiana, complained repeatedly to colleagues about the amount of time lost in pursuing individual rescue victims that Broderick had happened to see on TV, sometimes mistaking file footage for live coverage. "It was madness," Bosner said. "We'd get calls from Broderick or his staff shouting about a group of stranded people now on CNN, demanding that we find out where they were. Of course you'd find out they were pictures taken the day before."

Broderick's other interest was gathering disaster statistics, and he relentlessly pestered Bosner to provide exacting data on commodities delivered to the disaster zone and rescue sorties completed in the city. On Wednesday, Bosner got a call from HSOC asking him to run down a discrepancy in the rescue numbers coming from a particular neighborhood in New Orleans. One report put the number at thirty-six, while another had it at thirty-nine. According to Bosner, Broderick told him this detail was vitally important to Chertoff, who had an important press conference scheduled for later that day.

Bosner revolted. He flat refused to run down overwhelmed rescuers over such a picayune discrepancy. "Screw that," he said to himself. The HSOC called several times in the next few hours, and when they did, Bosner just lied. "Gosh, I tried three times and just can't get through," he said on one such occasion. Though Broderick later complained he just wasn't getting the information he needed out of New Orleans, it was Bosner's opinion that the ex-Marine was seeking an absurd level of granularity.

At the same time, Broderick and his staff at the HSOC realized that they were woefully behind and losing control of the response, and so they made a belated effort to catch up with some very basic information. Insung Lee, a senior watch officer at the HSOC, sent an e-mail message to several senior officials at FEMA, Homeland Security, and the White House, asking for "the inventory of all department agency operations/activity. . . . Are [there] any Federal powers or other processes that could be implemented to expedite the response or make it more efficient? . . . What are the plans for providing housing to . . . displaced people by hurricane damage?" Questions like these primarily caused the response to slow down still further.

As the hunt for ground truth continued, the Convention Center crowd that the FPS agents had observed overnight was now growing exponentially, nearly rivaling the assemblage at the Superdome in size. In a few hours, every news network would descend on the building with a fervor rarely matched anywhere else in the disaster zone. This story had everything: a mass of hungry people, squalling babies, old people, infirm people, dead people. The street outside the center was filled with garbage and despair, and as the day unfolded, people would cry, curse, and plead for help—all in front of the cameras. It was a mess. At 10:30 Wednesday morning, the Louisiana State Police dutifully reported that 25,000 people had gathered at the Convention Center. It didn't merit even a mention in the HSOC's morning report.

Although information about the situation in New Orleans was available from a variety of private and government sources, Broderick complained that he had no visibility in the city, and that he kept looking, without success, to FEMA to fill in the minute gaps in his knowledge. "We didn't realize until later Tuesday that there is no leadership in New Orleans," he would later say. "There is no communications from New Orleans. By Wednesday, we realize we've got a real problem."

Though FEMA generally shared whatever news it had with the Department of Homeland Security and with the White House, Broderick became convinced that the agency was deliberately withholding information from him. His staff sent out scores of bullying e-mail messages to FEMA officials complaining about the lack of information.

Though it was true that Brown and many FEMA managers had no love for the HSOC, Broderick's suspicions that FEMA was deliberately concealing the ground truth appear to be misplaced. While FEMA may not have been especially cooperative, it was clear the agency was flying just as blind as the HSOC. Marty Bahamonde and Phil Parr and the small contingent of FEMA officials at the Superdome knew absolutely nothing about the city they were sitting in. Parr, who led a four-person team of aid coordinators from FEMA's Region 6 office in Texas, should have been communicating Mayor

Nagin's needs to the staff in Baton Rouge. Though Nagin was in easy walking distance of the Superdome—the Hyatt was practically next door—"we didn't see him much," Bahamonde said. (Indeed, Nagin wouldn't even remember Parr's name when the two men met a few months later.) Parr thought his team was trapped by floodwaters at the Superdome, and he did not realize that the dry section of the city sat only about a block away from where they were camped. Nor did he recognize that FPS's main base of operations was about five blocks away, where supplies, communications, transportation, and a large contingent of well-armed men were available. Parr's inability to communicate kept him in the dark.

Nowhere was FEMA's blindness more on display than on the question of the buses needed to evacuate people from the Superdome. By Wednesday, nearly all of Louisiana's government was fixated on the FEMA evacuation buses, which Governor Blanco had verbally requested in her conversation with Michael Brown at the Superdome on Tuesday morning. After spending twelve hours fussing with the paperwork, FEMA delivered the request for 455 buses to the U.S. Department of Transportation at 1:45 A.M. Washington time on Wednesday. At the Superdome a couple of hours later, Phil Parr and Brigadier General Brod Veillon of the Louisiana National Guard put in a call to FEMA headquarters in Washington to find out when the buses would arrive. They were told that the buses would be in the city by 7:00 A.M. Veillon reported this to Jeff Smith in Baton Rouge. Finally, everyone thought, the massive evacuation of some 25,000 people from the overcrowded, uninhabitable Superdome was about to get under way. Though it was clear that 455 buses wouldn't be nearly enough, it was adequate rolling stock to at least start the process.

With this confirmation from FEMA, Governor Blanco's office put the brakes on its own efforts to round up school buses for the evacuation. At 10:30 A.M. Wednesday morning, Ty Bromell, one of the governor's aides, put out the word: "NO MORE CALLS FOR BUSES!!!" his e-mail message said in half-inch boldface type.

Though the buses still hadn't arrived at the Superdome by the time of the 11:00 A.M. videoconference, Reggie Johnson of the U.S.

Department of Transportation told participants that nearly half of the buses were already in the city, with the rest following close behind. "As was stated by [FEMA] in support of their evacuation of the Superdome, we have contracted 455 buses and it looks like we've got about 200 that are currently in place, with the remainder that should be coming in on a staggered basis," Johnson said. Nobody on that call—FEMA, HSOC, or the state—was in a position to contradict him.

Perhaps the bad situation at the Dome was about to turn around, but the news from around the region remained grim. Mississippi was also having problems with FEMA. At one point, Mayor Brent Warr of Gulfport arranged with FEMA for trucks of ice and water to be sent to local shelters where, it was said, evacuees had gone thirty-six hours with hardly anything to drink. He later discovered that the agency had ordered the trucks held at a distribution point at the Stennis Space Center, forty-three miles away, over a paperwork snafu. "The trucks were sitting for a day and half out there, idling, waiting to be told to come on into town," Warr told reporters. He said he got a similar runaround when he asked FEMA for generators to operate the city's sewerage plants.

In Louisiana, FEMA was falling further behind. For the third day, "Red October," the MERS disaster communications truck destined for City Hall, was instead parked in Baton Rouge, meaning that Mayor Nagin and the FEMA team at the Superdome were still sitting in near isolation. At Wednesday's videoconference, Dick Harmon, FEMA's preparedness director at Region 6 in Texas, said, "We understand that we can get them to within about two blocks of the Dome and then we've got water problems." Harmon added that FEMA was still studying the "feasibility" of putting the truck within walking distance of the Superdome.

Also at the videoconference was Lieutenant General Carl Strock of the Army Corps of Engineers, who said the corps had stumbled onto another levee breach in the city, at the London Avenue Canal, which he said his people were "looking at" but not actively repairing. This would further stall any attempt to drain the water from the city's streets. Strock also reported that a one-thousand-bed hospital the corps had been promising on the outskirts of the city still wasn't set up. Its mortician crews, who had been brought into the state before Katrina's landfall, still weren't in place.

But Jeff Smith seemed almost sanguine about other problems as he discussed the imminent evacuation of the Superdome with the buses that were said to have arrived. He thought it might be possible to get everyone out within twelve hours. He mentioned some problems—not enough food and water in the disaster zone, not enough attention being paid to St. Bernard Parish, hundreds of people still trapped in hospitals in the city. "I guess I could go on with this," Smith said. But he didn't. Instead, he offered FEMA some praise. "As with any operations there are little hiccups here and there but by and large we're very pleased with the support we're receiving," Smith said.

A short time later, Smith called down to General Veillon, who was at the Superdome. Five hours after the buses were due, there was still no sight of them at the arena. "I thought maybe they had gotten lost somehow," Smith said. He asked Veillon to take a helicopter up and hunt down the wayward bus fleet.

Veillon crisscrossed the city and its suburbs to the west, looking for the buses that Washington insisted were there. He never found them. But as he passed over the city's West Bank, he spied about thirty-five school buses idling in a mall parking lot—part of the fleet that had been wrangled by Governor Blanco's staff the day before. They had no air conditioning and were far less comfortable than the motor coaches FEMA was arranging, but they were available and they could move people. FEMA had argued against collecting the state buses, saying they were too uncomfortable and that much better coaches were on the way. But Blanco's chief of staff, Andy Kopplin, ignored FEMA's recommendation. "I never understood their argument," he said. "It seemed to me that if you were sitting at the Superdome, you'd take a ride on anything to get away."

Veillon landed and got the thirty-five inferior buses moving for the Superdome.

Michael Brown would later say that the case of the phantom buses was one of the most perplexing mysteries of the Katrina disaster, but in fact it was no mystery at all. Brown promised the buses to Blanco on Tuesday morning; early that afternoon, Jeff Smith filled out a formal request. The request was sent to Washington, where it was scrutinized (and modified) by a FEMA analyst. Then it was shipped back down to Baton Rouge that evening so Smith could look at the modification. Then it went back to Washington, where after several hours, it was transmitted to the U.S. Department of Transportation's overnight desk along with a request for three hundred ambulances. The ambulance request was later canceled because the Department of Transportation, in the words of one FEMA official, "doesn't do ambulances." And it was only then that bus contractors, some located thousands of miles from New Orleans, were given the word to roll.

All of these machinations were largely unknown by the state, which had not expected that some buses would be coming from hundreds, if not thousands, of miles away. And they were unknown to Reggie Johnson, on the Department of Transportation's dayshift, who simply confirmed what he had been told the day before.

The entire episode cut to the heart of the two biggest problems facing FEMA: As a part of the Department of Homeland Security, it had no real ability to call the shots from the ground of a disaster, and it was unable to tell whether the supplies it had ordered were in fact on the way. This lack of visibility added a complication to disaster planning that local officials in Louisiana and Mississippi found intolerable, primarily because their own first responders found themselves saddled with the consequences when FEMA goods didn't arrive. As Jeff Smith put it, the problem with FEMA wasn't so much that it failed to deliver but rather that it promised the help in the first place. "If something takes thirty-six hours to obtain, okay, fine, you develop a work-around," Smith said. "But when they tell you something is going to happen in twelve hours and then it doesn't, you're really put in a bind."

When General Veillon returned to the Superdome after his bus sortie, he heard the news pouring out of the portable radios among the evacuees. The word was that five hundred FEMA buses had already arrived in the city to take people at the Dome to a better place. Veillon knew better. "Goddam, this is going to get ugly," he said.

Neither were FEMA's mistakes proving helpful for Phil Parr at the Superdome. As the personification of the dysfunctional agency in New Orleans, the FEMA official was quickly becoming the object of scorn from National Guard officers. Soldiers blamed Parr for the lack of buses, the lack of food and water, and the general lack of supplies. Parr had not helped himself by confirming the imminent arrival of the phantom buses, but in truth, the ill will had been building for a day or more. City Hall was furious at FEMA for its poor early response—its inability to bring even a box of flashlights to the Superdome, which had been a standing request for days.

Veillon, in particular, had developed an intense dislike for Parr, primarily, he said, because the man cast himself as a FEMA hotshot but seemed to have no clout at all. "He talked a lot but he had nothing," Veillon said. Sometime early Wednesday, when Parr suggested that the Superdome might be evacuated by a squadron of nine Chinook transport helicopters, Veillon said he all but laughed in the FEMA man's face. "Helicopters? Why don't we just use the space shuttle?" Veillon sneered. "Hey, let's build a rope bridge across the floodwaters while we're at it. You want to evacuate with helicopters, bring 'em on."

Parr would later say the helicopter idea wasn't a fanciful plan but a real one, given initial approval by his agency but scotched at the last minute when the Pentagon decided to send its own man to New Orleans to coordinate aircraft, soldiers, and other supplies.

At any rate, the FEMA cadre at the Superdome was quickly wearing out its welcome. Parr needed National Guard help for everything, from making a phone call to navigating an occasional trip to City Hall across Poydras Street to scratching up a meal for himself and his colleagues. This had not been the plan. FEMA seemed to have forgotten about Parr. Veillon was right: Parr and his crew had nothing. They weren't the cavalry. They were refugees themselves, sleeping on the ground with the rest of the city's homeless citizens.

Meanwhile, Michael Brown was beginning to withdraw. As the

most recognizable face in FEMA, Brown should have been in the disaster zone measuring the agency's response, seeing for himself what the Gulf states needed, whipping up national support for the federal disaster effort, and giving the White House the ground truth. Instead, he was tethered to a desk in Baton Rouge, on Chertoff's orders. The FEMA chief had taken to spending hours in his hotel room, sending personal e-mail messages and trying to keep up with operations as best he could. Though Brown continued to work on some of the issues, he wasn't comfortable breathing over the shoulder of his deputies in Baton Rouge. By invoking the National Response Plan on Tuesday, Chertoff had effectively sidelined Brown. The FEMA chief was no longer calling the shots in this disaster; Chertoff and his deputy, Michael Jackson, were. Brown said that increasingly he was being overruled or ignored by Washington.

Marty Bahamonde, who was probably as close to Brown as anyone in the agency, attempted to keep his mercurial boss engaged by feeding him scraps of what he thought were news. But communications between the two men were sporadic and unsatisfying. "Sir, I know that you know the situation is past critical," Bahamonde wrote in an e-mail message to Brown on Wednesday. "Hotels are kicking people out, thousands [are] gathering in the street with no food or water. Hundreds [are] still being rescued from homes. We are out of food and running low on water at the dome."

Four minutes later, Brown replied. "Thanks for the update," he said. "Anything I need to do or tweak?" Had it been a phone call instead of an e-mail message, Brown's sarcasm would have been unmistakable. In print, it just looked callous.

If there was a single day when FEMA seemed at its most impotent, Wednesday was probably it. In Louisiana, Governor Blanco signed an order allowing her to commandeer buses, sending her whipsawed staff back to the phones. "They stupidly canceled buses when we still needed them," Chief of Staff Andy Kopplin told bewildered staffers, laying the blame squarely at the feet of FEMA. "If we can get 'em back we need 'em." In Jefferson Parish, the normally unflappable emergency director Walter Maestri burst into tears on television as he pleaded for evacuees to return to the blacked-out parish—with groceries to feed starving neighbors left behind. FEMA simply wasn't coming through with the food, Maestri said. "We cannot sustain this. This is overwhelming. People are starving."

In Mississippi, where fistfights broke out among survivors over control of the dwindling food stockpiles left over from a hurricane past, General Harold Cross, the commander of the National Guard there, asked FEMA for more. When he was told there would be a delay, he stepped around the agency and called the Pentagon's Northern Command himself. The next day, Pentagon rations arrived in Gulfport.

It was a scenario that would play out repeatedly in the upcoming days. Across the Gulf Coast, local officials were giving up on FEMA and striking out on their own. For Mississippi, the FEMA understudy was Florida. Within twenty-four hours of the storm, Florida's state emergency manager, Craig Fugate, began sending search-and-rescue teams into flattened Mississippi coastal towns, even before he was asked. Over the next few days, Florida's supply chain to Mississippi grew to include National Guard troops, food, water, medical supplies, communications gear, and 6,000 volunteers from all over the state.

By Wednesday, Fugate had opened a supply logistics center in the devastated city of Gulfport, even as FEMA struggled to simply place a medical team there. "You name it, we sent it," said Fugate. "Search-and-rescue teams. Law enforcement, diapers, food, water, ice, baby wipes. Communications gear, oxygen tanks, medicine. We basically said treat 'em like Florida counties."

For Louisiana, the savior state was Texas, which by Wednesday had opened forty-seven evacuation shelters and was preparing the Houston Astrodome for a flood of evacuees from the Superdome. Texas had a thirty-five-man water rescue team with its own boats that by Wednesday had already saved 1,100 people in New Orleans. It had also sent eight Blackhawk helicopters to the city, along with two Chinook helicopters and five fixed-wing aircraft. It sent a satellite phone communications suite, fifty game wardens with boats and trucks, four tanker fuelers, and fifty ambulances, along with 135 paramedics, nurses, and doctors. It deployed 300 military police and 120 combat engineers from its National Guard. It sent five airboats. The list went on.

And more was on the way. Not waiting for federal troops, which were said to be arriving in Baton Rouge Wednesday evening, Governor Blanco called on states to send soldiers and executed individual agreements on Wednesday to make this happen. Ultimately, other states would send about 20,000 troops to help Louisiana.

President Bush left his ranch in Crawford on Wednesday, trimming four days off the end of what had been a five-week vacation. On the way home, Bush ordered Air Force One to deviate a bit from the beeline and dip low over the disaster zone so he could see for himself the drowned city and the demolished Gulf Coast. The next day, White House aides would put together a DVD of television news segments that graphically highlighted the situation in New Orleans. "The president doesn't watch a lot of TV," one aide said.

Bush was aware that things were not going well on the ground. "He was already pissed off," said Dan Bartlett, the White House counselor who prepared the DVD. Then the president watched the video. And he got even angrier.

As had happened with Bush's father following Hurricane Andrew in 1992, FEMA's stuttering response, clear to just about everyone, was swiftly becoming a political problem for the president. In an unusual departure from standard procedure, the White House staff allowed reporters to call ahead from Air Force One to alert their desks that the flyover was going to take place, and let still photographers move forward so they could see the president looking grim and troubled as he gazed out the oval window at the calamity two thousand feet below. "It's got to be doubly devastating on the ground," the president was said to have murmured as the aircraft swooped over New Orleans.

When Bush returned to Washington early that evening, he didn't look rested or happy. Shortly after touching down, the president appeared in the White House Rose Garden to deliver a speech on Hurricane Katrina. Ringed by his cabinet, Bush said he had convened a task force, led by Chertoff, to focus federal disaster relief efforts. "This recovery will take a long time. This recovery will take years," Bush said.

The president spoke slowly and enunciated his words carefully. And yet his comments sounded more like a spelling recital than a call to arms. He reeled off a laundry list of generally incomprehensible statistics that had been cobbled by his staff from FEMA press releases: The government had marshaled 400 trucks to deliver 1,000 loads of supplies; it had shipped 13.4 million liters of water to the region; it had sent 134 generators, 135,000 blankets, and 11,000 cots. Bush spoke at length about the nation's supply of gasoline, saying he had granted "a nationwide waiver for fuel blends" that would moderate pump prices. He talked about dipping into the Strategic Petroleum Reserve.

Bush didn't mention any of the federal government's obvious shortcomings in responding to the disaster, and in fact, the comments overall struck many as flat and uninspired. Aides later admitted the speech wasn't the president's best.

As he spoke, Bush seemed oddly removed from the disaster, similar to the way he had appeared on the Air Force One flyover, as he viewed the devastation from an overstuffed aircraft seat in an air-conditioned cabin.

A short time after Bush's speech, the Pentagon's military contingent arrived in Baton Rouge, just as had been promised. Louisiana's Jeff Smith would later say it was the most disappointing moment he experienced during the entire Katrina ordeal. Blanco had asked President Bush for 40,000 federal troops to take control of the logistics and to oversee rescue efforts so the National Guard could work on law enforcement. Instead, she got about a dozen soldiers, as Lieutenant General Russel Honoré and a small staff strode into the state's emergency operations center and announced that the cavalry had arrived. But instead of a hero's welcome, Honoré was met mostly with hangdog despondency. "We were expecting the 82nd Airborne," said Bob Mann, a spokesman for Governor Blanco. "Instead, Honoré walks in with about a half-dozen people and a CNN crew."

Unlike FEMA, Honoré made no promises on Blanco's request for 40,000 troops. First, the general said, he wanted to survey the scene.

It was dark in Louisiana and really dark in New Orleans, where power had been snuffed out in the entire area. At the Superdome, the crowd was menacing. Just as General Veillon had predicted, the government's failure to produce the promised evacuation buses had put the crowd in a foul mood. People started mumbling about staging a riot, perhaps by burning the Superdome to the ground. Rumors spread like poison gas. Mayor Nagin and his police chief, Eddie Compass, contributed on this score. For days, the two men had been delivering fanciful descriptions to the press of the Superdome and the city at large. Nagin had spoken of the "animalistic" state of the Superdome's residents, of dead bodies piling up in dark rooms, of killings, rapes, and child mortality. Compass let fly with tales of sustained downtown gun battles, assassination attempts, and other accounts of derring-do. At the Superdome on Wednesday night, Compass sidled up to Phil Parr, in tears. "My guys are getting killed out there," he cried. "A girl, a child died in my arms."

Isolated from their agency and shunned by the locals, Parr started to get the creeps. Since arriving in New Orleans, he had left the Dome only once, and that was to go across the street to City Hall. He had no sense of reality beyond the fence and parking lots. If things went sour at the Superdome, the FEMA team would have no means to defend themselves. They had no safety net at all.

Parr had tried to secure a safety net. He had called for agents from the Federal Protective Service, whose job it was to protect FEMA employees during disasters, and who were bivouacked only blocks away, though Parr didn't know this. On Wednesday afternoon, David Tyndell, the FPS inspector from Denver, and ten of his agents had taken their SUVs to the Superdome but because of the water they were unable to find a way to drive up to the arena. "It was so frustrating—we were just three hundred yards away but we couldn't get there," Tyndall said.

The FPS agents decided to try to call Parr on their satellite phones but were only able to reach Baton Rouge. From there, the call was shifted to FEMA headquarters in Washington, which was able to track Parr down through a National Guard communications link. When Parr found out his cavalry had arrived, he tried to convince the Guard to send a highwater truck, but the soldiers said they had no equipment to spare. Finally, the FPS gave up, leaving Parr and his team with no protection of their own.

The Superdome crowd was girding for a long, hot night. The interior of the building was growing more cloying by the hour, and was heightened Wednesday evening when someone started a fire in the building, using damp paper as fuel. The blaze was more smoke than flame, and the city's fire department easily put it out, but the cavernous building filled with an acrid haze. As the National Guard later noted in its official history of the evening, the building was "uninhabitable by all but the hardiest souls."

As thousands of people spilled outside for fresh air, they began to press into the areas filled by soldiers, medical workers, and the FEMA contingent. The crowd was angry and frightened. Some began talking about taking matters in hand by starting a riot. Others gossiped incessantly about violent crimes that were said to be taking place in the building. In one corner of the property a scuffle broke out as a group of evacuees fell on a man and beat him unmercifully. The attackers said the man had been stalking little children. That evening, a Guard soldier who entered a darkened bathroom inside the Superdome was shot, and rumors began to spread that troops were beginning to kill civilians. It later turned out to be either an accident or an isolated event: The soldier was shot in the foot with his own gun.

Meanwhile, a small Superdome management crew, which had been husbanding the arena's lone, street-level generator and keeping dim lights burning inside the building, said it was pulling out. Though the generator was protected from floodwaters by a rank of sandbags, a local radio station was reporting that the water was expected to rise. If the generator failed, the Superdome would be plunged into utter darkness. Trouble indeed, the soldiers thought.

The National Guard commanders caucused, plotting a plan for withdrawal from the arena, should the lights go out or the crowd turn mutinous. They sketched out an area of the property where they would consolidate, if conditions warranted, to beat a retreat and abandon the Superdome to the crowd. A few hours later, a National Guard helicopter landed on a patch of concrete nearby. A thirty-man team of heavily armed, black-clad troops spilled out in full riot gear. The team was specially trained to put down urban unrest and fanned out into the crowd. Marty Bahamonde, seeing them, was reassured that the Guard had the muscle to keep the crowd in check. A short time later, he fell asleep on the concrete apron outside the Superdome.

9

GETTING CONTROL

Thursday morning, September 1, dawned to a cloudless sky, and it was already in the midnineties at 7:30 A.M. when Phil Parr awoke with a groan. The crowd was up as well, and just as disgruntled as it had been the night before. A few minutes later, Parr said, General Gary Jones of the Louisiana National Guard walked over and told him, "We can no longer guarantee your safety." He then pointed out a site on the perimeter of the property and said, "That's where we'll be making our final stand."

Parr called his small staff together. He ordered them to take off their FEMA T-shirts, lest they be targeted by the angry crowd. The FEMA squad and the thirty-five-member medical team under Parr's control began packing up for a hasty withdrawal. Bahamonde objected, telling Parr that FEMA had to stay and that he didn't see any threat. "It's not your call," Parr said.

That morning, the FEMA team boarded three box trucks and drove to Baton Rouge. Along the route they picked up an FPS escort. It was the first time Parr had seen the FPS since his arrival. It was also the first time he had seen downtown New Orleans.

Parr would later insist that the National Guard had urged the FEMA team to leave the Superdome, an assertion that the soldiers would deny. Bahamonde backed Parr, saying the Guard did in fact tell the FEMA team to withdraw from the arena. But even months later, Bahamonde didn't agree with the call. "It was paranoia" on Parr's part, he said. "They were the most peaceful 25,000 people in horrid conditions I have ever been around. There was no way they were going to attack anybody." Right or wrong, Parr believed it was a command decision, and he had to think of his men.

When Parr's team arrived in Baton Rouge it wasn't exactly to a hero's welcome. "Mike Brown was pissed that we left, and he said so," Bahamonde said. "He told me, 'Nice to see you, Marty. Now turn your ass around and get back to the Superdome.'" Brown was furious. "You could see it in his face," Bahamonde said. "He wore this expression like his face was going to crack."

Parr and Bahamonde didn't know it, but the FEMA Swiftwater Rescue teams that had been working in the western part of the city also stood down on Thursday morning, also in response to rumors of lawlessness. They retreated to a compound in suburban Jefferson Parish. By noon on Thursday, FEMA had completely withdrawn from the city of New Orleans.

Early in the morning, the HSOC had pushed out a list of available commodities by storage site, but it was still running late on the news: In a report just after midnight, it said that New Orleans hospitals were only half-evacuated—a fact that Louisiana's Jeff Smith had reported during the videoconference on Wednesday. Its dawn report offered nothing fresh. A pipeline was said to be leaking in Plaquemines Parish. The New Orleans police were said to be suspending rescue operations and returning to law enforcement. The levees in New Orleans were still unrepaired. Thursday morning, Kirstjen Nielsen at the White House responded to the stale news in an e-mail message to Frank DiFalco, Broderick's deputy at the HSOC. "We greatly appreciate the increase in information flow," she wrote. "However, sending us very stale sit rep [situation report] info that has already been updated [earlier] by the HSOC is not helpful. Is there a way to coordinate the info flow so we don't waste time reviewing such old dat[a] and your folks don't waste time sending us stuff?"

About midmorning, the White House sent the HSOC an e-mail message of a news clip about an incident, a shooting at the Superdome the night before. Four hours later, the HSOC would confirm that the shooting, of a National Guard soldier, had in fact occurred.

There were new things to report. FEMA put out a report saying that the availability of food rations for the disaster zone was "becoming critical." Municipalities and hospitals along the Gulf Coast were running out of fuel. Mississippi storm shelters still lacked generators, meaning there was no hot food available and no light after sunset. And there were recurring problems as well that may have bore repeating: As FEMA noted in one report, "distribution, communications and security" remained critical concerns in Louisiana.

On Thursday, Broderick's unit would once again miss the biggest news of the day: the growing humanitarian crisis at the Convention Center. Like the levee breaches three days before, information about the problem had been phoned or e-mailed to the HSOC for about thirty-six hours but was subsequently discounted or ignored as background noise. The first report of the Convention Center came in the early hours of Wednesday when the first FPS patrol relayed news of a "spontaneous gathering" up the command chain. The next report came at 10:09 A.M. Louisiana time, when a local federal official told the HSOC that 200 to 250 city bus employees had escaped flooding at their workplace on air mattresses and had taken shelter at the Convention Center. There were other reports floating around the system, from Marty Bahamonde's e-mail messages to the situation report from the Louisiana State Police. The news also poured in over the HSOC's myriad plasma TV screens as cable news networks reported the growing desperation of the crowds. Months later Broderick would tell congressional investigators he hadn't realized that the Convention Center and the Superdome were different buildings until early on Thursday morning, when he happened to be walking past a television set in the HSOC and saw the throngs of parched and hungry people outside the Convention Center, which looks quite different from the Superdome. "What is this Convention Center?" Broderick said. "Is that the Superdome?"

Once again Broderick was well behind the news and in desperate need of trustworthy eyes. He found a pair that had only just made it to the disaster zone: Wendell Shingler, the director of the Federal Protective Service. Shingler had pulled into Baton Rouge late on Wednesday after a long drive from Washington. "I was on the ground," he would later tell congressional investigators, "because I know my folks were going to be in some rough situations and they needed to be able to see me there with boots on the ground without the ranks and stars, walking through the water with them."

The first call Shingler got on Thursday came over his satellite phone at 9:00 A.M. It was Broderick with a simple order: "Your eyeballs on the Convention Center, and tell me how many people are there. Now!" Like a general inspiring his troops, Broderick heightened the importance of the mission by telling Shingler that Chertoff had a personal interest in the subject and that he was the only person who could be trusted to carry out the task. Shingler grabbed Chief Dwayne Andrews, hopped in an SUV, and hightailed it to downtown New Orleans. An hour or so later, they were perched on the Highway 90 overpass that arches over the Convention Center, looking down on what Shingler later described as a "sea of humanity." The crowd had bashed in the Convention Center's doors and had dragged hundreds of the building's stackable banquet chairs outside. And there they sat in the shade of the massive structure's porte cochere. There was no food, no water. "I jumped on the sat phone and called General Broderick," Shingler said, giving the HSOC commander his estimate that there might have been 20,000 people at the Convention Center, maybe more. He said Broderick seemed astounded by his crowd estimate.

After passing on the Convention Center information to Broderick, Shingler, with twelve backup agents, decided to walk along the edge of the crowd. The agents were immediately mobbed.

The people weren't violent, but they were scared, tired, hungry, and thirsty. They peppered the agents with lurid stories of gang activity and lawlessness that they swore were occurring inside the building. A group of unarmed National Guard soldiers had left the Convention Center on Wednesday night, and a Louisiana State Police SWAT team had arrived early on Thursday before the FPS, taking up a position behind the building. But the small FPS contingent were the only authorities the crowd could see. They begged Shingler and his agents to stay. Shingler was torn. He didn't have the force to bring order to this crowd. But he decided to leave a handful of agents behind to establish at least a rudimentary patrol.

"We kept saying, 'Just pass the word in the Convention Center that if you feel threatened, come on out, we'll be out here,'" Shingler said later. "I promised them we would not leave." He ordered six men to set up an observation post and told them to patrol with their blue lights blazing. "Smoke and mirrors" was how Shingler described the strategy, adding that the FPS was simply "trying to make it look like we were a lot bigger than we were." In fact, the FPS contingent in New Orleans consisted of only about sixty agents, though they were heavily armed.

Shingler spoke to the HSOC and to IIMG officials several times throughout the day, and he was convinced that Broderick would muster reinforcements. But Broderick didn't do this. Reinforcements never arrived.

For the first time since formally filing the paperwork to take charge of the disaster, Secretary Chertoff made an appearance on Thursday's 11:00 A.M. videoconference. Chertoff was stirred up, furious that the Superdome evacuation was still stalled after having been assured the day before that it was under way. Unlike previous videoconference appearances when he said little, Chertoff reeled off at least nine questions on this call. Chief on his mind were buses. He wanted to know the schedule for their arrival. He wanted to know when the evacuations would start. He wanted to know the security situation at the Superdome.

On this last question, Chertoff was told that the FEMA team at the Superdome had bailed out, primarily for security reasons. On the bus questions, there appeared to be some actual good news. General Veillon had taken another morning scouting trip in search of buses, and he happened upon a whole fleet of them, federally contracted motor coaches, lined up at a video poker truck stop about thirty-five miles west of the city. Landing in the helicopter, Veillon was told by a soldier on the ground that in accordance with the plan, the buses were rolling out in packs of ten under state police escort toward the Superdome. "Roll them all," Vellion said. "Now." And the buses rolled.

Though the arrival of buses sounded like good news, Reggie Johnson of the Department of Transportation threw a damper on things during the videoconference. There were 300 buses at the truck stop. The other 155 would not arrive until midnight. And even though it was clear beyond a doubt to everyone involved that New Orleans would need far more than 455 buses to evacuate the city, Johnson had not received any paperwork. "We have not received any other requests beyond that," he said. Louisiana's Jeff Smith didn't like the sound of this. "Midnight tonight is going to leave a very long void," Smith said.

Broderick also participated in the videoconference but limited his questions to a rumor that a riot had broken out in downtown Baton Rouge. Broderick said a university cop had told him about it. The men in Louisiana quickly shot the rumor down, but Broderick persisted until local officials promised—and then promised again—to fully investigate.

The Convention Center wasn't mentioned specifically, but there was plenty of conversation on the call about the wandering crowds who were increasingly jamming the city's dry parts of town. Colonel Henry Whitehorn, the superintendent of the Louisiana State Police, said he had driven around the city the day before and had been shocked by the number of homeless people who had sought refuge on the raised highways that cut through the city. "None of them had food or water," Whitehorn said. "They need it. We've got to have it."

Then came the bad news. A man from FEMA's Atlanta office acknowledged that the delivery of food was a problem. He said "sort of a small task force" was working on it. But the situation was so desperate that FEMA's own medical teams were short of supplies. "I just got a direct e-mail from Gulfport, Mississippi [medical] teams," said one FEMA official on the call. "They desperately need water, [food,] and supplies. They've run out."

All week, FEMA officials had been touting the resources that they were on the brink of bringing to the area. There were said to be trains coming for the evacuees, but they had yet to arrive and probably would not on this day, either, though Transportation's Johnson said a train would pull into New Orleans by evening. There were 45,000 FEMA trailers and mobile homes on the road and heading toward town. FEMA expected to have 400 phones delivered any time now. And two million meals were in transit to the disaster area. The problem was, none of this stuff had arrived, and FEMA seemed unable to say when it would.

But in the disaster area, the facts were these: Mayor Nagin and his depleted administration remained in almost total isolation, captive to swirling rumors that were bogging down disaster operations in all sorts of ways, even though FEMA had had a fully outfitted communications wagon lingering outside the city since the crisis began. The Superdome still had no portable bathrooms, even though officials there had made the request days earlier. Even FEMA's one-thousand-bed MASH hospital—the one that the agency had trumpeted since the first day of the disaster—remained incomplete. There was no food, no gasoline, no generators. In ways big and small, FEMA was failing. And the locals, hostage to the agency's promises, could only sigh.

Smith sounded weary. "We've still got people that need rescuing. We've got people that need food, water, ice. We need buses. Just get us the assets, please."

But little would change on Thursday, more than seventy-two hours after Katrina made landfall.

By Thursday, what Michael Brown had sensed was now reality: Chertoff had essentially placed his deputy, Michael Jackson, in charge of running the disaster. The first thing Chertoff did was to order

Jackson, a former deputy secretary of transportation, to set up an airlift plan from the city's Louis Armstrong International Airport so that evacuees could be taken out of New Orleans by airplane.

This was something FEMA had been working on for days but hadn't finished. It had lined up airlines to stage the flights but had been unable to work out destinations and schedules. Even when this was worked out, though, bureaucrats seemed intent on derailing the initiative. The Transportation Security Administration (TSA) suddenly insisted that all passengers and luggage be screened before any planes would be allowed to depart. FEMA and the Department of Transportation officials working on the airlift were stunned. "What are our priorities here, helping people or making sure they are not terrorists?" one FEMA employee complained to Jan Benini, the Department of Transportation official in charge of the operation.

Then a debate broke out about how the screeners would work in a city with no electricity. FEMA would have to fly in generators and then arrange separate flights for TSA equipment, a task that would further delay the evacuation. This was worked out when the TSA agreed to allow hand searches of bags and people, in lieu of screening gates and X-ray machines. But it still entailed an eight-hour delay while the agency flew in screening teams from Orlando and Houston. And then just when everything appeared set, Homeland Security decided that undercover air marshals would have to work the departing flights. This caused another delay. When it was all said and done, a relatively straightforward air evacuation initiative took nearly two days to even arrange.

As conditions at the Superdome degenerated, more and more evacuees were on the move—to highway overpasses, to the shadow of downtown skyscrapers, to the Convention Center. FEMA and the Department of Homeland Security seemed not to know this, though their own operations center had received the news from Wendell Shingler and also from Marty Bahamonde, who had told Brown the day before that the city's streets were crammed with wandering homeless. Moreover, despite Washington's assertion that relief operations were robust in areas of the city that could be reached by disaster workers, some 60,000 people languished in the city's Central Business District, an area of town that was easily accessible—even by passenger car—and had been, practically since Katrina passed through.

Despite the horrible conditions in New Orleans on Thursday, Washington officials remained in an eerie state of denial. At a press conference, Chertoff praised "the genius of the people at FEMA" in responding to the unprecedented disaster. "I think it is a source of tremendous pride to me to work with people who've pulled off this really exceptional response," he said.

The same day, the Department of Transportation ticked off its accomplishments in supplying commodities to the region without ever once mentioning the bus snafu. The National Guard said it had 11,000 soldiers on active duty in the affected states without mentioning that these were almost exclusively from Louisiana and Mississippi and that reinforcements from other states had yet to arrive in significant numbers.

In Washington that morning, President Bush gave an interview to Diane Sawyer of ABC News and went on the defensive when asked why he had been absent for so long. "I started organizing on Tuesday when we realized the extent of the storm," Bush said. "And I said, look, when I get back to Washington on Wednesday afternoon I want to have a report on my desk and a cabinet meeting for you to tell me exactly what your departments are going to do to alleviate the situation."

Despite Bush's efforts to portray the administration as being in control of the situation, in reality Washington remained far behind the curve. Local officials and the national media had been reporting for almost a full day that downtown New Orleans was swamped with tens of thousands of hungry and thirsty evacuees, including thousands at the Convention Center, yet Chertoff continued to insist that the dry, accessible areas of New Orleans were well stocked with basic commodities. And though senior Homeland Security officials, such as Matthew Broderick, had been clearly told that the Convention Center had been overrun by evacuees, Chertoff dismissed this news as rank rumor. In an interview late Thursday afternoon with National Public Radio, he was pressed a half dozen times to comment on the blooming disaster at the Convention Center. "As I say, I'm telling you that we are getting food and water to areas where people are staging," Chertoff insisted. "Actually I have not heard a report of thousands of people in the Convention Center who don't have food and water."

Michael Brown, too, seemed unaware of the problem, though cable news stations had been airing coverage of the Convention Center all day long. Late Thursday evening, Brown sat for an interview with *Nightline*'s Ted Koppel. In the interview, Brown vastly low-balled the number of people gathered at the Convention Center, saying it was only 5,000, when the estimates that day were in the range of 20,000 to 30,000. Then he insisted that FEMA was providing food and water there, backing down only when Koppel challenged him.

"I'm sorry, you're absolutely correct," Brown said. "We're getting the supplies to the Convention Center now." But in truth, FEMA was not.

It was an embarrassing day for Washington. And it was captured succinctly in an e-mail message that Dan Ostergaard, the executive director of the Homeland Security Advisory Council (a civilian group that advised Chertoff), wrote to Richard D. Davis, who sat on the council. Ostergaard headlined his message, "Katrina is a national disgrace." In the body of the message he wrote, "My subject line says it all."

After the embarrassing television appearance, Brown said he received a flurry of e-mail messages from boosters and friends, urging him to cut his losses and quit FEMA. "Do the right thing and resign now," Scott Morris, a Florida-based FEMA official wrote shortly after the show. "It's not too late to make it look like you are being responsible."

The Convention Center, like the Superdome, would become synonymous with lurid lawbreaking, and again, New Orleans police chief Eddie Compass was stirring the pot. Compass spread unsubstantiated reports that the Convention Center was the hideout for an armed gang that moved among the thousands of evacuees and had commandeered the building's third floor as a vast weapons armory. He said this shadowy force was picking off tourists who ventured too close. He also claimed that he had sent a force of eighty-eight police officers to the building to bring order to the place but that they had been beaten back by a better armed, highly organized thug army. Inside, he (and others) claimed, children were being raped and adults were being executed. Bodies were said to be stacked up like cordwood in the building's catering coolers. Many of these reports were accepted as fact by reporters and government officials.

These rumors prolonged the suffering at the Convention Center. After getting an earful from Compass, the Louisiana National Guard, in consultation with the city government, withdrew its plan to bring supplies to the building in the middle of the night, deeming the mission too dangerous.

As Thursday came to a close, a supply crisis was also bubbling in neighboring Mississippi. FEMA's top official in the state, William Carwile, had just received a report from FEMA logistics in Washington about the food, water, and ice flowing into the region. It was far less than what the two men had expected: Only 86 of the 900 trucks that had been promised to Mississippi were actually on the road. "Will need big time law enforcement replacements tomorrow," Carwile wrote to FEMA's deputy response director, Michael Lowder. "All our good will here in MS will be very seriously impacted by noon tomorrow. Have been holding it together as it is."

Despite his measured prose, Carwile was furious. After blasting FEMA's balky logistics office for not even giving him a heads-up on a problem that it had known about all day, he vowed to take matters into his own hands. "Fully intend to take independent measures to address huge shortfalls," he wrote.

Back in Louisiana, the military was starting to make its presence felt. General Russel Honoré's arrival on Wednesday night was actually the fulfillment of the wish that Michael Brown and Bill Lokey had expressed to Governor Blanco on Tuesday for a military takeover of the disaster. With Honoré came extra backing from the Pentagon and a fresh flood of food and helicopters, Louisiana officials said.

When Honoré arrived, state officials immediately put him in

charge of the most troubling aspects of the disaster response: marshaling buses for evacuations and feeding the wandering masses of New Orleans. Blanco wouldn't get the 40,000 troops she wanted, but other states were flying in modest numbers of soldiers to supplement what Louisiana had on the ground. Though the Louisiana National Guard had 4,020 boots on the ground and would have only 300 more by Wednesday, a flood of troops began moving in after Honoré arrived. Moreover, southern Louisiana, which had been subsisting on about 300,000 military meals a day since the crisis began, would be deluged with more than three times that amount on Thursday, as the Pentagon brought its own logistics forces to bear on the region.

With New Orleans said to be lurching toward anarchy, its streets flowing with armed bandits, and its own police force teetering on total collapse, one of the enduring mysteries of the fumbling U.S. response has always been why the Pentagon did not move more quickly to quell the unrest in the city shortly after the disaster began. And one of the reasons, civilian and military leaders said, was that the federal government believed—largely based on rumors—that it had to plan for a far more complicated military operation, one in which federal soldiers might have to kill American citizens, perhaps in great numbers. Such a prospect added serious political and tactical complications to what otherwise might have been a more straightforward relief effort.

If there was going to be bloodshed at the hands of U.S. soldiers, Washington officials and General Honoré were determined that those soldiers would be National Guard troops. Though Blanco had pleaded for regular army soldiers, she would not be accommodated until the coast was clear on the ground. To Honoré, that meant that the two magnets in the city for much of the supposed lawlessness—the Superdome and the Convention Center—would have to be subdued. And so while the 82nd Airborne cooled its heels at Fort Bragg, North Carolina, National Guard commanders cooked up a plan Thursday evening to take the Convention Center by force. Instead of dispatching fifty National Guard troops to bring supplies to the Convention Center, the military instead believed it needed a thousand heavily armed troops, specially trained to deal with civilian uprisings, Pentagon officials later said. Their belief was in large part based on the rumors being passed along by Compass, the press, and other officials that the sprawling building had been commandeered by a vicious confederation of street gangs.

Assembling such a force took time. Thanks in part to FEMA's inability to set up even the most rudimentary command and control structure on the ground, this planning proceeded under the assumption that the Convention Center was a den of lawlessness. "Some people asked why didn't we go in sooner," said Lieutenant General H. Steven Blum, the head of the Pentagon's National Guard command. "Had we gone in with less force, it may have been challenged, innocents may have been caught in a fight between the Guard military police . . . and we would put innocents' lives at risk."

The planning was also done in relative secrecy. Even Michael Brown did not know the details. That night, he sent an e-mail message to an old friend, erroneously saying that Honoré was in charge of the operation and that he planned to search the Convention Center "room by room," and "remove bodies, etc." The mission was planned for noon on Friday, which also happened to be the day that President Bush planned to visit the region for the first time.

Friday, September 2, dawned early in Baton Rouge for Michael Brown, if he even went to sleep at all. The FEMA boss was being sidelined by the state, by General Honoré, and by Chertoff, and he sensed that change was in the air. In the Baton Rouge emergency operations center, Brown had already blown up at Honoré and at state officials for leaving him out of the loop on their evacuation and logistics plans. And while he had been told of the upcoming raid on the Convention Center, he had not been given many details. Within a few hours, Governor Blanco would also sign a deal to bring in Brown's most famous predecessor, James Lee Witt, to offer his advice on managing the disaster. Witt's first question upon arrival, state officials said, was to ask why FEMA had not moved its communications trucks to New Orleans.

At 4:24 A.M. Baton Rouge time, Brown dashed out a short to-do list for his top two deputies, "unless I'm recalled today." A short time later, he left for Alabama and a rendezvous with Chertoff and President Bush. It would be the first time in three days that he would actually see the disaster area.

Just a few minutes later, in Washington, the HSOC sent out its daily situation report to Chertoff and the White House. It was old news, as usual, even wrong news. Long after it had been established that tens of thousands of evacuees had converged on the Convention Center, the HSOC reported that just 1,000 evacuees had taken shelter at the building, and that food and water were available. "New Orleans officers on scene and tactically prepared," the report said. (The HSOC attributed the bad information to Shingler, which he vehemently denied. "I told them 20,000 and never said anything about sufficient food. The 1,000 figure had been floating around the first day or so but not from me.") In Baton Rouge, Dave Tyndell, one of Shingler's lieutenants, was just about to finish a shift in the FPS mobile command center at 9:00 A.M. on Friday when Shingler burst in with a cell phone in his hand and said they had to go to the Convention Center right away. Shingler was clearly agitated, and stayed on the phone as they made their way to an observation post the FPS had set up on the overpass. When Tyndell and Shingler arrived, they could clearly see the sprawling crowd. "That's right," Shingler shouted in his phone. "At least 25,000. I told you before it was big."

At the same moment, Tyndell turned to see a man behind him trying to throw another man off the overpass. Tyndell leaped in to pull the assailant back just in time and wrestle him to the ground. The man about to be thrown off the highway started screaming that he had almost been killed over a bottle of water. Shingler again shouted into the phone. "You got to get these people out now!" he said.

That morning in Washington, President Bush faced the cameras on the White House lawn with Chertoff, looking grim. He had just finished a briefing with General Honoré and others and was furious about the stale, inaccurate picture he was receiving from New Orleans. As he strode across the White House lawn to meet the press,

Bush told Dan Bartlett how ticked off he was. "Tell them what's on your mind," Bartlett said, gesturing toward the waiting reporters.

Standing before the cameras, Bush spoke of the millions of gallons of water and tons of food that were speeding toward the disaster zone. He spoke of the "issue" at the Convention Center and said it was about to be secured by soldiers. "The results are not acceptable," Bush said of the federal effort. "I'm headed down there right now."

At the 11:00 A.M. videoconference, the mood was palpably lighter. The long-awaited contracts, based on requests the state had made several days before, were starting to kick in. The U.S. Department of Transportation had finally delivered a full complement of 1,100 buses, and many hundreds were already lined up in city streets. In addition, Transportation had also begun moving the first commercial aircraft into the New Orleans airport, to whisk evacuees out of the ruined city. At the Superdome, a promised shipment of Pentagon food rations had arrived, and the food stores, which had stood at 35,000 meals on Tuesday, were now at 90,000. That morning the National Guard dropped its rationing regime and allowed evacuees to take as much food as they pleased from scores of shipping pallets scattered about the concrete apron outside. Though the evacuees still outnumbered the available seats on buses and would continue to do so for hours, people lined up for a full city block as they awaited their turn to embark. So intent were evacuees on leaving the place that many wouldn't even leave the line to relieve themselves. The air outside the Superdome filled with the smell of urine.

On the videoconference call, Jeff Smith was effusive in his praise, though not for FEMA. "Texas has been extremely gracious and Texas is stepping up to the plate and helping us," he said. "Without them, we would be in—well, I won't say what we would be in, but thank you."

At almost the same time, the planned invasion of the Convention Center began to unfold. After assembling on a nearby highway overpass, 1,000 National Guard soldiers and 250 city police officers rode into the downtown area, toting rifles and tons of food and water. "The cavalry is and will continue to arrive," said General Blum.

Anyone looking for action would be disappointed. Instead of armed thugs, the soldiers found a dispirited crowd that was hungry, thirsty, and fully cooperative. Colonel Jacques Thibodaux, who commanded the Guard operation, said that as he rode down Convention Center Boulevard in a Humvee, he smelled somebody barbecuing chicken. "I realized right away that we weren't going to have any problems here," he said.

Indeed, the Convention Center fell without a shot being fired. There were no heavily armed thug forces, no third-floor hideaway. Soldiers searching the crowd said they found a scattering of weapons, steak knives mostly, and one rusty pistol that didn't appear to be operable. The place was secured within a half hour. By midafternoon the next day, it would be empty.

At about the same time, the HSOC sent out another report on the situation at the Convention Center, finally providing the correct figure for the estimated number of people at the site: 25,000. The report said limited food and water were available to the crowd.

President Bush's tour through the region was strange and slightly surreal. While at an airport hangar in Mobile, Alabama, even before he saw the first bit of destruction, Bush nearly started weeping. Then, though thousands of people had been absolutely wiped out by Hurricane Katrina, Bush singled out the losses suffered by one man— longtime Mississippi senator Trent Lott, whose vacation home had been heavily damaged in the storm. "Out of the rubbles of Trent Lott's house—he's lost his entire house—there's going to be a fantastic house," Bush said.

A few moments later, Bush stunned nearly everyone when he uttered the now-famous line that came to symbolize the federal response to Hurricane Katrina. With federal and local officials surrounding him, Bush turned to Michael Brown, who was standing there in his shirtsleeves, looking a little blue. "Brownie, you're doing a heck of a job," Bush said to the FEMA chief.

Bush also made a stop in New Orleans, where he took a quick tour of the 17th Street Canal levee breach and invited Mayor Nagin and Governor Blanco back to Air Force One. And it was here, Brown said, that he seemed to bond, if only fleetingly, with Chertoff, the man he had come to loathe. It was Friday afternoon and the two men were walking together, in their dress shoes, along the raised and muddy bank of the 17th Street Canal. Bush and his entourage and the local officials were up ahead of the two men, watching as massive Chinook and Blackhawk helicopters rolled by one after the other, dropping 3,000-pound sandbags into the levee breach. "And we're kind of walking along by ourselves," Brown recalled. "We were talking about doing catastrophic disaster planning, about how we really need to be doing that. We were saying look at these levees being broke—it could have been terrorism but this was a natural disaster and is worse than anything terrorists could have done. So we need to get it out of our heads that terrorism is the only problem out there that could have caused something like this. And for a split second I want to think that he and I are actually starting to develop a relationship, I can get his ear now and he can actually hear what I am saying because we are out there working in the dirt and everything else."

The moment passed. Bush had seen enough. The entourage walked back to the highway and loaded up for the short return to Air Force One.

On the presidential plane, Nagin took the first shower he had taken in nearly a week. In an adjacent cabin, Brown and several senior White House officials discussed a plan to get Blanco to turn over her authority as head of the state's National Guard to the federal government. The plan, which had been days in the making, was initially sparked by the widespread reports of looting and lawlessness as a way to hustle federal troops into the city. But at this late date, when the crime wave, such as it was, had passed, the initiative looked more political than practical. And that's exactly the way it was viewed in Baton Rouge.

A few minutes later, Bush put the proposition to Governor Blanco, asking her to give him control of the troops in the state. She didn't know it at the time, but the president had put the same proposition to Governor Barbour in Mississippi earlier in the day. Barbour turned him down flat.

Blanco wasn't inclined to do it, either. After a few hours on the ground in New Orleans, Bush returned to Washington. Shortly afterward, FEMA's "Red October" disaster communications truck finally pulled up on a grassy median strip outside of City Hall. As the Superdome crowd filtered into buses nearby, the driver began setting up a sophisticated communications suite for the use of the mayor and any FEMA officials who might happen by. "In retrospect, I wish I had done that four days earlier," Brown later said.

But by this time, Nagin had taken matters into his own hands. After directing his staff to loot a nearby Office Depot, the mayor had set up an Internet-based telephone, complete with a high-speed wireless network for dozens of computers.

James Lee Witt came to Louisiana, he said, to help Blanco puzzle through the confusing ways of Washington. But while he was at it, Witt tried—briefly—to rehabilitate Brown as well. After touring the state's operations center, Witt popped into the parking lot and rapped on the door of a small trailer that Brown had ordered for himself after "Red October" had left for New Orleans.

Inside, Witt found Brown in the back of the trailer, sitting, as he later described it, "with his chin in his chest." Witt was nothing if not relentlessly cheerful. He tried to buck up the FEMA boss. "I said, Mike, you need to come out here. You don't need to be in the operations center, you need to be walking around, you need to be visible," Witt said. "Now's not the time to be worried. Now's the time to get active."

For the next thirty minutes the men talked about the disaster and how, together, they would turn the situation around. And Brown did feel better. For a little while.

On Friday evening at about 11:20 P.M., a curious fax rolled into the emergency operations center in Baton Rouge. It contained no information about the sender, not even a phone number. A cover note simply requested that Governor Blanco sign the enclosed document.

Terry Ryder, the governor's chief counsel, picked up the document and thumbed through it. It was a so-called federalization agreement that would allow President Bush to take command of all soldiers in Louisiana, effectively taking away Blanco's authority to control even the Louisiana National Guard. Though this agreement represented a compromise of sorts, offering to appoint a "dual-hatted" commander who would technically report to Blanco and to the Pentagon, it still sidelined the state when it came to directing troops in Louisiana.

Ryder immediately got on the phone, calling up the governor and every other senior state official he could think of.

A short time later, Chief of Staff Andy Kopplin, whom Ryder had rousted from bed, was in the operations center, on the phone with his counterpart in the Oval Office, Andrew Card. Kopplin had not even read the document yet, but he had a central question to ask on behalf of the governor: "How does this give us any additional federal assets?"

In a calm voice, Card explained that the agreement would allow for the coordination of assets and speed up the flow of men and materiel. And Card said the agreement needed to be signed quickly. "He indicated there was a press statement that had been drafted for the president or at least the White House to make the next morning," Kopplin said. Card read the press release to Kopplin. "I asked for a copy of it, but he said it was a privileged document," Kopplin said.

The state officials were suspicious. A mysterious fax sent in the dead of night, pegged to a draft press release the White House wouldn't let them see. "It was a little strange," Kopplin said.

But the real question was what the state would receive in return. National Guard forces under the state's control had just that day finally arrived on the scene at the Convention Center. The Superdome was in the process of being evacuated. The flow of food and water seemed to have sped up with General Honoré's arrival. "We felt like we were turning a corner," Kopplin said. The agreement offered nothing in the way of more troops or supplies. And it wasn't as if the federal government had distinguished itself in its disaster response thus far.

Kopplin and other officials in Baton Rouge smelled a political game afoot. On Thursday, in advance of President Bush's visit, General Blum of the National Guard command had told Blanco that such a move was not necessary. The troops would come at the same speed and in the same numbers, no matter who was in charge, he had said. "It doesn't bring you another soldier, another federal asset," he told the governor.

On the phone with Card, Kopplin mentioned General Blum's advice from the day before. Card responded quickly: Blum? He just happened to be in the room at that very moment.

On the line, Kopplin could hear Card excusing himself so the two men could talk. But even this raised suspicions in Kopplin's mind. "It was a conference call—I had no idea who was in the room," Kopplin said.

Blum spoke up, but the discussion between him and Kopplin was stilted and strained. Kopplin later said he couldn't remember what the general recommended or whether he had even asked for advice. But sometime during that conference call, either at the beginning or at the end, Kopplin said Blum made his wishes clear. "There was no doubt in my mind that Blum was pushing for the document to be signed, too," Kopplin said.

Card said he needed an answer before 9:00 the following morning, and the call ended a few minutes later. After the call, Blanco declared, "I'm not signing anything in the middle of the night."

At around 2:00 A.M., General Blum called Ryder and urged the lawyer to get the governor to sign the paper. The discussion quickly got "rather tough," as Ryder recalled it. "He accused me of being political and he accused me personally of being responsible for the deaths in New Orleans by not telling the governor to sign," Ryder said.

In the end, Blanco's staff unanimously urged her not to sign. "It was a proposal to allow the federal government to claim credit for the corner being turned on the ground in New Orleans," Kopplin later said. "The specific question asked was, 'How does this give us one additional federal asset?' And they never convinced me it would give us anything."

Blanco took the advice of her staff. The press release was never issued. And President Bush never became commander in chief of combined forces in Louisiana.

At around dawn, General Blum called Terry Ryder back. This time, Ryder said, Blum called to offer an apology of sorts. "I apologize for the absolute goat screwing," Blum said of his conversation from the White House. "I hope you understand I was under political duress."

But Ryder didn't understand and doesn't to this day. "I'll never forgive him," he said.

On Saturday morning, a platoon of Arkansas National Guardsmen worked the street outside the Convention Center, preparing evacuees for boarding the commercial buses that were lined in ranks along Tchoupitoulas Street. It was a simple job: One by one, the unwashed, weary evacuees presented themselves and their ragged belongings for search and were allowed to pass after satisfying the three requirements for a bus ride. No pets. No weapons. No booze. After working all morning, the soldiers had collected a score of knives, most of them small, and a fifty-five-gallon barrel of liquor bottles, which they occasionally beat down with hammers. Whiskey leaked out of the barrel and ran in the gutters. "Man, I bet there's $20,000 worth of booze on the street right now," Sergeant James McDonald said.

As McDonald worked, he was approached by an elderly woman pushing a garbage bag of clothes in a shopping basket. He rifled through her goods and let her pass.

Instead, the woman hugged him. "God bless you," she said.

The woman moved on, and McDonald moved to the whiskey barrel, picked up a worn claw hammer, and began smashing bottles of cognac. "This whole scene is just unbelievable," he said. "This should've all been done by the time we got here."

By Saturday afternoon, the Superdome was evacuated and the Convention Center nearly so. There were still a few small ad hoc sites around the city to clear of evacuees, but for the most part, New Orleans was empty, its streets free of whatever criminals may have been roaming there.

In his Saturday radio address, President Bush said he had called up the 82nd Airborne for duty in New Orleans. For some at Fort Bragg, including at least a few of the commanders, this came as a surprise. The 82nd had been more or less ready to go for days but had heard nothing about leaving until Saturday; the final deployment order was issued just minutes after the president's address.

By Sunday afternoon, the 82nd Airborne was in New Orleans, bivouacked at Armstrong Park, just outside the French Quarter. A few nights later, a company of soldiers came marching down Bourbon Street, sharp in their desert camouflage and red berets. They had rifles, but the breeches were empty. The soldiers weren't allowed to carry loaded weapons on the streets of New Orleans.

Fierce fighters though they may have been, the soldiers of the 82nd Airborne were quick to make friends among the locals. Despite the curfew, the soldiers made no attempt to roust the crowds. "With everything these people have been through, we don't have the heart," one soldier explained.

When the soldiers walked into sight of Johnny White's, a grubby watering hole on Bourbon Street, a cheer went up. The customers at this bar had already learned that when the 82nd came, it always brought plenty of ice. Cold beer was in the offing, just moments away.

Part Three

FLOTSAM
AND JETSAM

10

THE BLAME GAME

As the aftermath of Hurricane Katrina ground into its second week, it was clear Michael Brown was all but finished calling the shots on this particular disaster. Though he continued to retain the public support of President Bush and Secretary Chertoff and was technically the man in charge on the ground, the momentum of control had shifted to Washington and New Orleans, even as Brown was still chained down in Baton Rouge. For practical purposes, Brown had been supplanted by Thad Allen, a vice admiral in the Coast Guard whom Chertoff had appointed as the deputy principal federal official, technically Brown's assistant. But while Brown sat eighty-five miles from the action, Allen headquartered himself in New Orleans, along with General Honoré, who was overseeing rescue and supply logistics for the entire Gulf region and directing the 7,000 troops from the 82nd Airborne and the First Cavalry Division. The men in New Orleans were now calling most of the shots.

Cut off from Washington and essentially ignored by Chertoff, Brown came to rely on Colonel John Jordan, a Pentagon military attaché, to keep him up to speed with disaster efforts.

Jordan obliged, sending out an e-mail synopsis to Brown and nine Pentagon officials of what was discussed at the two daily meetings that had eclipsed the daily videoconference in importance. Admiral Allen had started the two conferences, one at dawn, one at sunset. Though Brown attended some of these telephone briefings, he clearly did not dominate them the way he had when appearing on the early videoconferences. During the week of September 5, Brown passed one of the synopses sent by Jordan to Joe Hagin in the White House. "Joe, this is the raw data I receive each day—once in the a.m. and once in the evening," Brown wrote. "If this is helpful, let me know. I'll add you to the distribution list." But the document was hardly exclusive—Brown simply cut the nine other names who received the e-mail message before sending it on to Hagin.

In Washington, Chertoff didn't even pretend that Brown was in the loop. At a press conference on Saturday, September 3, a reporter asked Chertoff whether Homeland Security had gone overboard in preparing for a terrorist event at the expense of natural disasters. Chertoff's response was telling in describing where he now saw himself in the chain of authority. "I'll tell you my philosophy, since I guess it's my responsibility now," he said. "I think we have to plan for both, because I think they're both mutually reinforcing."

With New Orleans's population down to around 8,000 residents, FEMA now turned its attention to the city's dead. The agency started with the easy pickings—the hundreds of people it had been told were secreted in the Superdome and the Convention Center. "Between the Super dome [*sic*] and the Convention Center it looks like 200 homocide [*sic*] bodies," Scott Wells, FEMA's deputy coordinating officer in Louisiana, said in an e-mail message on Saturday.

The next morning, a FEMA mortician crew drove up to the Superdome in an eighteen-wheeled refrigerated truck and paused by the National Guard soldiers who were still on the scene. The crew told the officer in charge, Colonel Thomas Beron, that he was there to pick up the 200 bodies left behind after the arena was evacuated. Beron told the FEMA man that his numbers were wildly exaggerated. "But he was pretty insistent," Beron recalled, so he shrugged, untied the rope holding the Superdome's doors shut, and let the FEMA crew inside.

Trailed by a company of soldiers, the FEMA team prowled the trash-filled and stinking arena for about an hour, starting in the nosebleed seats and working slowly to the playing field below. They found no bodies at all.

Beron was waiting for the search team on the building's loading dock. Wordlessly, he opened the door to a walk-in cooler that held the sum of the Superdome's dead. There, laid out on bags of melting ice, were six bodies: a heart attack victim, three others who had died natural deaths, one apparent suicide, and one drug overdose. The FEMA crew fussed over the bodies for a few minutes. "Take them," Beron said. On the way out, they picked up four other bodies that had washed up on the streets nearby.

At the Convention Center, the scene was similar. Despite the lurid tales of wanton violence, the scores of dead that officials insisted were awaiting inside, the massive building yielded up just four bodies, only one of which, an apparent knifing victim, seemed to have met with a violent end. There were no dead babies, no adolescent girls with their throats cut, no bullet-riddled bodies at all. For all the hoopla, only ten people had died in the notorious evacuation centers. Another large evacuation site near the split of the city's two interstates yielded about thirty bodies, but it was impossible to say who among the victims had died there. In the days after the storm, the site had become an informal collection spot of sorts for the city's dead.

Though Mayor Nagin and even some state and federal officials had predicted a death count of 50,000 or more, the real number was a tiny fraction of that—about 1,100 in Louisiana and another 200 or so in Mississippi. Everyone would later agree that despite the hiccups, the massive local rescue effort had in fact worked fairly well. Hardly any of the victims had died a violent death at the hands of others. City coroner Frank Minyard reckoned there were eight gunshot victims during the storm and its immediate aftermath, and two of those were suspected suicides. "That's not even a good Saturday night in New Orleans," he said.

Despite conventional belief, the dead were not overwhelmingly black or overwhelmingly poor. Of the bodies that were identified within six months of the storm, about three-fourths of the victims had come from New Orleans. Of the identified, slightly more than half were black. Many victims had died in the wealthy neighborhoods of the city's lakefront district, and two-thirds of the victims were over the age of sixty.

Though the evacuation center victims were largely phantom, more than 500 bodies were in the city, scattered along its streets and hidden behind closed doors in bedrooms, parlors, and attics. In the days after the storm, the bodies would present FEMA with yet another complication it had failed to foresee. Under a normal disaster, the local government would be responsible for gathering the dead, but in this case the city would be of little help. Minyard's morgue and his fleet of death wagons were all in the basement of the Criminal Court building under several feet of floodwater. Minyard's staff was scattered to the four winds. The state claimed not to have the resources to handle the gruesome task. So it would be up to the federal government to take on the job.

On paper, FEMA seemed well enough prepared. Even before the storm had hit, FEMA had pre-staged two so-called DMORT, or Disaster Mortuary Response Teams, in the state—two thirty-man squads of body collectors that included pathologists, undertakers, and forensic dentists. The Pentagon had also sent nine Army mortuary units from the 54th Quartermaster Company out of Fort Lee, Virginia. The FEMA teams were trained and ready: Over the summer, the agency had made "casualty management" a priority, staging a series of exercises to ensure that everybody was familiar with the procedures. One of the training sessions had even been held in downtown New Orleans.

On that Saturday after the storm, Chertoff promised Governor Blanco that once the rescue operation wound down, collecting the dead would be a department priority. "Recovery with respect" is what he called it.

Alas, under FEMA's oversight, this seemingly simple task would take weeks to get going. Though floods were a standard fixture in every New Orleans disaster scenario, FEMA had never considered the possibility that the local morgue would lack the trucks or staff to gather the city's dead. A spokesman for the agency said that finding and collecting these bodies was below the station of its DMORT personnel. Even setting up a temporary morgue for the bodies—a task FEMA had anticipated—took ten days. And as FEMA cast around for a solution to all of this, bodies lay in the city's streets.

"Operational paralysis" is the phrase that Colonel Jordan, Michael Brown's military liaison, used to describe the fumbling progress in setting up a system to collect and identify the storm dead. In an e-mail message to Brown, he urged a speedy resolution, "or it will become evident to the media that [a] plan for collection is not in place."

Too late. In New Orleans, some of the storm victims, anonymous in life, were becoming famous in death as their bodies lingered in public view. More than one reporter had noted the body laying out on Fern Street in the Carrolton section, as well as the dead woman in the Lower Ninth Ward, whose body had been hung up by floodwaters on a section of chain-link fencing. Others among the visible dead got treated to lavish eulogies, as reporters found grim irony in the shabby treatment being afforded them. A Florida reporter wrote a first-person account about pitching in with neighbors to help bury a woman named Vera Smith, an apparent hit-and-run victim, in a shallow grave near her home in the Lower Garden District. Many others focused their attentions on Alcede Jackson.

Jackson was easily the most famous storm victim in the city. An octogenarian whose body, wrapped in a grubby blue blanket, sat for nearly two weeks on the porch of his Uptown home, Jackson was hard to miss: "ALCEDE JACKSON," someone had scrawled on a big sheet of Day-Glo posterboard that was tacked above the body. "Rest in Peace in the Loving Arms of Jesus." The New York Times, following a long line of journalists and photographers, described the death tableau on its front page. The Times didn't pretend to be delivering a scoop: "Anyone could see his body from the street, and many did," the story said.

FEMA's reputation was going from bad to worse. With nearly a million evacuees from the disaster area, the state of Louisiana complained that trailers and other housing help that FEMA had promised were slow to make it to the devastated areas, even though the agency had said that prefab homes were on the way. FEMA promised 300,000 trailers for the disaster area; alas, within days of promising this, it became clear that such a number was impossible to secure. "The trailer idea is worse than I originally thought," said an e-mail message that circulated among Vice President Dick Cheney's staff. "Per the data below, the last batch of the trailers that we are now purchasing will be coming off the production line in approximately 3.5 years."

"Temporary housing in Louisiana is a problem," said a summary of Louisiana's contribution to a videoconference during this week. "Have seen plans and discussed it, but have not seen any trailers." An idea to haul cruise ships into the disaster area to provide temporary housing for victims and disaster workers bogged down in negotiations between FEMA and the Pentagon over who was responsible for striking a deal. FEMA had started on this project just a few days after the storm, but the boats were nowhere to be seen. Brown was told that Pentagon procurement "doesn't allow for these quick decisions," to which he responded, "Why isn't red tape being cut?"

There were chronic shortages of food as well. A supply of German army rations that was flown into Louisiana was impounded by the U.S. Food and Drug Administration because it hadn't been properly inspected upon arrival. There was a sudden shortage of tarps to temporarily waterproof storm-damaged buildings and a continuing lack of generators for the area, which was still largely without conventional power. And this was in the places where help had actually arrived. Six days after Katrina's landfall, a FEMA assessment team wandered into St. Bernard Parish, about five miles from the French Quarter, and expressed shock that a population of several thousand storm survivors was in residence and clamoring for help. St. Bernard Parish had been obliterated by the storm, flooded to the eaves, its two evacuation shelters severely damaged by wind and water. And yet "the Rapid Needs Assessment Teams from FEMA had not identified this issue when they initially flew these areas immediately after the storm," a FEMA report on the matter concluded. "FEMA is getting water and [food] to the population to address immediate need."

The problems went on. A week after the storm, FEMA officials in Louisiana promised to hire 500 security guards to patrol the state's refineries, but they were told a day later by lawyers and procurement agents in Washington that the agency didn't have the authority to make such promises. On Thursday, September 8, FEMA still had no idea where many of the state's storm shelters were located; that same day, Washington officials expressed surprise that thirty-four bodies had been discovered in a nursing home in St. Bernard Parish, even though the facility had been listed on a roster prepared by the state before the hurricane had even hit.

As the Louisiana diaspora spread to other states, complaints about FEMA followed. At a videoconference, officials from Arkansas "expressed extreme frustration in receiving s[o]me assistance and level of support for the 50,000 evacuees that are being housed in the state," a synopsis of the meeting said.

Even as the criticism grew, the response from the Bush administration was muted. President Bush, who had been applauded for his decisive action and soaring rhetoric in the wake of the September 11 attacks on New York and Washington, continued to plod through public appearances in the aftermath of Katrina, larding his speeches with toll-free telephone numbers and meaningless statistics and promising to get the federal government moving. "Now, we have 3,000 people who are working around the clock to take the calls," Bush said just over a week after the storm, in a statement that sounded more corporate than compassionate. "We still have tens of thousands more people who need to be processed, so I ask for your patience if you experience problems in trying to contact FEMA."

During the week, Bush, Chertoff, and Brown discussed a new FEMA initiative to assist evacuees immediately by distributing thousands of $2,000 debit cards. Brown, who had all but disappeared from public view following Bush's much-lampooned "heck of a job" comment, surfaced on Thursday, September 8, to discuss the debit card scheme. "The concept is to get them some cash in hand which empowers [them] to make their own decisions," Brown said.

FEMA planned to distribute some 320,000 cards to evacuees who were now spread across the nation, starting with people in major evacuation centers such as the Houston Astrodome. Chertoff, who briefed the governors on the program, said the cards were intended to get people moving out of municipal arenas and other megashelters and into more permanent housing. But Chertoff and other federal officials skimped on the details about how the cards would be distributed. And the next day, a near-riot broke out at the Houston Astrodome as thousands of evacuees jostled and shoved among themselves for a chance at the money. Alarmed Houston cops placed the shelter, home to 20,000 evacuees, into forced lockdown.

FEMA canceled the debit card program two days later, but even this didn't come without a measure of confusion. In Baton Rouge, FEMA spokesman David Passey said the program was being scrapped in favor of "traditional" methods of getting money to storm victims, which during this disaster took about two weeks. But in Washington a short time later, FEMA spokesman Butch Kinerney didn't seem to know the debit card program had been scrapped. "That's not what I've been telling everyone all day," he told the Associated Press.

In Louisiana, local officials vented their anger at Washington. Jefferson Parish president Aaron Broussard flatly accused the federal bureaucracy of murder and demanded a congressional inquest. "Take whatever idiot they have at the top of whatever agency and give me a better idiot," he said. "Give me a caring idiot. Give me a sensitive idiot. Just don't give me the same idiot." But President Bush would oppose any sort of bipartisan or independent panel on the model of the 9/11 Commission. Instead, he promised to personally supervise a White House inquiry.

Deserved or not, much of the criticism for the federal response in Louisiana and Mississippi fell on Michael Brown. About ten days after the storm, someone in Washington leaked an e-mail message that Brown had sent to Chertoff on the day Katrina hit. Referring to Katrina as a "near catastrophic event," Brown requested reinforcements that would be able to "convey a positive image of FEMA" in the disaster zone. Understated and oddly bloodless, Brown's message concluded, "Thank you for your consideration in helping us to meet our responsibilities."

The *Times-Picayune* of New Orleans called for Brown's dismissal, saying he had all but disappeared in the days after the storm. The *Miami Herald* called Brown "the poster boy for what's gone wrong with an agency once lauded for its lightning reflexes." In Washington, the call was rising for Brown's dismissal as well. At an Oval Office meeting on Wednesday, September 7, House Democratic leader Nancy Pelosi bluntly demanded that Bush fire Brown. "Thank you for your advice," Bush said curtly. After the meeting, the Republican congressional leaders didn't dare shoot Pelosi down.

Demoralized, isolated geographically, out of the loop on many major decisions being made in Washington, Michael Brown nearly disappeared from public view. Politically speaking, he was a dead man walking.

Though the White House and Chertoff publicly maintained that Brown was performing up to expectations, the words from the top had a subtle hollowness. Chertoff, asked directly on CNN a week after the storm whether he still had confidence in Brown, ducked the question. "Look, I think Michael Brown's had a lot of experience," he said. "I think he's done a tremendous job under pressure." White House press secretary Scott McClellan simply maintained the president's support of Brown and then cut off debate. "There are over 75,000 people that are involved in all the response and recovery and law enforcement when it comes to Katrina," McClellan said. "And we appreciate the efforts of everyone."

Replacing Brown became more urgent in Chertoff 's mind as the days passed and as public debate moved on to questions about whether the Department of Homeland Security was prepared for other disasters, terrorist-inspired or natural. Suddenly, FEMA was viewed as a bellwether for Homeland Security at large. Despite the hype that surrounded the department's creation—and the huge slugs of money that it spent to counter terrorist threats—the press and many politicians openly questioned whether America was in fact safer, as President Bush often maintained was the case.

As Chertoff lurched into damage control, he cast around for a figure who could replace Michael Brown as the face of federal disaster response. He found a ready candidate in Admiral Allen. Unlike FEMA, the Coast Guard had performed well during the Katrina disaster, in part because it had been immune from the kind of budgetary deprivations and tinkering by department officials that had so devastated FEMA. Even the Bush administration's toughest critics had heaped praise on its performance and its single-minded focus on rescue missions.

But as the deputy PFO, Allen may have been causing as much trouble in the disaster zone as he was alleviating. Louisiana had never been under a unified or even a coordinated command, and this was the source of many of the problems in the state. Instead, throughout the disaster, state and federal agencies worked independently, under their own initiative, and sometimes at cross-purposes. The Coast Guard was one of the worst offenders: FEMA officials would later say the agency did almost nothing to keep other outfits up to speed on its activities.

In Washington, the hunt for a scapegoat was intensifying. Even staunch defenders of the Bush administration were critical not only of FEMA but of Chertoff as well. President Bush's poll ratings took a deep plunge, even among Republican voters.

Chertoff tried at first to highlight the overwhelming "disaster within a disaster" that he claimed was at the root of the problem. He pointed out that not even the Hurricane Pam scenario had envisioned actual levee breaches in New Orleans, only a less-catastrophic overtopping. "This is really one which I think was breathtaking in its surprise," he said at a press conference about a week after the storm hit. "We didn't merely have the overflow. We actually had the break in the wall. And I will tell you that really that perfect storm of combination of catastrophes exceeded the foresight of the planners and maybe anybody's foresight."

The reporters weren't buying it. "Why should we not have anticipated both events coming?" shouted one.

"You know, that's the kind of question which in court a judge usually sustains the objection to. It's called argumentative," Chertoff replied.

The reporters persisted. "It was unforeseeable that a Category 4 hurricane would knock down a levee designed to withstand Category 3 winds?" asked another.

The press conference came to a swift end.

Chertoff also continued to refer to Katrina as a double disaster, as if the hurricane's landfall were somehow a separate event from the levee breaches and the subsequent flooding of New Orleans. This was almost certainly not the case, and it hardly excused the Department of Homeland Security from falling down on its duty. Though Chertoff often invoked the double whammy of Katrina to explain why Washington had been remiss, the scenario was in fact embedded in the department's philosophy and planning, and had been a featured element in its TOPOFF exercises. In the three years prior to Katrina's landfall, the department had spent more than $13 billion on equipment and exercises that were supposed to fight both natural disasters and terrorists—often both at once. Several states spent their exercise money on drills that simulated a natural disaster compounded by a terrorist attack. Even in the midst of Katrina, Homeland Security had circulated to police departments around the country a report entitled "How Terrorists Might Exploit a Hurricane." This document had been put together by the department after Florida's 2004 hurricane season by a so-called Red Cell panel, a group of academics, pop-fiction writers, retired military officers, and musicians. Designed to spark what the department believed would be "out-of-the-box" thinking, the report began mildly enough, saying that it was unlikely terrorists would have the capability to exploit a natural disaster. But should they be able to, the report said, "they would have several opportunities."

Many people in Washington also were beginning to wonder aloud whether it had been wise to choose someone to head the department who had had no experience in state and local government. "Surely this would not have happened under Tom Ridge" became a common refrain. Ridge, the argument went, was a former governor and a seasoned politician, who understood that natural disasters were Politics 101, and that the quickest way for an elected official to lose his job was to muck up a calamity. "I doubt that Ridge would have been caught as flatfooted," said Clark Kent Ervin, the department's first inspector general and himself no great fan of Tom Ridge.

Nowhere was the pressure stronger to "stand up the response for the secretary" than on the ground in the disaster zone, where e-mail messages were flying back and forth between employees about the need to do whatever they could to make the department look good. What this meant above all was making sure that, whenever the media was around, the Homeland Security agencies were clearly in a leading role. Complicating their task, though, was the fact that other federal departments were also seeking to present a high profile to the TV cameras.

On the morning of Sunday, September 4, Jamie Zuieback, a spokeswoman with Immigration and Customs Enforcement (ICE), the parent agency of the Federal Protective Service and Homeland Security's main law enforcement arm, sent an e-mail message to Chertoff's press secretary, Russ Knocke, saying there were rumors circulating that the FBI was taking charge of the federal law enforcement response in New Orleans.

"Nope," Knocke replied. "We have the ball."

But word soon came back to Knocke that Zuieback was right. The FBI had pulled into town the night before in a fleet of black Chevy Suburbans with a mobile command center in tow, and had organized a hasty press conference to announce its arrival on the scene. Homeland Security officials were outraged. John P. Clark, the deputy head of ICE, fired off messages to senior officials at the department, including Matthew Broderick and his boss, Bob Stephan, demanding action. "I think DHS has one opportunity to turn this thing around. We can go into the areas, high visibility/full force, and lead a comprehensive security effort," he wrote. "Having failed in many aspects on preparation, emergency assistance and recovery, if we now turn our homeland security responsibility over to the FBI/DOJ, we might as well all await [the breakup of DHS]."

Stephan and Broderick encouraged Clark to "move out aggressively" and take the lead to bring in extra troops and make sure Homeland Security appeared fully in charge of federal law enforcement. "This is a good chance for us to be [the lead]," Broderick said.

But the rush for control blew up in their faces. White House and Justice Department officials slammed Homeland Security for playing politics while New Orleans suffered. "We're fully moving ahead and prepared to take orders from the FBI or simply work cooperatively with them," a chastened Clark wrote. "There have been no signs on the ground that there is any turf war brewing and I intend to ignite none up here. Already [I] have received some blowback on my first email on this, which circulated further than I anticipated, so I'll keep a low profile and stick to the business of steering our people down there."

As the debate over the federal response to Katrina raged in Washington, Brown, shunned by state officials and already stripped of much of his authority, took to spending long hours alone in his private trailer in the parking lot of the emergency operations center in Baton Rouge, picking at problems that were quickly becoming intractable. He had little communication with Chertoff and did not appear before reporters. Much of the White House staff brought in to help him cope with FEMA's public relations disaster withdrew. Worse, as the administration closed ranks around Chertoff, Brown's old friends at the White House asked him to stop calling. "I want you to start going through the chain of command," White House chief of staff Andrew Card told him.

And it was not just the Democrats who smelled blood. About a week and a half after Katrina made landfall, Brown decided to send a hospital ship called the USNS *Comfort* to New Orleans. A short time later, however, he got an angry phone call from Trent Lott,

Mississippi's powerful U.S. senator, who wanted the ship for his state. "Why don't you be a man?" Lott sputtered. "Why don't you act like a true leader and grow a pair of *cojones*? You need to use the *Comfort* in Mississippi."

Brown resisted, saying the *Comfort* needed to go to New Orleans, and pointed out that Mississippi governor Haley Barbour had said he didn't need the ship. Lott complained to the White House. Chertoff overruled Brown. The *Comfort* steamed into Pascagoula and dropped anchor.

Brown was pretty sure he was about to get relieved of duty, and told people so. On the afternoon of Friday, September 9, Chertoff tapped on the door to Brown's trailer in the Baton Rouge parking lot, let himself in, and sat down. He looked uncomfortable. "You're really tired," Chertoff said to Brown. "I want you to go back to D.C. and take as much time off as you need."

Brown smiled. "Oh, so this is the firing," he said.

Chertoff denied it. "I just want you to go home and get some rest," he said.

The conversation was over within a few minutes. Admiral Allen was now the principal federal official in charge of Katrina disaster response. A short time later, Brown outlined his immediate plan to a reporter from the Associated Press. "I'm going to go home and walk my dog and hug my wife, and maybe get a good Mexican meal and a stiff margarita and a full night's sleep," he said. "And then I'm going to go right back to FEMA and continue to do all I can to help these victims."

When Brown got back to Washington, he got his margarita. And he also got some advice, from a Republican lawyer with close ties to the White House. According to Brown, the lawyer told him to lay low, tap friends for a position in the private sector, and "exit gracefully" a few weeks later.

But it was not meant to be. On the following Monday, Brown was sitting in his office when he got a call from his old friend Michael Jackson, the deputy secretary of homeland security. Jackson asked Brown what his plans were. Brown recounted what the lawyer had told him to do.

"I don't think that's going to work," Jackson said. "I just think you ought to leave now." So Brown did. He called together his immediate staff and said, "I've had it, I'm out of here." By the end of the day, he was gone.

As the days passed, a subtle change came over the White House press operation. Administration officials began talking less about what President Bush had called the "unacceptable" federal response to Katrina and more about what local officials might have done to aggravate the problems. Bush, who had embarked on a relentless string of trips to the disaster area, began to make public comments about how Katrina had totally overwhelmed the city and the state. Chertoff did the same. Asked on CNN how he could not have known about the dire situation at the Convention Center during the height of the crisis, Chertoff laid the blame square on Louisiana. "You know, the very day that this emerged in the press, I was on a videoconference with all the officials, including state and local officials," he said. "And nobody, none of the state and local officials or anybody else, was talking about a convention center."

When he was running FEMA, Brown had refrained from criticizing Louisiana officials. But as a free agent, Brown now actively took part. He said he was specifically recruited by the White House to do so. A few days after he was cut loose, Brown said he got a call from Nicol Andrews, a FEMA spokeswoman who had been installed at the agency by the White House. According to Brown, she asked him to submit to an exclusive interview with the New York Times and "get some stuff out in the press," and "kind of plant some stuff for us." The "stuff" Andrews was referring to, Brown said, was an accounting of the failures by Louisiana officials to get on top of the disaster. "You need to tell the truth about how bad the state was," he said Andrews told him. Brown later noted, "And what was the purpose? It shifts the blame. And my problem was I'm so pissed off and had been so battered that I fell into that trap because I'm thinking this will help rehabilitate me."

Andrews denied pushing Brown to trash Baton Rouge. But whoever came up with the idea, it worked fairly well. Though Brown came off in the New York Times article as somewhat self-serving and unrepentant, the article lingered over his criticism of Blanco, contrasting what he described as her confused response with far more agile mobilizations in Mississippi and Alabama.

Baton Rouge was already clued into the White House strategy; its well-honed political radar had been up since the Sunday after the storm, when the *Washington Post*, quoting anonymous White House officials, said Governor Blanco had yet to declare a state of emergency in Louisiana. This was untrue: Blanco had declared a state emergency on Friday, August 26, three days before Katrina hit.

Though the *Post* later published a correction, it stood by the gist of the story, which was that the White House had embraced a political strategy of blaming the Katrina disaster on Blanco and her staff.

Baton Rouge saw the comment as evidence that the Bush administration was girding to do battle with the state's Democratic leadership. "That told me and everybody else down here that with respect to the White House, we were in the crosshairs," said Bob Mann, Blanco's communications director. "All of a sudden, we're getting the crap beaten out of us." In the ensuing days, Blanco's staff, not unacquainted with waging partisan wars, would devise its own catalog of Bush administration missteps. "Blanco declares state of emergency," the document said, "while Bush vacations at the ranch."

The day after the *Post* story hit, Bush made a trip to Baton Rouge. Blanco, who had planned to visit evacuees in Houston that day, abruptly canceled her trip when her aides got a last-minute heads-up from a reporter on the impending presidential visit. There was no question among her staff that the governor should be on hand. Going to Houston "reinforces the notion that she's not in charge," Blanco press spokesman Denise Bottcher said in an e-mail message to Andy Kopplin. Later in the day, in a real-time critique of the Bush visit, Bottcher urged the governor's handlers to push Blanco into the spotlight. "She's going to have to shove her way to [Bush] and glue herself to his hip," Bottcher wrote in an e-mail message. "When he moves, she moves—if he walks fast, she walks fast."

In late September, Michael Brown got a chance to defend himself before a hostile Congress. In his hours-long testimony before a

House committee investigating the Katrina disaster, Brown stuck to the script as he said the White House had outlined. "My biggest mistake was not recognizing by Saturday that Louisiana was dysfunctional," Brown said. He later admitted that blaming the locals for the dismal disaster response was unfair and only a partial recounting of what really had gone wrong. In his later testimony before the Senate and interviews with the press, Brown would heap much of the blame on Chertoff.

To be sure, state and local officials had made some grave errors as they prepared for and responded to Hurricane Katrina. In subsequent hearings and statements, Mayor Nagin and his top disaster chiefs would admit that they had started but never completed an agreement with the Orleans Parish School Board to commandeer school buses during emergencies, as neighboring Plaquemines Parish had done. They admitted they had considered drafting Amtrak to aid in evacuations but had never sealed the deal. There was little excuse for City Hall not to have stocked the Superdome with rudimentary supplies. Earlier that summer, Nagin's administration had forced the New Orleans Saints football team to set aside storage space for just that purpose. But while the space was there, the supplies were never purchased. The state and the city were reluctant to spend money unless Washington agreed in advance to pay for it.

Expenses for charter buses, meals, and bottled water—not to mention employee overtime and the like—are reimbursed only if the threatening storm actually hits. So when the day came to evacuate, bus drivers were not offered overtime pay to transport at-risk citizens. Instead of socking away food, Nagin told people to haul in their own.

City Hall made mistakes as well during Katrina's early aftermath. Though Nagin may have cut a heroic figure standing in the lobby of the ruined Hyatt hotel, he was essentially isolated from the very people who might have been able to help him the most. With spotty communications and only a low-level subordinate in place at the emergency operations center in Baton Rouge, Nagin might have been better served by dispatching a senior disaster official to convey the city's needs directly to Louisiana and FEMA officials. In neighboring Mississippi, local officials overcame poor communications between Jackson, the state capital, and the coast by instituting a runner system—dispatching cars on a routine schedule to physically convey information. This was never attempted in Louisiana. As it was, Nagin saw Michael Brown only once during the first four crucial days of the crisis.

The city also could have been a better shepherd of the resources it did have. In the run-up to the storm, instead of putting the entire police department on the clock, the city's cops were split into two shifts. The late shift was sent home to rest—a decision that created a big headache after Katrina hit.

Terry Ebbert, the city's homeland security director, said one of the signal horrors he witnessed during Hurricane Katrina wasn't something he saw but something he heard. On Tuesday, just a day after the storm hit, Ebbert said he was passing through the city's emergency operations center on the eighth floor of City Hall when he heard a man's shaky voice crackling over the radio. The man said he was in a darkened attic, standing in water up to his neck. He had no tools to break through the roof. He was alone and hysterical. He was a New Orleans police officer.

"It was one of the most chilling things I had ever heard," Ebbert recalled. As the officer pleaded for help and wept in frustration, a dispatcher asked him if he had his service revolver. "Now look for a vent and shoot it," the dispatcher said.

"All of a sudden, you can hear him firing," Ebbert said. "I understand he got away."

Lesson learned. Next time, Ebbert said, New Orleans cops will emulate utility companies, sending a sizable reserve of its first responders out of town before the storm hits. "Rescuing police off roofs is not exactly the best use of our resources," he said dryly.

For the state's part, the failure to invoke a critical element of its standing evacuation plan probably meant that some people were left behind when Katrina roared ashore who might otherwise have been convinced to leave. During the general pre-storm evacuation, Blanco's own transportation secretary, Johnny Bradberry, refused to assist the city of New Orleans in moving its vast population of indigents to safer ground, even though the state's own emergency evacuation plan demanded that he do so. And after the storm, the transportation department was supposed to "acquire, allocate and monitor transportation resources as the emergency continues." It didn't do this, either.

Bradberry later told Senate investigators that he knew this was his job. "We have done nothing to fulfill this responsibility," he admitted. "We had no plans in place to do any of this."

As a result, the post-evacuation plan for New Orleans was freelanced. And in its haste to rescue people off of rooftops in the early days of the disaster, the state and federal governments essentially ignored nursing homes. The result was that some seventy-five people—including several in nursing homes that were dry and easily accessible to rescuers—died.

Before Katrina hit, the state essentially told nursing home operators that they were on their own when it came to evacuating before the storm. Though this in itself is not unusual—most states leave it up to nursing homes to devise their own evacuation plans—Louisiana seemed almost to discourage evacuations by telling nursing home operators that the public "special needs shelters" were for the exclusive use of "non-institutionalized patients." In essence, the state told operators that if they wanted to evacuate, they would have to make private arrangements with other nursing homes in the region.

Perhaps as a result, the state's stunning success in evacuating the region—more than 80 percent of the residents left—was not duplicated in the nursing homes. Only nineteen of the fifty-three nursing homes in Orleans Parish and St. Bernard Parish—the two parishes where flooding was the worst—evacuated before the storm. The other thirty-four nursing homes had to evacuate after the storm passed—a migration that sucked up tremendous rescue resources once the area flooded. And for many nursing home residents, such as those at St. Rita's in St. Bernard Parish where thirty people died, the evacuation came too late.

In the end, the most precious commodity was buses. And for more than a day after Katrina hit, Louisiana's Jeff Smith said getting buses to the city was not a state priority. Smith didn't order buses until Governor Blanco specifically requested that he do so. At Tuesday's videoconference, more than twenty-four hours after Katrina made landfall, Smith hardly mentioned buses in his recorded conversations with FEMA officials.

But in his testimony before Congress, Smith said those who were critical of Louisiana's performance should consider the capabilities of their own local government. "Could your city evacuate 1.3 million people in under forty hours?" Smith asked rhetorically during one Senate hearing. "Does your city have a building that can house 40,000 people and the ability to provide them food and water and medical care for five days? Could your state find shelter for 273,000 people in a matter of days?"

The federal deficiencies were cascading, beginning with the Army Corps of Engineers, which had designed a flood protection system it judged shortly before the storm to be in "exceptional condition," only to watch it fail catastrophically at a level below its rated design strength. And when those levees failed, the federal government—or parts of it, anyway—failed to grasp the significance, to "connect the dots," as the 9/11 Commission had said about the attacks on New York and Washington in September 2001.

But the true errors were rooted in something more fundamental. Chertoff, who continued for days afterward to call Katrina a "set of catastrophes" as if the flooding were a separate event, would later explain to a Senate investigative committee that there are some disasters that simply do not warrant the attention of the secretary of homeland security. "I mean, if there is anything that FEMA does and has done over the last twenty years, it's been hurricanes," Chertoff said. "Even Michael Brown had been through four prior hurricanes the previous year."

But it was also becoming clear that disasters might not simply be segregated by the perceived severity of an impending disaster, that politics might play a hand as well. In the run-up and immediate aftermath to Hurricane Charley in 2004, which hit Florida during a presidential election year, the federal government was clearly better prepared to meet the immediate needs of the disaster. Within hours of the storm's landfall, FEMA and its partnering agencies had six Urban Search and Rescue teams deployed (twice what it had in Louisiana); twenty trailers of cots and blankets, portable toilets, sleeping bags, and tents (Louisiana had none); and an unspecified number of sea containers filled with building materials to perform quick housing repairs (Louisiana had none).

Two days after Hurricane Charley hit Florida, FEMA had moved 2 million meals into Florida and 8.1 million pounds of ice. *Four* days after Katrina made landfall, FEMA had distributed only 1.9 million meals across the disaster area and 1.7 million pounds of ice. Two days after Charley hit, FEMA had opened twelve disaster recovery centers and had offered living assistance to 19,000 people. In the Katrina disaster zone, FEMA did not open its first disaster center until four days after the storm hit, and that was in Alabama, far from the area that was hardest hit. "FEMA appears to have responded in a timely and effective manner three months before an election in Florida, a state governed by Jeb Bush, the President's brother," said the Republican-dominated House investigative committee. It added, "We cannot ignore the disparities between the lavish treatment by FEMA of survivors of Hurricane Charley." Regarding Katrina, the committee said, "FEMA, after all, speaks to a higher power, and that higher power was not only slow on the uptake but slow on the delivery as well. If the nightmare were over for Katrina survivors, this would be a matter for policy debate. But the nightmare for the survivors continues."

When he was called before the Senate investigative panel, Matthew Broderick was hard-pressed to explain why he did not know the levees and floodwalls in New Orleans had been broken for nearly thirty hours after they actually collapsed. His first response to the committee was to accuse Michael Brown of "running a parallel information system," which prevented him from realizing the gravity of what was occurring in New Orleans. But in fact, Broderick had plenty of information at hand to determine that a catastrophe was unfolding. He received early warning about the levee breaches and about the growing problem at the Convention Center. He simply failed to act on the information. As Senator Mark Dayton would remark, Broderick had not needed Brown to tell him what was going on in New Orleans as the disaster unfolded. "Well, the 'quick ground truth' was apparent if you turned on the television, with all due respect," he told Broderick. "You know, you don't need to send satellites over; turn on CNN." And as Henry Whitehorn of the Louisiana State Police would later remark, "I can't imagine anybody not knowing that in those days after the storm that there were thousands of people walking around in the city with no food or water. We told them over and over again. And they all knew that FEMA was the only agency that could provide what we needed."

Ultimately, the investigative committees in the House and the Senate, as well as the Department of Homeland Security's own inspector general, put the blame directly on the federal government. Hurricane Katrina, the House panel's majority report said, was "a national failure, an abdication of the most solemn obligation to provide for the common welfare." And as the commanding general of the federal disaster effort, Chertoff had fulfilled his responsibilities "late, ineffectively, or not at all."

The White House, which had reluctantly—and in the opinion of Congress, insufficiently—cooperated with the Capitol Hill investigations, offered up its own, thick "lessons learned" report. It was a curious document, scrupulous in pinpointing the many failures during Hurricane Katrina yet also insistent on pointing out everything that had gone right. White House homeland security adviser Frances Townsend singled out the state of Louisiana and the city of New Orleans in particular for doing yeoman's work during the disaster, especially in the hours leading up to landfall. It was an otherwise short list, however, and perhaps even misleading: In speaking about what had gone right, Townsend singled out the Department of Transportation and the Pentagon, two agencies that showed up late with buses and soldiers and offered help in a generally grudging fashion. She was less complimentary of the HSOC and suggested it be enhanced.

The White House report made 128 recommendations for reform, a few prudent, if obvious, recommendations for change among them. For example, it recommended that states negotiate their own disaster supply contracts and that the federal government agree up front to reimburse them. It also suggested that the Department of Homeland Security include natural disaster scenarios in its TOPOFF exercises.

Afterward, Chertoff dutifully said that he planned to implement all of the White House recommendations for reform, many of them before the 2006 hurricane system began. This time, Chertoff said, the federal government would ensure that a sufficient number of buses be on hand and that proper communications be in place before disaster struck. FEMA, he promised in an interview, would be completely integrated into the Department of Homeland Security. "You can't stovepipe FEMA away from the department," Chertoff said.

President Bush never directly criticized the state's performance during Hurricane Katrina. Indeed, on a trip to Baton Rouge a week after the storm hit, Bush approached Andy Kopplin, Blanco's chief of staff, and insisted that he had nothing but good things to say about the governor. "I want the governor to succeed and I'm not attacking her," Bush told Kopplin.

"I'm glad to hear that, Mr. President," Kopplin responded. "And with all due respect, you may not be attacking the governor, but your people sure are."

Shortly afterward, the Bush administration quit badmouthing the state, anonymously or on the record. In early October Chertoff demurred when asked by a House committee to highlight Louisiana's shortcomings. "I guess my own view is this: I've got to get my own house in order, and that's what I'm focused on," he said. "I'm not going to judge others."

White House counselor Dan Bartlett would later say that the Bush administration had never embarked on a studied campaign to smear Blanco or the state of Louisiana. "There was more suspicion and innuendo that something was going on than the reality would suggest," Bartlett said. "There were a lot of tired people, a lot of stressed people and everyone was feeling very defensive about being blamed. Were there things said that could be considered a political shot? I'm sure there were, on both sides. But it didn't come from the top. We were in crisis mode, not political mode."

But others in the administration say the effort was real and it was coordinated. The truth, however, is unlikely ever to be known.

As the days and weeks passed and the Gulf Coast moved into recovery mode, it was clear that FEMA needed more than a few tweaks to right itself. Just about everything the agency attempted—providing sufficient housing for returnees, moving evacuees from hotels to more permanent locations, lending a sense of order to the reconstruction efforts—collapsed in a heap of confusion. When it became known, for example, that many residents were refusing to evacuate the ruined city because federal rules barred people from taking pets to shelters, FEMA attempted—clumsily—to do something about it. Typical was an incident reported by the *Washington Post*. On Friday, September 9, nearly two weeks after the storm, FEMA called the retailer Petsmart and requested a truckload of cages to transport dogs and cats out of the region. The truck went out the next morning, but before it got to the disaster zone, FEMA called and canceled the order. The truck turned back.

Two days later, FEMA called again and renewed the order. The next day, FEMA called to say it was not sure. Each time FEMA called, it was a different official. And each time, the official gave no reason for the change. So it went for a full week—until Friday, September 16, when $28,370 worth of crates finally rolled into the disaster zone. But by then, the urgency in getting out of the city had passed.

And then there was the question of the bodies. On Sunday, September 11, FEMA's contractor, Kenyon International, threatened to walk off the job because FEMA continued to stall on signing a formal contract with the company. "Our intent was to leave as soon as we could," said Robert Jensen, Kenyon's president, as he ticked off the various, maddening ways that FEMA had managed to complicate the simple process of gathering the dead and identifying them.

And on Tuesday, September 13, Governor Blanco got a measure

of revenge against Washington when she called a press conference to excoriate the federal government for its utter incompetence in handling the matter of the dead. As she reminded reporters at the time, Chertoff had promised more than a week earlier to get the process moving, quickly and efficiently. "No one, even those at the highest level, seems to be able to break through the bureaucracy to get this important mission done," she said. "The failure to execute a contract for the recovery of our citizens has hurt the speed of recovery efforts. I am angry and outraged."

So the state would come to the rescue, Blanco said, stepping up where Washington had failed so miserably. Louisiana would sign a contract with Kenyon. Collection of the bodies would begin. "I could not bear to wait any longer," she said.

11

DO IT YOURSELF

The cavalry made it to Jefferson Parish about a week after Katrina hit. On Tuesday, September 6, Walter Maestri was standing outside his office when the phalanx of black Chevy Suburbans bounced into the parking lot and jerked to a halt. The doors opened, and grim-faced men with automatic rifles spilled out onto the asphalt at a dead run, rushing to surround Dan Griffith, FEMA's designated envoy to the parish. Maestri laughed. If Griffith's men were looking for action, they were going to be disappointed in this beaten-down suburb of New Orleans. Jefferson hadn't notched a violent crime since before the storm. "It looked like a scene out of a movie about the Mexican revolution," Maestri said with a chuckle. "Even the president doesn't travel with that kind of security."

Maestri, Jefferson Parish's director of homeland security, decided to cut Griffith a break. Maybe this is how FEMA operates, he reasoned, armed to the teeth and prepared for any contingency. Griffith needed an office, and Maestri obliged, setting up the little federal army in a building just down the way from the parish's West Bank operations center. And then Maestri didn't see Griffith so much anymore.

As the days unfolded, it started looking as if all Maestri was going to get out of this FEMA man was a good laugh. Never mind that
the agency had put out a press release more than a week before, touting the millions of gallons of water, tons of food, and piles of electrical generators it had on hand; Maestri was getting nothing for his
parish, and Griffith was no help. "He's a nice guy but that's about it,"
Maestri said.

Two days later, Jefferson Parish was still wasted. It had hardly any
power or utilities to speak of, its businesses were shuttered, and its
people continued to suffer. The parish was down to a single day of
emergency food and water for its beleaguered residents and had yet to
receive a single shipment of fuel from the federal government. Instead, parish trucks and equipment were operating on the gasoline
and diesel fuel that Maestri's staff had managed to wheedle from the
master of a Navy ship down at the river docks. Making matters worse,
the parish sewerage system, utterly dependent on electric pumps to
function, was still idle, meaning raw sewage was starting to bubble up
through the manholes in the streets.

Of the things he needed—food, fuel, and generators—the lack of
generators burned up Maestri the most. For more than a year, FEMA
had smugly touted the mountain of emergency supplies it had stockpiled in the region in case of disaster. The agency had specifically
assured him that the generators for Jefferson were at hand. The summer before, FEMA had sent a crew of technicians to Jefferson Parish
to visit every single sewer lift station and dope out exactly how many
of each type of generator Maestri would need to keep his sanitation
operating in the event of disaster. FEMA had vowed to reserve 150
generators for the parish—and assured Maestri that his order was a
priority.

But when disaster did strike, the cavalry idled. Maestri was bitter
as he dialed in to the daily conference call with state emergency managers on Thursday morning. When it was his turn to talk, he got to the
point.

"This is Walter," he barked into the phone. "I'm about to have a
medical catastrophe in this parish. The lift stations are not working,

the matter is going into the streets and we're gonna have a medical disaster. FEMA tells me and they've told me since they arrived on the scene three days ago they're coming. I don't know what's going on but not one generator through that system has arrived here."

As the others on the call clucked in sympathy, Maestri launched into a litany of FEMA's shortcomings and broken promises. Food and water shipments had trickled off to nothing. FEMA had yet to arrange a single fuel delivery since the storm. Fires were breaking out all over the parish, but when Maestri asked FEMA if he could tap the sixty firefighters from Kansas the agency had standing by, he was told Jefferson Parish was not a priority for the reserves. "They say they're FEMA assets," Maestri said of the firefighters hanging around Griffith's office, just a few steps down the road.

Jeff Smith, the moderator of the call, sounded weary as he told the callers that he had complained to Vice President Cheney about FEMA's inability to provide temporary shelter for refugees. "I blew my top this morning," he said, almost apologetically. Smith asked Maestri if Dan Griffith was aware of the food shortages. "He's next door, he comes over periodically," Maestri said. "We requested it, have requested it, been requesting it, and nothing's coming."

Then there were the generators. "Whatever happened to these FEMA genpacks—these pallets of generators that are supposed to be pre-positioned across the country and can be flown in a moment's notice?" Maestri asked. "They ballyhooed all of that [in] all these other exercises and at the national hurricane conference, and now when we are on our knees, nothing's available."

The men on the conference call had no answer. "Good question," Smith said, just before he adjourned the call.

As FEMA floundered and local politicians went adrift, some people took matters into their own hands. In New Orleans, they speak in reverent tones of the "Cajun flotilla," the steady stream of fishermen from the west of the state who crowded city boulevards with their mud boats and air boats and rescued hundreds, if not thousands, of people. St. Bernard Parish president Henry Rodriguez likes to say the Canadians saved his neck of the woods—a cadre of

Mounties was among the first outside groups to make it through the muddy lake that had been the town of Chalmette in the early days after the storm. In downtown New Orleans, some Immigration and Customs Enforcement agents cleared the city by making individual deals with helicopter pilots to let evacuees take pets along on the journey, despite FEMA's rules that barred animals.

All over town, people strode into the vacuum left by official Washington and got the job done. They commandeered supplies to help themselves and others, they staged large, ad hoc rescue operations in their own neighborhoods, and they worked things out without federal help. In government, such initiative was less common, but it existed there, too. From the most elevated bureaucrat in Washington to the lowest city pump operator, some people damned the rules and just got to work. In Plaquemines Parish, during the hours leading up to Katrina's landfall, parish president Benny Rousselle didn't leave evacuees to sit because he had no bus drivers at hand. Instead, he checked for drivers licenses and flipped school bus keys to the person with the most relatives on board, telling them to drive north and drive safe. "You know, we sent out at least four hundred buses," Rousselle said. "Where are they today, I don't know."

In the Mid-City district of New Orleans, after the winds receded and deep water crept in behind it, a man named Carl LeBoeuf saved himself and then returned to the neighborhood, offering a workaround for the federal government's ban on rescuing pets. If people would evacuate their flooded neighborhood and leave with the rescuers, LeBoeuf promised to care for the neighborhood critters at his brother's home in Metairie. For several days, LeBoeuf and his brother donned straw hats and waded a mile or so through the shin-deep waters of Esplanade Avenue, gathering dogs on leashes, putting cats in hatboxes, and even balancing a few goldfish bowls in their arms in an effort to get their neighbors to leave. "I'm like Ace Ventura here," LeBoeuf said as he slogged through the brown water, his brother pulling two dogs on leashes, while he toted a pet carrier containing Lucky the cat and a plastic bottle where an agitated lovebird known as Booger fluttered inside. "We come in twice a day and we always talk a few more people into coming out," he said.

Two days before Katrina hit, Pastor Vien Nguyen hadn't needed the mayor or FEMA to tell him that catastrophe was spinning away in the Gulf and that it was time to leave. At a Saturday vigil mass on August 27, he laid it on the line to his parishioners at the Mary Queen of Vietnam church in eastern New Orleans. "I skipped the homily and told people to get out," he said.

And get out they did. Of the 4,000 or so parishioners living within a mile of the church, Nguyen estimated that 3,500 made their escape in the hours before the storm. But when fifty parishioners showed up for Sunday's late mass, Nguyen made his second command decision: He opened up a shelter of last resort, just as Mayor Ray Nagin had done thirteen miles away at the Louisiana Superdome. And then Nguyen put the screws to his mother: "I said, 'Mom, you're going to have to leave. I won't have time to take care of you.'"

In Father Nguyen's piece of eastern New Orleans, the shelter of last resort wasn't an overcrowded and undersupplied building but a well-stocked, two-story parochial school that he oversaw behind the sprawling tin-and-steel-beam church. And as Katrina bore down on New Orleans on Monday morning with lashing gusts and rain, Nguyen stood in an open doorway on the lee side of his rectory, watching the tempest rage. Evacuees called incessantly during the storm, and when they did, Nguyen held the phone receiver out the door where the wind shrieked and wailed. Nguyen thought he was watching the worst of it: With its labyrinth of levees and pumping stations, this part of eastern New Orleans hadn't seriously flooded in the thirty years the priest had lived in the city.

But in the early afternoon, when the wind died down a bit, the remaining parishioners noticed something odd: The water in the church's parking lot seemed to be rising. Nguyen marked the water level and confirmed the rise. Then he hopped in the parish van and prowled the neighborhood for people in distress.

He found a number of people in distress, scores of them actually, and he dropped vanloads of them at the parish schoolhouse behind Mary Queen of Vietnam. When the water rose above the van's headlights, he commandeered a rowboat. And when the flood current became too much to row against, Nguyen commandeered a power boat. In the end, Nguyen had about 150 people in his shelter, and on Tuesday, he issued orders to conserve supplies. "All cooking will be communal," he said. "We'll ration water and we'll wait for help."

Like many of his parishioners, Nguyen was among the original Vietnamese "boat people" who came to New Orleans after the fall of Saigon in 1975. Many of these fresh immigrants were placed in a run-down public housing complex known as the Versailles Arms. Today, the complex includes many older residents, and the surrounding Versailles neighborhood is now dominated by first- and second-generation Vietnamese households. Set hard against the dirt levees that form the back boundary of the city's hurricane control structure and bisected by a series of drainage canals, this area of tract homes and weathered shopping strips has taken on many of the characteristics of a Southeast Asian village. The signage is Asian, the Saturday market is clotted exotic vegetables and live animals, and the fertile aprons of nearby drainage canals are painstakingly terraced with microgardens that evoke the watery paddies of the Mekong Delta.

Versailles sits along a depressed strip of U.S. Highway 90 that is known for its auto salvage shops, massage parlors, and gritty industrial yards. The area hosts the old city dump, a jumble of fishing camps, and a stretch of deserted roadway notorious for illegal drag racing contests. Indeed, the area is popular with people engaged in all manner of illegal activities. It is not unusual to see piles of discarded automobile tires and construction trash mysteriously appear along road shoulders here, and it's not unheard of to find a few bullet-riddled bodies mixed in with the debris. Though things have improved somewhat in recent years, City Hall's reach in this area remains theoretical in many respects, and so there was little surprise among the Vietnamese priests when Mayor Nagin's push to enlist preachers in his evacuation plan before the storm didn't quite make it to Mary Queen of Vietnam.

But Father Nguyen is used to this; he has been filling the community power vacuum for years. A short and cheery priest whose honeyed voice and open demeanor belie his canny grasp of the city's Byzantine political culture, he was determined to meet Katrina head-on. In the ensuing days, when New Orleans teetered on the brink of anarchy and the city's social structure seemed to dissolve with Katrina's storm surge, Father Nguyen employed a mixture of guile and understated political threat to hold his flock together and get an outsized amount of help for his little slice of the disaster zone.

Unlike the Louisiana Superdome, Father Nguyen's church was packed with supplies when Katrina made landfall. The power winked off at 4:00 A.M., but the telephone worked and he had a battery-operated radio to keep tabs on the situation. In the late afternoon on Monday, he caught a brief report about looting in the city, and he immediately selected a posse of wranglers from the people camped out in the school. "I told them to go out and get the boats, even if they belonged to a neighbor," Nguyen said. "You wouldn't be able to loot this area without a boat." By nightfall on Tuesday, dozens of pleasure craft were lashed together with lines and bobbing in the parking lot behind Mary Queen of Vietnam.

Help arrived late Wednesday afternoon in the form of an out-of-town fire rescue team and a crew of Texas wildlife agents in boats. The firefighters offered to take the evacuees, who now numbered 350, to the city's Convention Center, where they said buses were already taking people to a shelter in San Antonio. After conferring by cell phone with Vietnamese community leaders there, Father Nguyen agreed to move his flock, but he stayed behind with the family of one woman, a stroke victim, whom the rescuers judged too fragile to move. The parishioners loaded up in the boats. And the priest thought his Katrina adventure was just about over.

But just before dawn on Thursday morning, Nguyen awoke to hear two men outside the rectory shouting his name. One of them was a man Nguyen was almost certain had evacuated the day before. "I thought to myself, 'What a stubborn person he is, refusing to evacuate,'" Nguyen recalled. And he was right, the man had left with the rescuers. But instead of taking the people to Houston, the rescuers had simply dumped everyone into a dry parking lot along Chef Menteur Highway and moved on. The rescuers had left no provisions for the 350 people in the parking lot. So there they sat, in the dark, on a hot piece of asphalt, outside a small grocery store about a mile from Mary Queen of Vietnam.

The two men outside the rectory had come back in a small flatboat they had commandeered. Nguyen packed the craft with food and a fifty-five-gallon drum of building materials and tools so the parishioners could build an outhouse for themselves in case help was slow to arrive.

In the early afternoon, Nguyen traveled to the grocery store on Chef Menteur Highway, where he found his flock boarding National Guard trucks to the Convention Center. He admonished them to look out for each other as they waited for buses, to set up their own security, and to share their food. The next day, Nguyen prepared for his own escape, also on the back of a passing truck. After strapping the ailing woman to a mattress and putting her on the back of a pickup truck to meet a nearby ambulance, Nguyen and the woman's family hitched a ride with another rescuer and rode to Lafayette. Nguyen left clutching a small duffel bag filled with the final offering he had collected at the church's Mass on the Sunday before Katrina hit. He got to Lafayette around midnight, determined to reconstitute his flock and reconstruct his neighborhood.

The Convention Center group was dispersed but not necessarily to San Antonio. Instead, the congregants were broken up and placed on buses destined for a half dozen cities around the South. In ensuing days, Nguyen traveled in a borrowed car to Baton Rouge and Houston, Austin and San Antonio, Little Rock and Fort Smith and Pine Bluff in Arkansas, and Dallas and Atlanta. He picked up the evacuees he could find and took them to a series of Vietnamese churches, on the unflooded West Bank of New Orleans, where they immediately set about plotting their return to Little Vietnam.

A few weeks later, the floodwaters had receded from eastern New

Orleans, and on October 5, Mayor Nagin opened the area for what he called a "look and leave" tour. The mayor said the neighborhood was still uninhabitable and forbade residents to stay overnight. Nguyen and a few dozen of the hardiest parishioners left the West Bank at dawn to make the trip. They took chainsaws and crowbars, generators and food. Almost immediately, the neighborhood started looking better, as residents swept up the rubble. After three days, forty men from the neighborhood, including Nguyen, decided to defy Nagin's decree and stay overnight. "What were they going to do, arrest a priest?" Nguyen said. The following day, he celebrated his first Mass at Mary Queen of Vietnam; three hundred worshippers showed up.

The following week, eight hundred congregants celebrated mass. One week after that, Nguyen arranged for the archbishop of the diocese to visit, and two thousand people turned out. Nguyen took lots of pictures of the crowd. They would come in handy in upcoming days. Mayor Nagin's "look and leave" decree was still in effect; it wouldn't be lifted for months.

Once settled in, Nguyen called his local councilwoman, a Catholic as well. He told her the neighborhood was piled with debris and was hardly fit for the archbishop and the two thousand people he had attracted to Versailles the day before. Two days later, a large crew showed up from the Army Corps of Engineers to begin hauling off mountains of trash. They stayed for weeks, even as nearby neighborhoods remained clotted with wreckage from the storm.

The next week, Nguyen visited the local power utility, Entergy New Orleans, which had just declared bankruptcy and said it wouldn't have the power on in Versailles for at least four months. City Hall had ordered the company to concentrate all of its efforts on providing power to the city's business district. But executives at the cash-poor company said they might be able to help if Nguyen could "justify the load" for the neighborhood. Nguyen broke out the pictures of the eight-hundred-person mass. "It's a bankrupt company—they want people who pay their bills," Nguyen recalled. The company asked Nguyen to guarantee one hundred paying customers; the priest promised five hundred. Less than two weeks later, lights began winking on in the neighborhood. By Christmas, the entire area had power. Months would pass before residents of nearby neighborhoods could say the same.

About two weeks after the storm hit, Mike Lala was squatting in a French Quarter parking garage siphoning gasoline from his white SUV to his green pickup truck when the chest pains came on. He dropped his pistol, staggered back to his restaurant, climbed three flights of stairs, and fell down dead.

And that's where he remained for two long, sultry days, while his girlfriend, her son, eight dogs, and fifteen cats lived on at the N'Awlins Cookery, their French Quarter restaurant, where the entire crew had taken refuge from the storm. Lala's girlfriend called the police, but they were no help. Only FEMA was allowed to move bodies, the cops said.

Then Brobson Lutz came along. Lutz had been the city's health director from 1983 to 1985. Though now a private physician, Lutz retains the title of assistant coroner for infectious diseases—a position more honorary than actual, since it carries no salary at all. But the title does come with a "dinky little badge," as Lutz calls it, which gave him just enough authority to operate as a body catcher in a town where FEMA was said to be calling the shots.

Though crawling with all manner of cops and first responders in the days following Katrina, New Orleans had tremendous trouble keeping up with the hundreds of dead bodies the storm had left behind. For weeks, they littered porch stoops and sidewalks while disaster workers attended to what they said were more important tasks. The city wanted the state to do it, the state wanted FEMA to do it, and FEMA wanted to lay the task off on the Pentagon. But in truth, nobody really wanted the job.

But Lutz didn't mind. Though he had no real authority to move Mike Lala's body, he arrived at the N'Awlins Cookery, flashed his badge at three New Jersey firemen idling outside, and commandeered their services to wrap the body in clear plastic sheeting and push it into a waiting ambulance, breaking all sorts of sanitation rules in the process. From the Cookery, the ambulance took Lala's body to Lutz's private office Uptown, until the doctor could figure out what to do. But at least it was out of the dim and funky-smelling restaurant, and away from the people and pets living there. "You take care of the living by taking care of the dead," Lutz said.

With no power or gas, with garbage piled up in the streets and a much reduced population, New Orleans seemed to revert to the mid-nineteenth century in the days and weeks after the storm. And Lutz, fifty-eight years old, seemed to have followed the city back in time as well, serving as the local doctor, coroner, pharmacist, and psychiatrist to a host of dazed French Quarter denizens.

He strung up a white banner across his French Quarter residential compound—which includes the former home of the playwright Tennessee Williams—and spray-painted FRENCH QUARTER HEALTH DEPARTMENT IN EXILE in black letters. He told all comers that the city wasn't the cesspool of disease the federal government claimed, reserving special ire for Mike Leavitt, the secretary of health and human services, for declaring the city a health disaster. New Orleans was fine, he said, and to prove it, he drank the supposedly tainted tap water himself. Lutz even made up a commemorative T-shirt marking the passage of Hurricane Katrina. "I drank the water," it said on the back.

After the storm, Lutz began clearing putrid refrigerators from the blacked-out apartments owned by neighbors. But the plodding pace of body retrieval gave him darker work to do.

Lutz's evacuation of Mike Lala was followed the next day by a trip to Maison Hospitalerie, an upscale nursing home in the French Quarter, where he helped a group of FEMA men in white moonsuits remove the bodies of four residents who had been crammed into a closet off the rear courtyard. The bodies, loaded into an unrefrigerated Penske rental van, were badly decomposed, making it difficult to match them to the names that had been scrawled on the door of the closet in bold purple pen. The authorities had known for days that the bodies were there, but the FEMA men only came after Lutz complained about the agency's unresponsiveness on a national cable television show. When they arrived, Lutz ordered the FEMA crew to go to his office and retrieve Lala's body as well. Meekly, the FEMA men obeyed.

Operating with a gang of California paramedics who had holed up in a shotgun house a block down from his compound, Lutz became a neighborhood do-gooder, collecting bodies, dispensing medicines, and taking canned peas to semidelirious neighbors. The paramedics, delighted to be busy, cooked meals, fetched gasoline for the generators, and embarked on sundry expeditions directed by the man they simply called "Doc."

"FEMA said they didn't have a spot for us, that we didn't have a special requisition number," Jeff Kennedy, a paramedic in the crew, recalled. "We said, 'That's okay—we know how to help.'"

Providing help required medical supplies, which were readily available in the ruined city if one knew where to look. Happening on a case of FEMA-supplied tetanus shots preloaded into syringes, the California crew turned to Lutz to scrounge the needles they would need to administer the doses. Lutz discovered that needles were available at a looted Walgreen's drugstore in an area of the city called Algiers. So he and the paramedics hopped into an ambulance and roared across the river to check it out.

They arrived to find the Walgreen's parking lot jammed with New Orleans police officers trying to fill prescriptions in advance of paid leaves the city had recently awarded. The cops had commandeered the store, and presiding over the prescription desk was the Fourth District's narcotics chief, who was trying to fill requests based on his street knowledge of the drug trade.

"He was doing a pretty good job—he'd managed to find a lot of the stuff he needed," Lutz said. By the time he arrived, most of the narcotics and all of the Viagra had been snapped up. The demand remained for Viagra, Lutz said, "but all they knew were the little blue pills." So he joined the narcotics chief behind the counter and "fixed them up with the Levitra and the Cialis" until those stocks also ran out.

In gratitude for figuring out the Viagra substitutions and for identifying the generic equivalent of a popular medicine for high blood pressure, the narcotics chief presented Lutz and the paramedics with a shopping cart and told them to take what they pleased. They quickly filled the basket with hypodermic needles, bandages, rubbing alcohol, and swabs. And on the way out, Lutz snagged three hundred doses of antibiotics for his own in-house pharmacy.

Lutz had been well known in New Orleans before the storm, both for his public position as health director and because he had long done health-related segments on the local talk radio station. In the French Quarter he was something of a bon vivant, often seen walking the streets in a seersucker suit and dining at the famous high-French bistros, Antoine's Restaurant and Galatoire's, where he was occasionally called upon to attend to patrons who suddenly took ill or had a bit too much to drink. "You get called on at Antoine's and they pick up your check and pay the next one when you come back," he said. "I helped a woman at Galatoire's one night and all I got were two after-dinner drinks."

Now New Orleans offered brisker trade. On most mornings in the early days of the disaster, Lutz was often found hosting a steady stream of storm-weary holdouts who needed minor treatments or prescriptions filled. In between these visits, he consulted with the paramedics, who administered tetanus shots from a trailer on the banquette outside the French Quarter house where they were staying.

In the afternoons following the storm, Lutz often donned a suit, hopped on his bicycle, and made the rounds of the two French Quarter watering holes that stayed open through the disaster, Molly's at the Market and Johnny White's Sports Bar and Grill. Sometimes, he took a few paramedics to dispense personal hygiene products to the largely unwashed and drunken crowd that congregated at the darkened and grubby establishments.

It was at Johnny White's that Lutz ran into Maggie Smith, a boardinghouse operator with a bad abscess on her arm. Smith, who had once heard that people taking penicillin weren't allowed to drink, immediately told Lutz that she was allergic to the drug. Lutz gave her another antibiotic and told her she could keep ordering drinks.

The same afternoon brought a crisis of a different sort. An evacuee called, saying he had heard that his guesthouse had been broken into. Springing into action, Lutz dashed home, returning with a huge chrome revolver he had borrowed from a friend—"a cowboy gun," he called it. A loitering fireman had a shotgun, and the two men and a skinny paramedic formed a posse and set off for the house.

The house had indeed been entered and the cash drawer up-ended, with a few possessions scattered about. The men searched the place, but it was empty. They returned to the front to secure the door, as Lutz labored over a hand-lettered sign that he drove into the door-jamb with a ten-penny nail. CLEARED BY SHERIFF LUTZ, it said.

One evening after dark, Lutz decided to pay a visit to Mike Lala's girlfriend, Connie Tenhaaf, and her son, Damion. "I bet what Connie would really like is a cold beer," he said.

Grabbing two Coors longnecks and a carton of cold milk, Lutz and two paramedics hopped in an ambulance and made their way through the darkened streets to the N'Awlins Cookery. The street was pitch black but hardly quiet; a massive generator hammered away on the corner, lighting up the windows of a hotel that the local police had commandeered.

Inside, the room was surreal, lit by scores of candles that used to decorate the tables of the eatery. The place reeked of dogs and death; pets moved furtively through the shadows, just flashes of snout and tail.

Lutz sat at a courtyard table with Connie and Damion, watching closely as the two struggled to string sentences together. Connie talked mostly about Mike Lala, how she loved him and missed him already. "Y'all need to get out in the fresh air more," Lutz said.

Connie declined the beers, but her eyes lit up at the carton of milk. "Cold milk," she cooed, "it was Mike's favorite drink. Well, that and Beefeater's."

Lutz nodded sagely. "Acid reflux," he said.

On Tuesday, August 30, a few hours after the world first learned that the New Orleans levees had crumbled, the phone rang on Douglas Doan's desk at the Department of Homeland Security in Washington.

A very angry man from Wal-Mart was on the line. Ray Bracy, the company's vice president for federal and international public affairs, had been bounced from desk to desk all morning, and by the time he was kicked over to Doan, he was ready to explode. He got right to the point. "The National Guard is looting Wal-Mart," he bellowed, "and I want to know what you're going to do about it."

Doan was surprised at the heat coming through the line. Like many Americans, he had watched in horror at the images being televised from New Orleans. As Bracy and two other Wal-Mart executives on the line ranted, Doan got the gist: National Guard troops and first responders didn't have the supplies to give to the people they rescued, so they were breaking into local Wal-Mart stores, removing diapers, baby formula, and bottled water by the case and passing it on to survivors. In essence, Wal-Mart was involuntarily serving as the region's FEMA warehouse, while the real federal disaster agency struggled with supply bottlenecks and logistical snafus.

As Doan listened, he began to see a solution emerging, though it was contrary to the letter of federal procurement rules. Wal-Mart's supply and distribution system was the envy of the world. Could it be harnessed to provide the goods that FEMA seemed unable to deliver? "I have an idea," Doan said to the angry executives. "First, I think we should stop calling this looting and start looking at this as an unusual procurement."

An unusual procurement: It wouldn't be the first time Doan had applied unorthodox principles to a seemingly untenable problem. A West Point graduate, Doan had been an Army intelligence officer, but he had grown bored with the military after a few years. So he left the Army and started an investment banking business with his wife. He had been an early backer of George W. Bush's presidential bid in 2000, and after the Department of Homeland Security was created, he took a job there in the Office of the Private Sector.

His job description was to help American businesses work out their security problems, but he turned the assignment around and spent most his time trying to enlist U.S. entrepreneurial know-how to help the government solve its own security troubles. One of his first acts after joining the department in 2003 was to connect big-box retailers like Wal-Mart and Target with U.S. Customs officials looking for ideas to improve the security of the global shipping industry. "Companies like Wal-Mart wrote the book on supply chain security," he said. "Why should government reinvent the wheel?"

That same year, Mexican melon farmers and U.S. importers complained that their produce was literally cooking on their trucks because post-9/11 border security checks had created day-long customs delays, under the blistering southwestern sun. Doan's solution: The melon growers should have their own road. Doan then helped the farmers to clear a mountain of red tape to enable the roadwork to begin, then he got Customs to man it.

Even in his private life, Doan was a maverick. A cigar fanatic, in 1999 he cultivated the first cigar tobacco in Virginia in 150 years. The cigars, called Virginia Blues, defied the skeptics who said the tobacco would never equal Caribbean imports. They are critically acclaimed smokes that are said to rival the quality and price of some of the best Cuba has to offer.

The Wal-Mart executives knew Doan's reputation as a problem-solver, and their anger was quickly replaced by curiosity. Bracy asked Doan to explain what the phrase "unusual procurement" meant. "Well, it's not Plasmatron television sets walking out the door, it's emergency supplies," Doan said. "So the challenge I have for Wal-Mart is: Can you guys keep the supplies of these goods flowing to those stores so the National Guard has whatever it needs?"

There was silence on the line as the executives considered Doan's query. Marauding National Guard soldiers aside, the retail giant was facing a number of logistical problems of its own. One hundred twenty-six of Wal-Mart's stores, including twelve in the New Orleans metropolitan area, had been shuttered in advance of Katrina's passage. Two distribution centers in the region were idled as well. More than half of those stores had no power, a handful were flooded, and eighty-nine had sustained at least some storm damage. The hurricane had also knocked out Wal-Mart's computerized system for automatically updating store inventory levels in the area.

But unlike much of the government, Wal-Mart had a comprehensive contingency plan. Jason Jackson, the retailer's director of business continuity, was camping out in Wal-Mart's emergency command center in Arkansas five days before the storm hit. By Friday, August 26, when the hurricane passed across Florida, he had been joined by fifty Wal-Mart managers and support personnel, ranging from trucking experts to loss-prevention specialists. After Katrina knocked out Wal-Mart's computer system, Johnson set up a unit to field phone calls from stores to determine what they needed. He also alerted a replenishment team to reorder likely demand items, such as mops, bleach, bottled water, and generators. Even as Bracy and Doan were talking, Johnson already had scores of Wal-Mart trucks moving into the disaster zone, some under police escort, carrying more than forty generators and several tons of dry ice to deliver to stores that had no power but millions of dollars of perishable food in inventory.

Theoretically speaking, Wal-Mart should not have been facing its problems all alone. For that matter, no Fortune 100 company was supposed to be cut off from the government during an emergency. That lesson was already supposed to have been learned after the September 11 attacks in 2001. Many big firms affected by the terrorist strikes on New York and Washington, like AT&T (which lost a major communications node during the attack on the World Trade Center) and FedEx (whose delivery air fleet was grounded with the rest of the nation's civilian aircraft), couldn't find anybody in the government capable of resolving their issues. Other companies, like the Home Depot, which had boots that were resistant to the intense heat of the smoldering pile of debris in Lower Manhattan, couldn't reach anyone to offer their vital supplies.

To avoid a repeat of these problems, the chief executives of the nation's leading companies worked with government leaders and the Central Intelligence Agency to establish CEO COM LINK, a secure communications network that in thirty minutes could connect the heads of the country's largest firms with senior White House or Homeland Security officials. The system had been tested on the first anniversary of the September 11 attacks and again in August 2004, when intelligence agents uncovered a supposed al Qaeda plot to bomb Wall Street.

So when Katrina struck, many leading CEOs ordered their minions to identify any problems and inventory those resources they had to share with the government, and then they sat by their phones for three days waiting for Secretary Chertoff to call. He never did. Chertoff never explained why he didn't call, and some Homeland Security officials say the secretary, on the job only six months when Katrina hit, didn't know about the program. Others offer a more prosaic excuse: Everyone simply forgot. Whatever the reason, companies found themselves struggling, just as they had in the old days, to find someone willing to help them or to accept their offers of help.

The member companies of the International Bottled Water Association, for example, repeatedly called the Department of Homeland Security offering to send truckloads of free drinking water into the region soon after the storm. "Nobody called back," said Stephen Kaye, a spokesman for the organization, which has a history of responding to disasters. It eventually used church groups to ferry 10 million bottles into the disaster zone.

But Ray Bracy had managed to get through, and now the government was asking for help. After talking it over, he and his fellow executives agreed to Doan's plan. While FEMA's contractors floundered, Wal-Mart would push the disaster supplies to the Gulf Coast. Unlike FEMA, the company had the ability to track every liter of bottled water delivered to and taken from its stores. But here was the question, Bracy said: Who would be paying the bill?

Doan was brisk. "Let's sling hash, serve beer and run a bar tab later," he said. The government would pay. "It's a simple accounting problem. Right now, people need help." Doan and Bracy struck a gentlemen's agreement that Wal-Mart would keep scrupulous track of the goods shipped and received, with the billing pegged to pre-Katrina prices, to avoid allegations of profiteering. But the entire system rode on Doan's promise that he would reimburse Wal-Mart. Though he didn't have the details worked out, Bracy couldn't imagine this would be a problem.

Like magic, a pesky commandeering situation became an elegant force of good. "We were taking unprecedented steps and operating outside the normal government procurement system," Doan said later. "Furthermore, we both knew that there would be lots of scrutiny of our efforts some time in the near future. But I was a firm believer that you can't get in trouble for doing the right thing."

Over the next two weeks, officials tapped Wal-Mart to deliver a great deal more than bottled water, diapers, and flashlight batteries. When the Port of New Orleans sent word that the tires had been ruined on its entire fleet of emergency vehicles and it could no longer guarantee the safety of its stevedoring operations, Wal-Mart sent replacement tires within hours. Wal-Mart also helped supply chainsaws and generators for countless rescue operations.

By Doan's reckoning, the Wal-Mart delivery system worked far better than FEMA ever could have hoped to in the early days of the disaster. As first responders coped with the torrent of storm survivors that clotted the Superdome and the Convention Center, most of the baby food, diapers, batteries, and bedding distributed by National Guard troops came not from FEMA's contractors but from Wal-Mart. Though shippers on the federal tab reported a litany of problems getting goods through the city's drenched and menacing streets, Wal-Mart trucks were a common sight in the disaster zone. Wal-Mart worked when FEMA did not.

Moreover, when the calls went up in Washington over Homeland Security's disappointing performance, Doan saw the deal with Wal-Mart as a shining example of a big, bloated bureaucracy showing a little creativity in getting the job done. When the time came to cut the checks, Doan was sure Wal-Mart would be among the first to get paid. "This was a good news story and I was expecting that the department would be shouting about it," he said.

Doan was wrong. Instead of applauding the supply deal, Homeland Security's auditors were horrified, and they were furious that the department was on the hook for supplies that had been distributed by nondepartmental agencies such as the National Guard. Janet Hale, Homeland Security's undersecretary for management, who had overall responsibility for the department's procurement system, phoned Doan personally to deliver an extended lecture on the subject. The department had detailed and unyielding regulations that governed all procurements, she told him. There were long-standing contracts in place to handle emergency supplies—deals that had been signed long before the storm. As Hale put it to Doan, "junior" employees such as himself do not hammer out their own procurement deals.

The next day, a team of lawyers arrived at Doan's office to take a statement. They told him they might pursue legal action against him for signing off on the Wal-Mart deal. Infuriated by the intrusion and by the insinuation, Doan settled in at his computer and silently typed out a three-line statement. "I did it," the statement said. "I would do it again. The president would agree with it."

Doan signed the statement and handed it to the department's general counsel. And then he sat back down at his desk and turned away.

Homeland Security's senior officials never viewed the Wal-Mart arrangement as a success story. Nor did they fully understand that the Wal-Mart supply chain had been responsible for pushing the exact emergency supplies that were needed most. Quietly, they cut Wal-Mart a check for $300,000. And then they never mentioned the transaction again.

Though angered by the department's response to the Wal-Mart deal, Doan was undaunted. A few weeks later he went to New Orleans in search of a way to help local restaurants survive the aftermath of the storm. Doan hammered out a plan to serve 26,000 meals a day to the residents of St. Tammany Parish, who had no way to cook for themselves because the power was still off. Preparing the food would be a syndicate of local restaurants that were also hurt by Katrina. The idea struck him when he saw storm victims being served peanut butter sandwiches that had been trucked in from Florida and canned beans from Ohio, at a cost of $14 a day. Louisiana is the culinary capital of the nation, Doan reasoned, and there was no reason to subject its citizens to the inferior grub that was being hauled in on tractor-trailers.

With little prodding, the local chefs came up with a better menu than peanut butter and beans. For $13—a savings of $26,000 per day—they whipped up a menu featuring seafood pasta and beef with a red wine mushroom sauce. The plan was brilliant on its face: better food for storm victims, a helping hand for local businesses struggling to survive the disaster, a better deal for the government. But Janet Hale nixed the idea. It was a violation, she said, of long-standing contracts for peanut butter sandwiches and canned beans.

So Doan quit, unrepentant. "If 9/11 represented a failure of imagination, then four years later we have yet to learn our lesson," he said.

12

REINDEER GAMES

In the wake of Hurricane Katrina, the White House decided it could no longer be complacent in the face of natural disasters. On Thursday, September 15, President Bush ordered the Department of Homeland Security to evaluate the ability of states and big cities to respond to a disaster. He also appointed his homeland security adviser, Frances Townsend, to investigate the failure of the federal response and find ways that Washington could be sure it would never happen again.

Broderick and his team at HSOC joined this effort and quickly began calling governors, mayors, and police chiefs to demand information about their emergency plans. The exchanges sometimes bordered on the farcical. "Broderick's guys kept calling, demanding to see our evacuation plans," said Gil Kerlikowske, Seattle's chief of police. "I asked, 'What am I evacuating from?' I told them we have different plans for different scenarios. Is it a dirty bomb at the port? Wildfires? An eruption of the volcano? A meteorite? They said they'd get back to me and then called a week later, demanding to know where my evacuation plans were, and the whole conversation would repeat itself."

Meanwhile, the Pentagon's contingency planners drew up a new set of plans designed to give soldiers a greater role in responding to local catastrophes. Admiral Timothy J. Keating, the commander of the U.S. Northern Command, or Northcom (which was created after the September 11 terrorist attacks to defend the continental United States from terrorism), had been telling lawmakers and top military officials that active-duty forces should have complete authority to respond to catastrophic disasters. Keating talked of using Northcom officers to train and certify the competence of governors to handle domestic emergencies. He crafted PowerPoint presentations for the White House that set 10,000 casualties as the trigger for the military to take over from the civilian authorities. He was ready to take the lead where FEMA had so clearly failed.

A second chance for redemption came in the midst of this effort. Hurricane Rita entered the Gulf on Tuesday, September 20, and by the next day had became a Category 5 storm, projected to make landfall near Houston and that city's collection of oil refineries. In anticipation of Rita's arrival, Governor Rick Perry of Texas recalled all emergency personnel from Katrina recovery efforts, including almost 1,200 members of the Texas National Guard.

In contrast to Katrina, the pre-storm preparation was extremely focused and relatively smooth. State and local officials marshaled buses and other resources, and asked in advance for federal help, which they received with unusual promptness. In Louisiana, Governor Blanco made her request for federal troops in writing, so as to avoid the supposed ambiguity of her repeated verbal demands for help during Katrina. She asked for 15,000 soldiers. She got them.

In New Orleans, Mayor Nagin very reluctantly suspended his plan to bring residents back to the city, while the National Guard went door to door in some of the city's poorest neighborhoods to warn the few remaining people that another storm was on the way. The city of Port Arthur, Texas, population 60,000, provided municipal and school buses to transport several thousand residents with no means to evacuate on their own. The Texas and Louisiana National Guard flew thirty-nine missions before the storm to evacuate several thousand patients from hospitals in towns from Beaumont, Texas, to Lake Charles, Louisiana. Galveston, the Texas coastal city that sat on a barrier island and had been wiped off the map in 1900 by a killer storm, became the first city in the state to order a mandatory evacuation, telling its 60,000 residents to start packing on Tuesday evening, four days ahead of the storm's projected landfall. Corpus Christi and Port Arthur followed in rapid succession. Along the coast of Texas and Louisiana, refineries and pipeline operators shut down their businesses, and hundreds of roughnecks evacuated offshore oil rigs. The price of crude oil rocketed to nearly $70 a barrel.

At 9:30 A.M. on Wednesday, Mayor Bill White of Houston ordered mandatory evacuations from low-lying sections of the city while urging voluntary evacuations from flood-prone neighborhoods and mobile homes. "Don't follow the example of New Orleans," he pleaded.

In contrast to previous hurricanes, the problem in Houston under Rita's threat was that too many people took to the road. Houston, some fifty miles inland and on far higher ground than New Orleans, isn't nearly as vulnerable to a hurricane strike. Texas's emergency management coordinator, Jack Colley, estimated that 1.3 million people probably needed to evacuate from the projected strike zone, but with the devastation of Hurricane Katrina fresh in people's minds, some 3 million Texans fled, including many who lived far inland and on high ground—and many who took every car in the driveway. State authorities tried belatedly to coordinate this mass exodus, but in the end, everyone simply left when they pleased. And everyone suffered as a result.

The evacuation quickly become a traffic horror story, with highways clogged for one hundred miles north of Houston. Northbound Interstate 45 and westbound Interstate 10 ground to gridlock Wednesday and remained that way on Thursday. Drivers ran out of gas in twenty-hour traffic jams, or looked in vain for a place to stay as hotels flashed "No Vacancy" signs all the way to the Oklahoma and Arkansas state lines. State police and National Guard trucks carried gasoline to motorists whose tanks had run dry. But they couldn't keep up with demand. With temperatures in the nineties, cars stalled and tempers frayed. Some people got fed up and turned back, intensifying the backups.

On Thursday, September 22, Governor Perry implemented his own contraflow plan along Interstate 45, opening eight lanes of traffic heading north for 125 miles. Though the traffic eased from gridlock, it was still slow going. The contraflow lanes eventually had to merge back into regular configuration after all, and when they did, a monster traffic jam developed.

About sixty people died during the evacuation, including twenty-three nursing home residents who were killed when someone's oxygen tank exploded near Dallas and blew apart their bus. Others died from heat exhaustion and heart attacks after spending long hours in their cars without water or air conditioning. Spectacular traffic accidents took other lives.

As the people stampeded, FEMA stockpiled essential provisions such as food, water, bedding, and satellite telephones to an unprecedented level. The agency moved in 165 truckloads of ice, 185 truckloads of water, and 98 truckloads of food—about seven times the supplies it had on hand in Louisiana when Katrina struck. The military reserved twenty-six helicopters for search and rescue. Thousands of National Guard troops across the country were on standby, ready to assist if asked. Six naval vessels—the USS *Iwo Jima*, USS *Shreveport*, USS *Tortuga*, USS *Grapple*, USNS *Patuxent*, and USNS *Comfort*—were nearby, should Texas need assistance. The Coast Guard had forty aircraft and nine cutters on standby. And the federal government flew commercial jetliners into the gritty refinery town of Beaumont, near the Louisiana border, to evacuate three thousand hospital patients in advance of the storm.

President Bush, with Secretary Chertoff in tow, made a conspicuous show of his involvement, visiting FEMA headquarters in Washington and Northcom headquarters in Colorado on Friday, and embarking on a full schedule of hurricane-related activities on Saturday, which included spending the morning at Northcom headquarters as Rita made landfall and then hopping down to Texas to observe relief operations after the storm blew past.

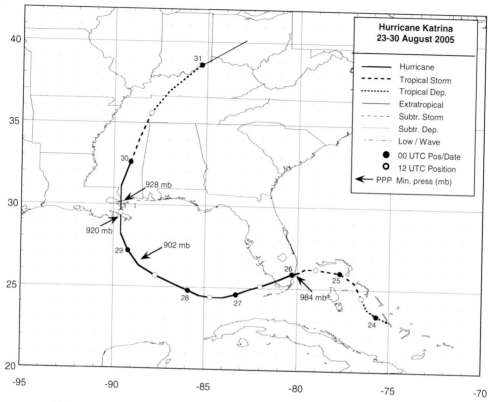

This map shows the course of Hurricane Katrina as the storm swept out of the Atlantic Ocean, passed over Florida, intensified in the Gulf of Mexico, and struck Louisiana and Mississippi on Monday, August 29, 2005. (NATIONAL OCEANIC AND ATMOSPHERIC ADMINISTRATION)

Over the course of several sessions beginning in July 2004, Federal Emergency Management Agency officials, with local leaders, began work on Hurricane Pam, a comprehensive plan to deal with a catastrophic hurricane striking New Orleans. FEMA canceled most of the follow-up sessions scheduled for the first half of 2005. (FEMA)

FEMA director Michael Brown *(far right)* greets Tom Ridge, the secretary of homeland security *(left)*, and Tommy Thompson, the secretary of health and human services, as they arrive in Fort Myers, Florida, to tour areas affected by Hurricane Charley, August 17, 2004. (FEMA/MARK WOLFE)

Michael Chertoff, a federal appeals court judge and a former Justice Department official, succeeded Tom Ridge as secretary of homeland security in February 2005. (PHOTOGRAPH BY BARRY BAHLER/DHS)

On Saturday, August 27, 2005, New Orleans mayor C. Ray Nagin, Councilman Oliver Thomas, and Louisiana governor Kathleen Blanco urged residents of low-lying areas to leave their homes and seek higher ground. The following morning, Mayor Nagin would order a mandatory evacuation of the city. (AP PHOTO/CHERYL GERBER)

Jeff Smith, Louisiana's deputy director of emergency preparedness, coordinated the state's response to Hurricane Katrina. (COURTESY OF THE GOVERNOR'S OFFICE OF HOMELAND SECURITY AND EMERGENCY PREPAREDNESS)

President Bush and Deputy Chief of Staff Joe Hagin participated from Crawford, Texas, in the final videoconference before Katrina hit, on Sunday, August 28. On the video screen is Max Mayfield, the director of the National Hurricane Center. (WHITE HOUSE PHOTOGRAPH BY PAUL MORSE)

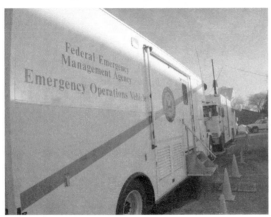

FEMA deployed Mobile Emergency Response Support (MERS) trucks to Louisiana, to be used as communications centers on the ground. The agency, however, was unable to get any of the vehicles into New Orleans for several days after the hurricane hit. (FEMA/DON JACKS)

Marty Bahamonde, a FEMA public affairs official, was the only person from the agency on the ground in New Orleans when Hurricane Katrina slammed into the city. On a helicopter ride on Monday afternoon, August 29, he surveyed the damage and reported the dismal news back to Washington. (FEMA)

From the helicopter, Marty Bahamonde took this photograph, showing vast tracts of the city underwater. (FEMA/MARTY BAHAMONDE)

A retired Marine general, Matthew Broderick was in charge of the Homeland Security Operations Center in Washington, which served as a conduit for all information coming out of the impact zone. (BARRY BAHLER/DHS)

The Louisiana Superdome was the shelter of last resort for those New Orleans residents unable or unwilling to leave the city before the hurricane. Eventually, 25,000 people would take refuge there under conditions made more arduous by the damage to the roof caused by the storm. (FEMA/Marty Bahamonde)

A former New York City fire chief, Phil Parr was FEMA's top official at the Superdome.

The New Orleans Convention Center, about twelve blocks from the Superdome, was also overrun with evacuees seeking shelter and food, and quickly proved inadequate.
(FEMA/Win Henderson)

Wendell Shingler, head of the Federal Protective Service, was in charge of providing security for federal buildings and Homeland Security personnel after the storm.
(Marc Raimondi/ICE Public Affairs)

On Friday, September 2, President Bush made his first visit to the region. He is shown here in Alabama, where he met with *(left to right)* Senators Trent Lott and Thad Cochran of Mississippi, Mississippi governor Haley Barbour, Alabama governor Bob Riley, Michael Brown, Michael Chertoff, and Alphonso Jackson, the secretary of housing and urban development. It was on this trip that Bush praised the FEMA director, saying, "Brownie, you're doing a heck of a job." (White House photograph by Eric Draper)

Vice Admiral Thad Allen of the Coast Guard *(left)* and Lieutenant General Russel Honoré of the U.S. Army were put in charge of the post-Katrina relief effort.
(FEMA/Jocelyn Augustino)

Two weeks after the storm, one breach in the London Avenue Canal had been temporarily repaired with sandbags.
(FEMA/Bob McMillan)

President Bush and Governor Rick Perry of Texas conferred in the aftermath of Hurricane Rita, September 27, 2005.
(FEMA/Ed Edahl)

Craig Fugate, the director of the Florida Division of Emergency Management *(left)*, and Governor Jeb Bush during a briefing for Hurricane Wilma, October 21, 2005. (AP/PHIL COALE)

Secretary Chertoff testifying before the Senate Homeland Security and Governmental Affairs Committee, February 15, 2006. (© KEN CEDENO/CORBIS)

A float lampooning Michael Brown that rolled during the 2006 Carnival celebration in New Orleans, in the run-up to Mardi Gras. (COURTESY CHRISTOPHER COOPER)

The entire Washington establishment was doing everything it could to show that it was engaged and ready. Of course, anything less would have been political suicide.

For its part, the Department of Homeland Security started asking questions early and often, driving state officials mad as they worked to prepare for the storm and bring order to the evacuation. "At one point, I think I turned the volume down on Broderick," said Steve McCraw, Governor Perry's homeland security director. "The guy was just out of control with his questions. It's all well and good to find out about traffic flow rates but not when you are in the middle of preparing for disaster and trying to move three million people."

Washington imposed its will on the states of Louisiana and Texas in ways that the local officials didn't appreciate, inserting federal assets into the response without advising or consulting the states. On Wednesday, Chertoff dispatched Homeland Security agents to Houston and San Antonio and appointed Admiral Larry Hereth of the Coast Guard as his principal federal official to direct the federal response. On Thursday, Admiral Keating of Northcom activated a joint task force to coordinate the Pentagon's response to Rita. A military press release said the task force would "command and control active duty military forces committed to Hurricane Rita relief operations in support of FEMA and the State of Texas" and "ensure unity of effort between the state and federal responses."

One problem: Neither Texas nor FEMA had requested the Pentagon's help. And just as Blanco had balked at the White House's federalization bid, so did Texas. "The military decided to activate itself," McCraw said. "It's not that we weren't grateful for the help, but this isn't the way it was supposed to work. We expressed our concerns but rather than fight them while trying to get ready for a killer hurricane we either incorporated them into our plans or worked around them."

Hurricane Rita made landfall at 2:30 A.M. local time on Saturday, September 24, just east of Sabine Pass on the Texas-Louisiana line. It roared ashore as a Category 3 storm, packing 120-mile-per-hour winds, a foot of rain, and a fifteen-foot storm surge. In the end, it steered clear of Houston and crashed instead into a relatively unpopulated piece of Louisiana, near Lake Charles. About two million people lost power. In New Orleans, a modest surge easily topped the temporary fix the Army Corps had made to the Ninth Ward floodwall, and the neighborhood flooded again. But this time there was nobody around to get stranded on rooftops or overpasses.

Rita swamped roads, washed out bridges, and damaged buildings, but it was not the disaster that had been feared. Officials in Washington congratulated themselves for a job well done. But they had created a monster.

Four weeks after Hurricane Rita passed, Hurricane Wilma barreled out of the Gulf, bigger and meaner than any tropical storm in recorded history. It was the sixth major hurricane of the record-breaking 2005 season and the third to attain Category 5 status. At its peak on Wednesday, October 19, Wilma was the most powerful Atlantic storm ever recorded, with 185-mile-per-hour winds, a tight eye, and a low pressure center that gave it the potential to ruin a city. Wilma had devastated the coastal areas of Mexico's Yucatan Peninsula and was taking aim at the west coast of Florida, where a potential 3.65 million people stood in its path.

Even as Wilma was raking Cancun, Craig Fugate, Florida's emergency management director, activated his emergency operations center in the state capital, Tallahassee, for the eighth time in fourteen months and began preparing for the worst. This was becoming routine.

A bear of a man with a cult following among firefighters, police, and politicians, Fugate was an all-too-familiar figure to Floridians. He was the chubby, goateed face of disaster. If he wasn't on TV responding to trouble, he was on TV admonishing residents to be prepared. He had risen from local firefighter and paramedic to become director of the state's division of emergency management in 2001, and in just four years he had created perhaps the finest response system in the country, capable of preparing Florida for everything from tornadoes to terrorists. Even the smallest details fit seamlessly into his design: He had even standardized the state's firehoses, from Key West to Pensacola. The state of New York, by contrast, has at least six different types of hose connections, meaning that Albany fire-fighters have a tougher time helping Manhattan in an emergency.

Under Fugate's guidance the state coordinated purchasing of supplies, like chemical-biological protection suits and gas masks, so that emergency services, police, and National Guard units could train and work together, just as they would during a real event. While Fugate hadn't ignored the emerging terrorist threat, he knew from hard-won experience that hurricane response was his bread and butter.

"No one in the country knows more about preparing for and responding to hurricanes than Craig Fugate," said Bruce Baughman, the former FEMA operations chief who ran Alabama's emergency management agency.

Fugate had a no-nonsense air about him and plenty of home-spun quirks, such as his habit of wearing a tattered orange University of Florida Gators baseball cap when a disaster was at its peak and a clean blue Gator cap when it was under control. He spoke of preparing for tropical storms and other catastrophes as if he were organizing a barn dance or church supper, rather than an emergency response. "Disasters," he said, "are always a come-as-you-are party." An avid reader of history, Fugate often saw parallels between disaster response and the great military campaigns of yore. He liked pushing forward in a mobile command vehicle to the worst-hit spots in the immediate aftermath of a storm. "That's General Patton's idea," Fugate said. "At a certain stage a general has to get out to the field to make sure his colonels have all the tools and support they need to fight the battle."

His method of operation was to worry about people first, not bureaucracy or budget overruns. The fundaments of his emergency management philosophy are simple; they are known as "Craig's Rules" and are posted in every county's emergency operations center: "Rule 1: Meet the needs of the disaster victim. Rule 2: Take care of the responders. Rule 3: See rule 1."

Though Florida had been hammered by four successive hurricanes in August and September 2004 and by Hurricanes Dennis, Katrina, and Rita over the course of 2005, none of these storms were anything like Wilma. Marco Island looked set to be washed out to sea. Tampa could be deluged and even Orlando was at peril. Fugate was on the phone constantly with Governor Jeb Bush.

In his seven years as the governor of Florida, Bush had made sure the state had all the tools and money it needed to build a hurricane response operation that was without peer. He kept a pool of money set aside for Florida's National Guard, so that if he ever needed them in a pinch, he could break the bank and get the support he needed. There would be no need to wait for a federal disaster declaration before asking the Guard to wheel out its soldiers, helicopters, and planes. Bush's staff watched with a sense of nervous amusement as the governor marched up and down the halls of his office from meeting to meeting, screaming "Wilma!" in a Fred Flintstone voice and shaking his fist in the air.

All the frantic activity in the days before landfall wasn't just because of Wilma. There was another storm brewing at the same time, a political tempest blowing out of Washington that threatened a federal takeover of Florida's disaster response. The Department of Homeland Security was seeking once again to appoint a principal federal official to oversee the preparations and response to the storm, while the Pentagon was poised to seize control of logistics and the National Guard. Active-duty soldiers and teams of Homeland Security agents were standing ready to flood into Florida. At the same time, Matthew Broderick, who had just been promoted to a new post, chief of operations, was using his new authority to try to whip Fugate and other Florida officials into coughing up more information for Secretary Chertoff, who was himself increasingly getting down into the weeds of Florida's hurricane preparations.

Florida didn't want the help. Fugate had developed a tried and tested formula to deal with the ravages of big tropical storms. The federal government would do more harm than good, he feared, by introducing untested players with unclear roles at the last minute; Wilma was no time to experiment with a new regime. Fugate knew the capabilities of the state better than any outsider did. And he didn't want Washington running a response by remote control.

But in the aftermath of Hurricane Katrina, the Bush administration was under tremendous pressure to perform. The bungled response in Louisiana and Mississippi had added significantly to public misgivings about the administration's ability to keep the country safe. The mishandling of intelligence before the war in Iraq, the deteriorating situation overseas, and mounting U.S. casualty figures were also taking a heavy toll on President Bush's approval ratings. To compensate, federal agencies were increasing their involvement in all potential natural disasters, just to be sure they wouldn't get caught flatfooted again.

Many governors and National Guard commanders grumbled about what they saw as an effort by Washington to supplant the states in the first-responder role. The most strident complainer of all was Governor Jeb Bush, the brother of the president. On September 30, in an op-ed article in the *Washington Post*, Bush blasted such a federal takeover as dangerous. "Just as all politics are local, so are all disasters," he wrote, adding that the most effective response starts at the local level. "As the governor of a state that has been hit by seven hurricanes and two tropical storms in the past 13 months, I can say with certainty that federalizing emergency response to catastrophic events would be a disaster as bad as Hurricane Katrina."

Governor Bush assiduously presented his case. "The federal government cannot replicate or replace the sense of purpose and urgency that unites Floridians working to help their families, friends and neighbors in the aftermath of a disaster," he observed. "If the federal government removes control of preparation, relief and recovery from cities and states, those cities and states will lose the interest, innovation and zeal for emergency response that has made Florida's response system better than it was 10 years ago."

The article caused a stir, but it did little to change thinking at the Department of Homeland Security. When Chertoff was asked by Congress in mid-October to explain the fervor of his actions during Rita compared to Katrina, he replied, "I am quite sure that I, if anything, overcompensated for Rita. And I will probably, frankly, continue to overcompensate."

But even as Chertoff outlined his plans, Jeb Bush pushed back. Bush pressed his point in his testimony to the House Committee on Homeland Security on Wednesday, October 19. "The most effective response is one that starts at the local level and grows with the support of surrounding communities, the state and then the federal government," he said. "The minute you try to turn that pyramid upside down and have folks from . . . the Pentagon or other places outside the state calling the shots, it would be an unmitigated disaster."

Governor Bush didn't have to wait long for confrontation. He learned on his flight back to Tallahassee that day that Washington was indeed continuing to push for control despite his objections. The Department of Homeland Security had readied three hundred satellite telephones and had drawn up plans to distribute them to mayors, county officials, and Homeland Security agents already based in the state so they could report directly to Broderick in Washington, in order to give Secretary Chertoff steady doses of ground truth. Jeb Bush and Craig Fugate were getting cut out of that loop.

The final straw came the next morning when General Douglas Burnett, the head of Florida's National Guard, received a call from the commander of the Fifth Army at Fort Sam Houston in San Antonio, asking where he could start flying in equipment to establish a joint task force command. Burnett was completely taken aback. "Who could have come into Florida who had more experience with hurricanes than the state team and the National Guard?" he said later. "Did we need a three-star general from Texas to come to direct our response? No, we did not."

Florida went into open rebellion. General Burnett called Northcom headquarters to complain. Governor Bush called Michael Chertoff, telling him the federal government's unilateral actions were "insulting" to him personally, to Craig Fugate, and to all the citizens of Florida.

But still the message didn't seem to get through. Broderick and his subordinates were calling state emergency officials in Tallahassee almost hourly in the days before the storm demanding answers to trivial questions. How many tourists were on Marco Island in August?

What was the rate of traffic flow out of the Florida Keys to the mainland? This was followed by second-guessing Florida's long-standing operating procedures—for example, asking why the state was evacuating coastal residents only a few miles inland rather than hundreds of miles away.

The state emergency coordinators dubbed Washington's constant requests for information "reindeer games," a reference to the movie of that title in which the phrase described a pointless exercise. The questions got so annoying that Fugate kept a set of costume antlers in his office and would hold them in his lap before videoconferences, ready to put them on in case Washington's picayune inquiries got out of hand.

Fugate had had his first run-in with Homeland Security a month earlier, just before Rita passed over the Florida Keys en route to Texas. During a videoconference, he recalled, top Homeland Security officials pressed him for trivial details about his evacuation plans and demanded explanations for his every action. He lost his cool. "I told them in no uncertain terms that I had moved more people during [the 2004] hurricanes than had ever been moved before, and that I would be happy to sit there answering their stupid questions, but that I had a job to do." Several FEMA employees at the headquarters in Washington were listening in on the videoconference, and they erupted into a cheer. "It was a beautiful moment to hear of someone who knew what they were doing tell these DHS guys off," said Leo Bosner, FEMA's union boss.

The confrontation over Wilma came to a head at the daily videoconference on the morning of Friday, October 21, three days before the storm was expected to make landfall. Fugate essentially pulled off the equivalent of a boardroom coup. He announced to the assembled officials the creation of "Wilma Command"—a unified "incident command" in accordance with Homeland Security's own National Incident Management System, or NIMS. This system had been mandated by President Bush in the aftermath of 9/11 to ensure that all levels of government were working from the same playbook during a disaster. Its bedrock principle: one incident, one commander—no matter how many agencies send help. NIMS, while simple in concept, had yet to be mastered by many states. But Fugate knew what to do.

He said the Wilma Command team would include himself and General Burnett of the Florida National Guard. It would also include Justin DeMello, FEMA's federal coordinating officer (FCO) in Florida, who had a reputation for working more closely with state officials like Fugate than with FEMA headquarters in Washington. Then Fugate reached off-camera and pulled Governor Bush into the frame. "I'd now like to introduce the incident commander," he announced, "the governor of Florida." Fugate said later he wanted everyone to realize that Tallahassee—not Washington—was in charge. "Craig had out-maneuvered them and they knew it," said DeMello. "There was nothing for them to say as under the NIMS they are required to support the incident commander."

DeMello, a former California firefighter, had been sent to Florida in October 2004 to assist the state with long-term recovery after that year's four-storm hurricane season. He and Fugate were now working well together in the run-up to Wilma, consolidating control by making sure that everything Washington sent to Florida was put under Wilma Command, or not sent at all. To this end Fugate confiscated the three hundred satellite telephones that Homeland Security had moved down to Orlando for its own emergency reporting teams and redistributed them to the state workers who would normally serve the public after a storm, handing out flyers about filing claims and getting food and water.

Fugate then ordered that any people or equipment sent into the state from outside of Wilma Command would be arrested or confiscated. "If you want to help, Wilma Command is happy to find a place for you," he told Homeland Security officials during one phone call. "If you are not going to be part of Wilma Command I'm sure we can find a building somewhere in Tallahassee to put you."

Homeland continued lobbying Florida to allow Secretary Chertoff to name a principal federal official under the National Response Plan. Joshua D. Filler, Homeland Security's director of state and local government coordination, called Fugate late on Friday to make one more pitch. He told Fugate how important it was that Secretary Chertoff name a PFO, which could be a big benefit in leveraging the assets of the Department of Homeland Security.

Fugate responded, "Josh, first, I don't need to create confusion over who is in charge here. I don't need an extra body hanging over my shoulder so you guys can look good. And second, if I get in trouble I don't need the assets of DHS; I will need the assets of the entire federal government. Under law, the FCO has that power, not the PFO." Deputy Secretary Michael Jackson called Fugate again on Saturday, but to no avail. No PFO was appointed. Northcom never called up the Fifth Army.

But Homeland Security officials continued to press ahead with plans to use employees of the department—such as Customs inspectors, federal building guards, and law enforcement agents—as their eyes on the ground. They sent a Customs plane aloft to feed live video images back to Washington.

In the end, Wilma, like Rita, fell short of being the disaster everyone had feared. It entered Florida through the Everglades as a Category 3 storm, missing the west coast's more densely populated areas. Instead of breaking up, however, the storm maintained its strength when it hit the Miami, Fort Lauderdale, and West Palm Beach areas. The storm knocked out power to millions, but property damage overall was light.

Wilma Command had organized successful evacuations of vulnerable areas, maintained order, and ensured there were enough police on hand to prevent traffic snarls. Within hours of the storm's passage, Fugate had moved his mobile command truck to the parking lot of a Broward County shopping mall, and with DeMello at his side, he pushed supplies and relief workers into the most affected areas of South Florida.

Meanwhile, FEMA diverted its water trucks into staging areas where they could be outfitted with satellite devices to better track deliveries. But the process was cumbersome and slowed down deliveries, yet again making the agency an object of public scorn. Fugate and DeMello moved to cut FEMA red tape at every opportunity, in one instance helicoptering down to a FEMA staging area in Homestead to fire a FEMA truck dispatcher who was holding up deliveries of ice and water over quibbles about paperwork. "Don't feel bad," Fugate gently told the crestfallen federal worker. "It's not your fault. You've been trained to serve bureaucracy, not victims."

When Wilma's winds died and the rain passed, Fugate and DeMello took a National Guard helicopter to Marco Island to survey the damage. The island's fire chief, Michael Murphy, was waiting at the landing zone with a handful of emergency responders. He said the island had dodged disaster when the storm swung south, and that all was normal, save one minor oddity: A cadre of Homeland Security agents had been skulking around the island's emergency operations center with no apparent mission. "It was strange," said Murphy. "I walked up to one guy I saw and asked him about something when he put his hand in my face and said, 'Don't tell me. I'm from Homeland Security. Go talk to the FEMA guy.'"

Fugate shot a glance at DeMello and shook his head. He was furious. "Unbelievable," he said. "Washington managed to sneak in some spies after all."

DeMello was equally perturbed. "Those people are not reporting to us," he said. "And if they're not reporting to Wilma Command, what are they doing here?"

In the first week of recovery, Wilma Command had moved more ice, food, and water into South Florida than during any of the four major storms of 2004. Still, it fell short of Governor Bush's pledge that supplies would be on the ground within twenty-four hours of the storm's passage. Many Floridians, especially on the east coast, didn't even bother to lay in bottled water in advance of the storm, and their expectations for immediate relief ran high. When many distribution centers didn't open on time with sufficient ice, water, and food, the outcry was immediate and fierce. Moreover, power outages had knocked gas stations off-line in a third of the state. So while Florida had plenty of gasoline, there was no way to pump it into cars and cans. At the few stations that had maintained power, lines stretched for miles. A few impatient patrons began waving firearms around, prompting a police callout at all working gas stations.

With Michael Chertoff at his side two days after the storm, Governor Bush accepted responsibility for the criticism, saying the delays and confusion were exclusively the fault of the state. "If anyone wants to blame anybody, blame me," Governor Bush said. "I'm not going to criticize anybody and I'm not going to let anybody criticize FEMA for something we accept responsibility for. . . . We did not perform where we want to be."

Later that evening, Craig Fugate sat in his command center and tried to console his boss via cell phone as they discussed what went wrong. "Perhaps it was overambitious," Fugate said, pulling the brim of his tattered orange cap down over his eyes. "But we can try again next year."

After the call, Fugate immediately ordered his logistics team to get more supplies on the road. It would be another day before a sufficient number of distribution centers opened. And that's when Fugate switched to his blue cap.

The events that unfolded in Florida during those four days in late October 2005 were emblematic of the larger struggle that was raging between Washington and the states ever since Hurricane Katrina left a trail of destruction through the Gulf Coast.

Local officials from across the country were already under pressure from Homeland Security officials to vet their emergency plans through the department, while the Pentagon began its own campaign to seize more of a role in disaster response. Long-forgotten plans were being dusted off and reassessed, and lawmakers were fretting about vulnerabilities and whether efforts to address them went far enough.

At stake was what to do in the aftermath not just of killer storms, but of all disasters—natural and man-made. Those who favored giving Washington a lead response role said that only the federal government and the military had the resources and experience to deal with major catastrophes. President Bush had already suggested that federal troops should be more engaged in disaster efforts, and in October 2005 he suggested that the armed forces might be enlisted to enforce quarantines in the event of a flu pandemic.

Admiral Keating, the commander of the U.S. Northern Command, also advocated giving active-duty military forces complete authority to respond to catastrophic disasters such as Hurricane Katrina, and he intended to float this idea at a meeting of the Western Governors Association in Scottsdale, Arizona, on November 8. When word of Keating's plans reached Major General Timothy J. Lowenberg, the head of the Washington State National Guard, he immediately went on the offensive, sending e-mail messages to his colleagues across the country, urging that they resist this effort.

"Although usually couched in terms of 'support for governors,' " Lowenberg wrote, "the Northcom proposals would bring about a fundamental change in the emergency governance of states impacted by large scale disasters. Some might liken this to a policy of domestic regime change."

Lowenberg said that Hurricanes Katrina, Rita, and Wilma represented "the finest hour" for the National Guard, and he told governors they should make this clear to Admiral Keating. Lowenberg added a warning: "If they politely listen to his offer of 'assistance' without asserting their constitutional and statutory authority, they will only encourage his proposals."

National Guard generals at the Pentagon also fretted about Northcom's impending power grab. In its short existence, Northcom had already raised plenty of hackles among this group. Admiral Keating's predecessor, Air Force general Ralph "Ed" Eberhart, had aggressively organized joint exercises with cities and states across the country, but he also encouraged National Guard units to spy on their communities and report back to Northcom on any "actionable intelligence" they might discover.

Keating had been most concerned with protecting the U.S. coastline against enemy infiltration, but Katrina had pushed disaster management onto Northcom's agenda—a move that was almost certain to cause conflict with the National Guard, which had traditionally shouldered such duties. "Keating spent his whole life pushing aircraft carriers around the place. What does he know about civilian authorities and responding to disasters?" scoffed a senior National Guard officer in Washington.

Ultimately, Keating did not attend the Western Governors Association because of a scheduling conflict. But the governors spoke out anyway. "Those closest to disaster, those closest to the emergency, are best equipped to deal with it," Governor Jon Huntsman of Utah said in a speech to his colleagues. If local and state authorities cannot handle the demands of a disaster, they can reach out to the federal government for help, he said. "It should not work the other way around."

Washington was not convinced.

13

A CIVIC RESPONSIBILITY

The body floated on a six-foot tide through a poorly secured side door and into the cavernous warehouse on Claiborne Avenue. It came to rest just next to the Royal Barge, an oversized Mardi Gras float that had been part of the Rex entourage for years. Death up close was an unusual occurrence even for an organization as storied as Rex, which had been parading city streets on Fat Tuesday since 1872—the longest run of any Carnival krewe in the city. During the span there had been a few extraordinary years when Carnival was canceled, the 1979 police strike being the last. World war had forced cancellation a few times, as had a year during Reconstruction following the Civil War, when "local unrest" made parading too dangerous. Some—actually many—had argued Katrina was such an extraordinary event that the city should cancel its pre-Lenten celebration. After all, the city was broke, and holding a big municipal party costs millions in police overtime and other city services. There was also a question of probity: How would it look to the politicians up north if the city, in the wake of such death and destruction and heartbreak, were to hold its annual debauch as if nothing had happened? "It's a two-edged sword," said Mayor Nagin. "It'll send out the signal that New Orleans is not dead, that we've honored our tradition of 150 years. But it also sends the signal that we're okay, and 'There they go again, partying when they have serious challenges.'"

The mayor was of two minds, first supporting the idea of holding Carnival and then spontaneously coming out against it. In the end, he was shouted down by other local politicians for his waffling. Though New Orleans was now a FEMA town, utterly dependent on the federal government for everything from trash pickup to police cars and places to live, this was one decision the city could make on its own, without interference from the federal government. And so Nagin reluctantly agreed that the show would go on, even if in somewhat stunted form.

So the Rex organization called Henri Schindler, its chief designer, to oversee the restoration of its near-complete parade floats and bring order to its flooded den. When Schindler made his first trip in October, the body was gone. "It's not something the organization likes to discuss," he said.

The Rex den is nothing fancy, just a sprawling tin warehouse uptown from the Superdome and the spaghetti of elevated roadways that connect Interstate 10 to the main bridge over the Mississippi River. The den took in at least six feet of water when the city's floodwalls collapsed, and when the water retreated, cops from the Sixth Police District commandeered the building, filling the front of the warehouse with soap, snack food, and other sundries for officers who had been washed out of their homes. The cops had disposed of the dead body but had left most of the other rubbish where it lay. When Schindler's design crew returned, the den was stinking with a slurry of mud and plaster, garnished with bits of twinkling foil and blooming mold. Dozens of papier-mâché orchids that normally adorn the floats were in ruins. The floats themselves were all ringed with black bands showing where the water had stood at various stages before the city was pumped dry. "What's stuck to the floats is pretty gross," Schindler said.

Short and cherubic, Schindler is a native New Orleanian with round wire glasses and a Dutch boy haircut that belies his sixty-five years. Since childhood, he had devoted much of his life to celebrating Carnival and guarding its traditions against the steady creep of commercialism and crass modernism. Schindler is a traditionalist, shunning the foppish colored lights and out-of-scale designs of the less-storied parading krewes in favor of gossamer confections that draw heavily on mythology and hark back to the years when floats were pulled by mules, not farm tractors. The 2006 Mardi Gras was no exception: The theme was "Beaux Arts and Letters," and it was vintage Schindler. The float dedicated to the works of former New Orleans resident William Faulkner featured a sinister-looking purple mosquito trimmed in glittery foil, a tribute to the author's first novel by the same name. A tribute to the novelist Walker Percy was cast as a baroque movie theater in the style frequented by the title character of *The Moviegoer*. The float paying homage to the folk artist Clementine Hunter was expertly rendered in flat representations of the rural South, cleverly evocative of what the artist had called her "memory paintings." And all of the floats were trimmed lavishly with oversized papier-mâché orchids and lush foliage and glittery pieces of trembling foil.

Most of Rex's twenty-one themed floats, constructed on a fleet of antique city garbage wagons that were outfitted with wood-spoke wheels, had been near completion when the storm hit. And the flood hadn't been kind. The water had warped many of the wooden float wheels, rotted the canvas underpinnings, and shot the plaster full of cracks. Many sported beards of black mold. In a break with tradition—Rex floats typically remain out of public view until Fat Tuesday—crews moved the entire fleet to the parking lot of a nearby dairy, where they were doused with bleach and given a good scrubbing. The cure removed most of the grime ring but also some of the paint. Even after a vigorous scrubbing, some of the flood rings peeked out here and there. "We'll just have to make do," Schindler said.

All of New Orleans was just making do. On September 15, two weeks after the storm, President Bush came to New Orleans, in an attempt to ignite the still-stuttering effort to help the Gulf Coast region. Standing in the symbolic center of the blackened city in front of the St. Louis Cathedral, which had been lit up white hot with generator-fired klieg lights by a White House advance team, Bush spoke to the nation and promised, "We will do what it takes, we will stay as long as it takes, to help citizens rebuild their communities and their lives. And all who question the future of the Crescent City need to know there is no way to imagine America without New Orleans, and this great city will rise again."

But in fact, as the months passed, New Orleans changed little. In the first six weeks after the storm, FEMA spent $1.5 billion on trailers and mobile homes, yet an estimated 600,000 evacuees remained in hotel and motel rooms. An estimated 14,000 people still lived in municipal shelters, in a situation that Admiral Thad Allen, the top federal official on the ground, called "a bridge to nowhere." By March, Congress had appropriated $85 billion to aid in the rebuilding effort, but local officials complained that Byzantine rules, coupled with FEMA's ham-handed oversight, meant that much of the money was locked up and unavailable. Nowhere was this more apparent, perhaps, than in Hope, Arkansas, where in a massive staging yard sat one of the largest agglomerations of trailers the world has ever seen. For weeks, row upon row of shiny white mobile homes stood empty and unused. These weren't the trailers with wheels that could be moved around with ease. These homes were the cream of FEMA's housing options—single-wide trailers with separate bedrooms and full-sized baths. The trailers sat. And a few hundred miles away, some 98,000 people in Louisiana and Mississippi crammed into undersized hotel rooms or shivered in tents.

According to a study by Congress, FEMA had spent almost $900 million for 25,000 mobile homes to house evacuees from Katrina but had only placed about 1,200 of them by the following April. They were held up by a rule that FEMA apparently had forgotten when it made the purchase: a regulation that only camper-style trailers could be placed in floodplains. Even President Bush was appalled. "Do something with them," the president said.

So FEMA came up with a plan—not a plan for distributing trailers but for storing them. But first the agency needed a way to keep the trailers from sinking into the Arkansas mud. So it spent $6 million on gravel.

Across the country, newspapers brimmed with reports that FEMA was operating at something less than peak efficiency as it sought to rebuild the Gulf region. The so-called blue roof program, a scheme to provide temporary waterproofing of damaged structures by wrapping roofs in a sheet of blue plastic, was costing some $3,000 per structure, though the actual price paid to the laborers performing the task was a fraction of the amount. The rest was going to middlemen—beneficiaries of massive no-bid contracts that FEMA had allotted to a handful of national companies, which in turn hired smaller firms to do the work. "Needless bureaucratic churning" was how Secretary Chertoff characterized the rich contracts, and he and top FEMA officials promised to rebid the work along more equitable lines. But months passed, and the contracts remained in place.

In New Orleans, people seethed over the slow pace of debris pickup, the lack of housing, and the Bush administration's stubborn refusal to say exactly how strong the rebuilt levee system would be. As the conduit for most federal aid in the region, FEMA received special scorn. In December, when the agency sent about one hundred senior managers from Washington to visit St. Bernard Parish, president Henry Rodriguez, Jr., met the visitors on the porch of his own FEMA trailer. "I appreciate y'all coming down to visit but I want to say, you're all a bunch of goddam idiots," Rodriguez bellowed.

Even as Louisiana and Mississippi burned with rage, complaining bitterly about the pace of federal recovery, President Bush tried to regain his standing as the commander in chief of federal disaster response. In the six months after Katrina, Bush made ten trips to the storm region. In most cases, he skirted the truly demolished portions of Louisiana, such as St. Bernard Parish and the all-but-abandoned sprawl of eastern New Orleans. In January, Bush displayed impatience with critics who said the administration continued to fiddle while New Orleans burned. "I want to remind people in that part of the world, $85 billion is a lot," Bush said.

But in fact, it wasn't nearly $85 billion that was being directed toward the disaster zone. Nearly a billion dollars was going to other states, to pay for housing evacuees. Some $17 billion of the money was used to pay federal flood insurance claims, which were at least partially backed by the premiums homeowners had been paying for years. And despite early accounts that most New Orleanians in low-lying areas had flouted disaster by failing to maintain such insurance, in fact the rate of compliance in the city was among the nation's highest.

And much of the federal reconstruction money came with strings attached. A large portion was in the form of loans that would eventually have to be repaid. FEMA also reckoned that the state of Louisiana owed Washington about $1 billion as its share of the overall costs of the recovery effort and began sending dunning notices to Baton Rouge. The first installment, for $158 million, wasn't itemized. When the state requested an itemization, FEMA balked.

And then there was the big chunk of recovery money that went into FEMA's own pocket—"administration" expenses that paid travel costs, upkeep, and salaries for the agency's own workers in the field. The amount was not insubstantial: In a report it submitted to Congress in February, FEMA said that a whopping $7.7 billion of the $29.7 billion spent to date had gone toward such expenses—an overhead rate of 26 percent.

And yet President Bush pronounced himself satisfied. On a January 2006 trip to Bay St. Louis, a Mississippi community that had essentially been leveled, Bush looked past the man-sized piles of debris that still littered the roads, the unaddressed destruction that had rendered the town's major federal highway impassible, and the thousands of people still living in tents and substandard dwellings while they awaited government trailers. "There's going to be a building boom down here—there just is," he said, adding that the private sector would be leading the charge to rebuild. On the same day, Bush told local leaders in New Orleans that the city looked great—though his own tour was confined to the slim area of the city's central business district that hadn't flooded. "I will tell you, the contrast between when I was last here and today . . . is pretty dramatic," Bush said. "It's a heck of a place to bring your family."

In fact, beyond the unflooded "sliver by the river," where only about 20 percent of the pre-storm population resided, the city was no place to take a child. For one, there were no schools or playgrounds in this area, and very few open gasoline stations or stores. A huge portion of New Orleans didn't even have electrical service, let alone running water or gas. Streets were crammed with uncollected debris, and homes stood vacant, their doors having been kicked open by soldiers, looters, pet rescuers, and mortician crews. Ruined homes became crude marquees for voicing frustration or conveying simple messages. COME ON FEMA, HELP US, said one spray-painted appeal on a house outside of the suburban community of Belle Chasse. MAW MAW, CALL CHAD appeared on a home near the community of Poydras in the parish of St. Bernard.

Even in the populated, electrified areas of the city, the basic measures of civilization—mail and newspaper delivery, garbage service, working stoplights—were in short supply. In January, there were just twenty-nine available hospital beds in the city—a pittance even for the sharply diminished population. In January, the wait for an ambulance was estimated to be an hour.

Perhaps even more distressing, at least psychologically, was the stubborn lack of progress in making even cosmetic improvements to the cityscape. After the hurricane, thousands of homeowners turned out to drag ruined furniture from their residences and take moldy walls down to the studs. But from that point, it seemed, practically everyone had stopped. From a redevelopment standpoint, New Orleans seemed locked in amber, as Washington dithered over the overarching questions that would drive the rebuilding of the city. Would the federal levee system be restored to a level that could handle the biggest of Gulf hurricanes? The Bush administration refused to answer directly. Would the government create a revolving land bank that would allow the city to cash out individual landowners and bundle large tracts of properties for redevelopment? The Bush administration killed a bill in Congress that would have accomplished this.

Would the federal government continue to offer flood insurance to New Orleans property owners? The FEMA maps that would answer this question were promised but then delayed. At this point, after having disappointed so many times, even FEMA's acting director, R. David Paulison, admitted, "We have a tendency to overpromise."

The city government of New Orleans rocked along through the fall and winter as an employer of last resort, keeping about 5,000 of its 8,000 workers on salary, with the help of a $50 million loan that Mayor Nagin had secured from a banking syndicate. FEMA claimed that federal rules barred it from helping the city stay afloat, and Nagin's own accountants projected a $140 million deficit by May. Unlike the federal government, New Orleans was forbidden by statute from running deficits, and bankruptcy loomed as a distinct possibility. The city's bond rating, never stellar, sank to junk status.

It was no exaggeration to say that the spring of 2006 was perhaps the worst time to hold municipal elections, but the city staged one anyway. Nagin, a heavy favorite for reelection before Katrina, now seemed in danger of losing his post—and he reacted accordingly, becoming more tentative when presented with sticky decisions that would govern the city's redevelopment. With many of the city's black residents evacuated to other states, the white gentry in Uptown began to believe it might have a shot of electing one of its own, for the first time in more than thirty years. The white patrons who had supported Nagin's run for office in 2002 deserted him in droves.

Though skin color had long loomed large in New Orleans politics, Katrina opened new chasms between the races, beginning practically as soon as the storm made landfall. White citizens flashed with anger at City Hall's failure to bring the looting under control, a crime spree they mostly blamed on black residents. White citizens were also enraged at City Hall's ultimately abortive attempts to forcibly evict New Orleanians from the storm-wracked city, even from the unflooded sections of Uptown. For their part, black citizens were furious over the city's inability to bring succor to the mostly black evacuees at the Superdome, the Convention Center, and the interstate overpasses. And they remained deeply suspicious of any attempts to rebuild the city, fearing it would lead to the redlining of black neighborhoods.

Such suspicions weren't completely misplaced. To Nagin's embarrassment, one of his top appointees, a white Uptowner named Jimmy Reiss, gave a rambling interview to the *Wall Street Journal* in early September, in which he crystallized the view of the city's power elite regarding a new vision for the rebuilt city. Speaking in the coded words of race politics, Reiss declared that the city's white industrialists and employers wouldn't tolerate a city that didn't have a lower crime rate, better schools, and far fewer indigents. "Those who want to see this city rebuilt want to see it done in a completely different way: demographically, geographically and politically," said Reiss, whose first act after the storm was to helicopter a heavily armed, private security force into the city to protect the gated neighborhood where he lived. "I'm not just speaking for myself here," he warned. "The way we've been living is not going to happen again, or we're out."

In early March, on the final day of qualifying for the April 22 mayoral election, Nagin found himself opposed by no fewer than twenty-two candidates, all but two of whom were white. In short order—and sometimes in the face of prudence—Nagin, who had been swept into office on the shoulders of white, Republican-leaning New Orleanians, began defining himself as the black candidate in the race. He began to subtly change his stance on topics such as redevelopment of the city. Though professional planners urged New Orleans to shrink its footprint, and even to bar redevelopment of certain neighborhoods that were flood-prone or economically unviable, Nagin, in the face of intense resistance from black residents against redlining any neighborhood, refused to rule out any area for rebuilding. He also advocated creating a casino zone within the city—a plan that had reasonably strong support in the black community but had been repeatedly rejected in the past by the city's white elite.

But it was in his unusual and somewhat unbalanced rhetoric that Nagin most clearly telegraphed his new political strategy. In a speech delivered on Martin Luther King Day, Nagin mused aloud about

God's purpose in visiting Hurricane Katrina upon New Orleans, concluding it was vengeful punishment against the nation for prosecuting an unjustified war in Iraq. Then the mayor said that a rebuilt city would be "a chocolate New Orleans. This city will be a majority African American city. It's the way God wants it to be."

A short time later, Jimmy Reiss, still part of Nagin's administration, gave $5,000 to one of the mayor's white Uptown opponents. Reiss's wife contributed $5,000 more. Other patrons followed in droves. And Nagin, who had captured 85 percent of the white vote in 2002, now had to rely on a strong black turnout if he was to survive.

On April 22, Nagin finished first in the crowded field, with 38 percent of the vote. The city charter calls for a runoff if no one wins a majority; Nagin's opponent would be Lieutenant Governor Mitch Landrieu, the scion of one of the city's most prominent white political families. Many political analysts gave Nagin little chance of winning reelection, but in the runoff on May 20 he bested Landrieu, 52 percent to 48 percent. He closed his victory speech that night with a quote: "As Gandhi once said, 'First they ignore you. Then they laugh at you. Then they fight you. And then you win.'"

The 2006 Mardi Gras was almost as unusual as the election. Fat Tuesday, February 28, dawned cloudless and temperate; for the first time in recent memory, the Krewe of Zulu rolled on schedule. Though the city's only majority-black krewe of substance had imported genuine Zulu warriors from Africa to march in the parade, the mood was subdued; about a dozen of its members had been killed in the storm, and many others had been washed out. Several of its fifteen floats passed through the city only half-filled with riders.

At his Gallier Hall reviewing stand, Mayor Nagin masked as General Honoré, dressed in full Army regalia, all the way down to the jaunty black beret. Governor Blanco joined the festivities as well, but she didn't mask.

Carnival often features political satire, and the 2006 season may have been unrivaled for its bite. Not since the Krewe of Comus portrayed President Ulysses S. Grant as a tobacco grub during its 1873 parade had Washington come in for such a symbolic horsewhipping. The target of much ire this time was FEMA and Michael Brown, whose bobbing head was perched high atop a float called "Department of Homeland Insecurity." One krewe also took a vicious swipe at Washington's chief levee builders, "The Corpse of Engineers," and featured a skeleton wearing the agency's signature white hard hat, consulting blueprints that called for a mixture of iron, mud, and Jell-O for the city's levees. "They have quite a sense of humor down here," said Dan Hitchings, a civilian corps official on loan to the New Orleans office from Vicksburg. Another float featured Nagin, Blanco, and Brown tending a boiling green roux simmering in a pot that looked suspiciously like the Superdome. Above and ahead of the trio, placidly sailing a small boat in a sea of fire, was a horned and smiling President Bush, piloting the "ship of state." The float was called "The Inferno." The Krewe D'Etat offered the most subtle and detailed portrait of Brown, bloated and dead-eyed, reclined and gazing idly into a hand mirror as the Superdome floated downstream on an angry sea. "Anything I can tweak?" the cartoon Brown said.

But perhaps the most striking tableau of the Carnival season was the one presented by Muses, an all-female club that parades a few nights before Fat Tuesday. It was the last float in the parade, lit up, studded with white blossoms, a ghost float completely devoid of riders. At the front of the barge was a Grecian bust, clearly shedding a tear; at the back, a simple black-lettered banner. WE CELEBRATE LIFE. WE MOURN THE PAST. WE SHALL NEVER FORGET, the banner said.

By January the forecasters at the National Hurricane Center in Miami were already predicting the 2006 hurricane season would be more active than usual. Though it wasn't likely to top the record-breaking 2005 season, Max Mayfield constantly reminded his staff, "It takes only one to make a bad hurricane season."

As a mild winter gave way to spring along the Gulf Coast, and the June 1 start of hurricane season drew closer, disaster officials across the region started getting nervous. The biggest threat remained in Louisiana, where the state's tattered system of floodwalls remained in a half-completed state and where an estimated 50,000 citizens were sweating it out in decidedly storm-vulnerable trailers. True, the Army Corps of Engineers was beavering away on closing the ragged gaps in New Orleans's floodwalls and putting massive steel swing doors on the mouths of its three outfall canals. It was unlikely the system would be without flaw. The corps was also junking many of the city's substandard I-wall flood control structures, which had cost more than $100 million to construct just a decade or so before, replacing them with sturdier T-walls. But much of this work would extend far beyond the hurricane season.

Indeed, the outer edges of the city, along with the outlying parishes of St. Bernard and Plaquemines, would likely not be protected in the 2006 hurricane season. Katrina had done nearly $158 million worth of damage to the hurricane protection system in these two parishes; there was no hope of work being completed in these areas in time. Though the corps had proposed a series of stopgap protection barriers, nobody knew how they might hold up to even a brushing encounter with a hurricane. Moreover, there were many known flaws and vulnerabilities in the existing hurricane protection system extending west of the city, in areas that were relatively untouched by Katrina. Congress hadn't appropriated the money to deal with these problems.

This would turn out to be the least of the state's worries. In early April, in a declaration that caught both Washington and Baton Rouge by surprise, the corps said that protecting Plaquemines Parish from a strike by a middling-sized hurricane would cost a whopping $3.5 billion more than had been budgeted, while raising floodwalls around the rest of the region would cost an additional $2.4 billion. Bringing eastern New Orleans up to storm code alone would cost an additional $710 million, the corps said. Together, these substandard areas were home to some 210,000 people; reconstruction ground to a halt, as citizens and state officials wondered whether Congress would be willing to pony up such a vast sum. There was little Governor Blanco or anyone else in Baton Rouge could do. The state of Louisiana belonged to Washington.

In the end and after deep conversation with the White House, the corps cut its projected extra costs down to a more reasonable $2.5 billion, though protecting the lower coast of Plaquemines Parish, it said, would cost $1.6 billion more. The White House rejected the revised cost figures for Plaquemines and accepted the rest. In May, Congress began debating the extra White House–backed money, bringing the total for rebuilding the New Orleans area flood system to a whopping $5.8 billion. By late May, its passage was hardly assured. And this amount, the corps' Dan Hitchings said, wouldn't address some of the long-identified design flaws that had been a part of the area's flood protection configuration since its inception. "We aren't going to be changing the system in its configuration," he said.

The city also unveiled its new hurricane plan for the 2006 season, which was blessed by Homeland Security. The plan called for shutting the Superdome and all other shelters of last resort in the city. Instead, Mayor Nagin said he would press the Convention Center into service, not as a shelter but as a depot for evacuation buses. The plan comported with Washington's new thinking about hurricane preparation, which emphasizes evacuation over shelters and calls for getting everyone out of town before a storm hits. But 100 percent evacuation is hardly a realistic goal, and without shelters, the stragglers would be scattered and completely at a storm's mercy. The Dome, bad as it was, had served as a central collection area, which made it easier to feed and shelter those left behind.

In Texas, homeland security director Steve McCraw watched the goings-on next door in Louisiana and shuddered. In March, he and his counterparts from several other states had traveled to Washington for a two-day meeting at the Department of Homeland Security with Secretary Chertoff and George Foresman, the department's new undersecretary for preparedness. There, Chertoff extolled the department's plans to hire new contractors with radio frequency tags and satellite technology that would allow Washington to track shipments of ice, water, medicine, and emergency generators from the time they were ordered to the time they were delivered—something that had been sorely lacking during Katrina. Chertoff said FEMA would soon be getting more money to hire 1,500 new employees, filling the many top positions that had been left vacant for years. Chertoff also said the department was creating two-man and six-man "reconnaissance teams," equipped with the latest in streaming video and foolproof communications, to hunt down ground truth during a crisis.

One piece of news was greeted with enthusiasm in some circles of Homeland Security: Matthew Broderick decided to retire in March. Broderick was to many the personification of the department's dysfunction, and his promotion to director of operations rankled. Some people in Homeland Security said Broderick was being pushed out at the behest of the White House, but if this was true it was never made public. Broderick simply said he wanted to spend more time with his family, and that he had contemplated retirement for some time. In a statement released to the press, Secretary Chertoff said, "Matt worked tirelessly to ensure the integration of the department, always demonstrating coolness in crisis and energy and integrity in the execution of his duties, under the most difficult circumstances. . . . He has left an indelible mark on the department and on our country."

Apart from Broderick's departure, little else gave McCraw much comfort; Chertoff was offering familiar rhetoric and nothing concrete. Moreover, it seemed to McCraw and others that in some cases, Chertoff was heading down the wrong road, adding layers of bureaucracy to a system that already groaned with complication. On the second day of the meeting in Washington, he spoke up. "It's not what I need," he told Chertoff. "I think it's a good idea that you are reviewing plans around the country and working on fixing FEMA and you all have my support in that endeavor. But speaking for me and my group in Texas, what we need—and we need it sooner rather than later—is for Washington to send one person—just one person—who is familiar with the capabilities and plans of the federal government so that we can incorporate that into our planning for this year's season."

It was a fine idea that went nowhere. A few weeks later, Chertoff appointed a host of federal coordination officers and principal federal officials, signaling his intention to stick with the troubled National Response Plan, which even the White House had criticized as over-wrought and cumbersome. In theory, when both a principal federal official and a federal coordinating officer are assigned to a specific incident (as was the case during Katrina), the FCO coordinates the response from other federal agencies, while the PFO delivers progress reports to the homeland security secretary. But in reality, few if any of the people on the ground understood how the two positions were supposed to work in tandem. Even Admiral Allen, who took over from Michael Brown in New Orleans, complained about the confusion until Chertoff finally appointed him to both positions, several weeks into the recovery. That simple act begged the question why two coordinating positions were even needed when one seemed to suffice.

In a report released in November 2005, Homeland Security's inspector general, Richard L. Skinner, noted that during the most recent TOPOFF terrorist response exercise in April 2005, the National Response Plan had proved to be a disaster within a disaster, sowing uncertainty and delay during mock bombings and bioweapons attacks. He reserved specific criticism for the PFO-FCO, structure, saying it sowed confusion as emergency responders struggled to divine the difference in responsibility between the two positions. Four months later, Skinner repeated the charges in his scathing critique of the federal response to Katrina: "As the PFO assumed a greater role in the response operations, the new lines of command and authority created confusion," he wrote. "For example, a state official told us the PFO was coordinating directly with local government officials without the knowledge of the state. In addition, the PFO duplicated planning and reporting activities."

But Chertoff showed a remarkable deafness to all of this criticism. If anything, he aggravated the problem by creating a raft of new positions never envisioned in the National Response Plan that were variations on the complicated scheme. In addition to naming PFOs and FCOs, Chertoff appointed deputy PFOs, "Super PFOs," as well as so-called federal preparedness coordinators, who were supposed to help local officials plan for disasters. The Super PFOs, an elite cadre, would be appointed only in the worst catastrophes. Deputy PFOs would always be appointed during disasters but without any clear delineation of their role. State officials could only shake their heads at this breath-taking exercise in bureaucracy-building. "Their house is burning and they're spending their time picking out window curtains," Florida's Craig Fugate said with disgust after the March meeting.

Steve McCraw said all he wanted was a single point of contact with the federal government. Instead he got three and perhaps more. So with the 2006 hurricane season approaching, McCraw took mat-ters into his own hands. He pressed ahead with his own plans that relied on local retail chains such as Wal-Mart and Home Depot to provide disaster supplies and associated commodities. The state also planned its own hurricane disaster exercise in May to test plans that would involve local, not federal, responders. And while he would hardly turn down help from Washington, McCraw was determined to avoid becoming dependent on the federal government, the way Louisiana had during the Katrina catastrophe. "Whether the federal government is ready or not, hurricanes will be coming," McCraw said. "And Texas has to be ready."

Craig Fugate observed that relying less on the federal govern-ment "may be perversely a good thing that will get states back in the game, forcing them to build capacity rather than just doing the bare minimum," but the problem was that many states—the poor ones, the inexperienced ones, the smaller ones—might not have the fore-sight or the capacity to take such initiative. Not every all-hazards re-sponse system was as well developed as those in Florida, Texas, Alabama, and California. Indeed, many states had taken the lead of the federal government in recent years and dismantled their natural hazard response systems to prepare for terrorist attacks. In this en-deavor, they received a great deal of encouragement from the federal government, which dispersed some $13 billion in grants to help states prepare for disaster, virtually every dime of it to combat ter-rorist threats. "That's probably the thing that makes me the angriest: Every federal grant these days deals with terrorism," Louisiana's Jeff

Smith said. "It's not a question of getting turned down for other help—other help just doesn't exist."

In some cases, the Department of Homeland Security knew full well how woefully unprepared some states and localities are for disaster. In November 2005, the department began to audit the disaster plans of seventy-five major cities and all fifty states. Though the agency never made the results public, some of the information leaked out. The study began with a self-assessment, and three states, Oregon, Hawaii, and West Virginia, immediately confessed that their outdated disaster plans weren't up to snuff. Additionally, twenty-one states said their evacuation plans were subpar. And one state, Wyoming, which had abolished its department of emergency management some years back, didn't respond at all.

After the self-assessment exercise, Homeland Security sent in teams of contractors to review local emergency plans, state by state. Among the states that passed muster were Louisiana and Alabama. But as Alabama's Bruce Baughman noted to federal auditors, the review didn't really measure anything. "It's just paper," he said. "It doesn't mean crap. Good plans do not mean smooth execution."

But Secretary Chertoff didn't need a study to confirm his long-held assumptions about national preparedness. Like Tom Ridge before him, Chertoff was convinced that the federal government was the only entity with the capacity to deal with large disasters. If anything, Katrina reinforced this sense. While Chertoff and Homeland Security officials continued to speak publicly about state and local responders taking the lead role during disasters, they were in fact designing a response system that could be micromanaged from Washington, especially during catastrophic events.

Indeed, the "all-hazards" approach to disaster response increasingly took a back seat to a new paradigm. Frequently, the administration referred to two kinds of disasters: garden-variety calamities which could be handled by the states and "catastrophic" events where the federal government took charge, leaving local responders to serve as little more than Hollywood extras. To add muscularity to the federal response, the White House still supported the idea of giving the

Pentagon a larger role, dispatching troops regardless of whether individual states requested them. In the view of White House homeland security adviser Frances Townsend, the system of providing resources only at a state's request didn't work in large disasters. In those situations, she advocated fuller federal control.

The fear among many emergency managers and governors was that this approach might make matters worse, especially if the trigger for a bigger federal response were pegged to a somewhat arbitrary event, such as a levee breach, as opposed to an overtop. "If the federal government assumes control of first response to catastrophes, I believe it will add needless layers of bureaucracy, create indecisiveness, lead to rampant miscommunications, and ultimately cost lives," said Governor Rick Perry of Texas.

In mid-March, FEMA held its annual meeting of federal coordinating officers, its first big post-Katrina gathering. Justin DeMello, who had worked alongside Florida's Craig Fugate during Hurricane Wilma, had recently been named as a top FCO to help the Southeast get ready for the 2006 hurricane season. DeMello had hoped that the meeting would address the problems experienced between the FCOs and the various levels of Homeland Security's bureaucracy. But over the three days not once did any senior department official come to speak to the group. Instead, a stream of FEMA officials cooed about how the department was going to make national response better. "All we got was the same old bad ideas dressed up as breakthroughs. I didn't hear anything positive," said DeMello.

In fact some of the changes being proposed deeply worried him. He was particularly concerned by Chertoff's plan to send federal SWAT teams to disaster zones to hunt down ground truth for Homeland Security. DeMello felt that unless the teams were under control of the officials on the scene of the disaster, the information could be used by Washington to try to direct the response by remote control. He was also troubled by the fact that Homeland Security officials in Washington would be the only ones able to track the movement of ice and water with the new satellite system. Why, DeMello asked, couldn't top FEMA officials on the ground also follow the vital blips on a computer screen? The answer was that access had to be restricted for "security reasons."

"What they are proposing is a return to a Katrina situation where you'll have Washington reacting to information that it didn't tell the state about," DeMello said. "DHS believes it can manage a response thousands of miles away in Washington. So in a nutshell what you will have is DHS micromanaging the entire response operation from the cube of ice on the ground to the policy decision of how to ship the ice. You can't do it that way. It is a recipe for delays and infighting and disaster."

In the middle of the conference, DeMello got a call from Denver offering him a job as the director of the city's emergency department. He took it on the spot. "I decided then I was no longer going to be a party to DHS's bullshit," DeMello said.

Signs of America's broken disaster response system were evident as the nation prepared for the next presumed large-scale disaster, a pandemic breakout of bird flu. The subject was on President Bush's mind in early October, about a month after Katrina hit. And judging from the president's words, planners in Washington had not devoted much time to the subject. Bush seemed almost to be thinking out loud as he discussed the subject at a Rose Garden press conference. "The policy decisions for a President in dealing with an avian flu outbreak are difficult," he said. "One example: If we had an outbreak somewhere in the United States, do we not then quarantine that part of the country, and how do you then enforce a quarantine? And who best to be able to effect a quarantine?"

In contrast to a hurricane or terrorist attack, there would be no central focus for federal support in the event of a fast-moving flu outbreak. In such a situation, the answer to Bush's question is simple. Local law enforcement would have to do it—barring luck or coincidence, there would be nobody else on the ground.

In preparation for a possible flu outbreak, the federal government began training with local officials, but the early returns were not especially encouraging. In March 2006, in a secure room at the

National Guard's Readiness Center in Arlington, Virginia, General H. Steven Blum, who headed the Pentagon's National Guard Bureau, conducted a series of "tabletop" exercises in which participants tried to manage a flu epidemic. Taking part in the exercise by secure video link were disaster managers from sixty-five local offices around the country. It was the largest exercise of its kind ever conducted.

The drill included a few realistic elements designed to get creativity flowing. There were fake broadcasts from an ersatz cable news network that chronicled the flu outbreak as it spread rapidly from rural Brazil into the United States. The Centers for Disease Control predicted that 35 percent of the general public would be infected by the disease, along with 35 percent of the soldiers in National Guard units.

As the disease moved through the country, response took on the eerie feel of Hurricane Katrina during the worst days. Everyone did his own thing: Some states ignored federal instructions and set up their own quarantine regimes. Others failed to make provisions for body pickup and garbage removal. Local hospitals devolved into chaos as staff doctors and nurses took ill. And as the states fell down, the federal government proved woefully unprepared to step in and prop them up. Under this scenario, participants didn't have the one true luxury afforded to Louisiana. With everyone battling a common scourge, the states couldn't call on other states to back them up.

Throughout the exercise, General Blum kept shouting for common response. "I gotta tell ya, we all gotta be on the same page here," he bellowed. "Rethink what you are saying and doing. If you as a state don't handle this correctly I'm not sure what Washington is going to be able to do for you." His shouting did no good. In the exercise the locals failed. Washington failed. And millions of people would have died.

Within hours of Michael Brown's resignation, he was replaced on an acting basis by R. David Paulison, a popular former Miami fire chief. Paulison had come to Washington in November 2001 to serve as fire administrator, the nation's top firefighter. The search for a permanent replacement for Brown began in earnest the following January.

Among the first candidates considered was Craig Fugate, Florida's disaster chief. Fugate was reluctant to consider the job, but Governor Jeb Bush encouraged him to at least hear the administration out. So in January Fugate visited Washington. By the end of the day, he had heard enough to know he wasn't the man for the job. "They wanted a liquidator, not a director," Fugate said.

The search for Brown's replacement would extend over four months and would include some of the brightest lights in the business: Alabama's Bruce Baughman; Ellen Gordon, the former emergency manager of Iowa; Richard Andrews, a former homeland security adviser to Governor Arnold Schwarzenegger of California; Dale W. Shipley of Ohio and Eric Tolbert of North Carolina, two former FEMA officials who also served as the top emergency managers in their home states. The administration struck out with all of them. In March, Secretary Chertoff acknowledged that the search for Brown's replacement was going slowly. "You've got to be able to attract people," he told a Senate committee. "And I will not deny that certainly I think when there is a lot of negative publicity, it doesn't make a lot of people want to migrate."

With the list of credible candidates disappearing, it looked as if Paulison might get the job by default. And indeed, that's what happened. It wasn't that much of a stretch: Though he may not have had the same depth of experience dealing with large disasters as some of the other candidates, Paulison was solid on paper. Moreover, he had a decent relationship with Chertoff. And on April 6, President Bush nominated Paulison for the job. "I'm going to personally make sure we don't have another response like we saw in Katrina," Paulison said upon his appointment. "FEMA's been tested. We've been retooled. We're ready to go."

But despite his assurances, the future of FEMA remained uncertain.

Exactly three weeks after Paulison accepted his new title, Senators Susan Collins and Joseph Lieberman dropped a bombshell: FEMA, they said, should be scrapped. Their seven-month investigation into what had gone wrong during Hurricane Katrina revealed a "bumbling bureaucracy" incapable of meeting the demands the storm had placed upon it. "We have concluded that FEMA is in shambles and beyond repair and that it should be abolished," said Collins.

In partisan Washington, the conclusion represented a rare meeting of the minds. "Sometimes an organization—private or public—becomes so dysfunctional or disreputable that you have to dissolve it and begin again," said Lieberman. Both senators said the new agency should be rebuilt from the ground up, left within Homeland Security but divorced bugetarily from the parent department and made immune from the internal "taxes" that had brought FEMA to its knees.

The White House rejected the idea out of hand as too radical. Other critics said it didn't go far enough. As hurricane season approached, the only thing certain seemed to be that FEMA wouldn't undergo any dramatic change without a protracted fight between those wanting to remake FEMA inside the Department of Homeland Security, and those who wanted to see the agency restored to its former status as an independent cabinet-level agency. The wrangling would likely go on for some time.

For FEMA employees, the Collins-Lieberman idea simply added a demoralizing subtext to the uncertainty that already faced the agency. Leo Bosner, the FEMA veteran and union chief, summed it up: "I feel like I've been walking down a dark alley at night and suddenly I'm attacked and beaten by a gang of muggers. And as I lie on the ground bleeding with a broken arm and a broken nose, I hear one of them say, 'Hey, this guy's in pain, I feel sorry for him. Let's put a bullet through his head and put him out of his misery.' Am I supposed to feel grateful to this guy?"

For his part, Michael Brown became a disaster consultant, working under his old patron Joe Allbaugh. He managed to rehabilitate himself somewhat, making a series of public apologies for his mistakes during Katrina and showing up with fair regularity on television. And it wasn't uncommon for people to approach the former FEMA chief to say they had revised their opinion of him, viewing him more as a scapegoat than the source of all of FEMA's ineptness.

And he had one iron defense: FEMA continued to flounder long after he left.

But all wasn't completely forgiven; Brown was forced to cancel a consulting contract he struck with St. Bernard Parish after word of the deal leaked out and public outcry ensued. Brown still served as a consultant to the storm-tossed parish, but it was a pro bono job.

The legacy of Hurricane Katrina was clearly on display in April 2006 when Secretary Chertoff took the podium at the annual National Hurricane Conference in Orlando, to make the case that the state of the national emergency response system was strong.

Chertoff told the emergency responders who had gathered for the conference that every level of government—federal, state, and local—had different and reinforcing responsibilities when disaster strikes, and he quickly ticked off the specifics, from evacuation to stockpiling supplies to removing debris. Then he changed tack.

"At the end of the day, we know the responsibility for emergency preparedness isn't solely in the hands of government," he said. "Individual citizens also have an important role to play. Indeed, I believe they have a civic responsibility to take some sensible steps to get ready for hurricane season, especially if they are able-bodied. . . .

"People should be prepared to sustain themselves for up to 72 hours after a disaster—because first responders might not be able to reach every single person within the first day. That means individuals—especially those in the Gulf states—need to have an emergency plan and an emergency kit with adequate supplies of food, water, and other essentials like a flashlight, first-aid, and medicines."

In the end, Chertoff unwittingly defined the most important lesson of all to emerge from Hurricane Katrina: When disaster strikes, we are all on our own.

Sources

This book is the result of more than one hundred interviews, the review of more than ten thousand pages of documents, personal notes, and e-mail messages. In writing it, we traveled from Washington, D.C., to Louisiana, Texas, Florida, and Alabama. We have relied on dozens of sworn depositions, some of which have never been made public; nearly one hundred hours of interviews on tape; congressional testimony; firsthand notes from sources; and other corroborating information, such as photographs and paperwork, that supports what people have told us.

Some of the individuals we interviewed, such as former FEMA director Michael Brown and FEMA spokesman Marty Bahamonde, had to endure many hours (over a period of months) sitting patiently answering questions, and even more time on the phone as we tried to understand where they were and when, and what they were doing. Bruce Baughman of Alabama not only provided a wealth of information and experience but also worked hard to make sure the information in the history section of the book was accurate. Craig Fugate of Florida completely opened up access to the state of Florida's response during Hurricane Wilma as events of that storm unfolded. James Lee Witt and Joe Allbaugh also graciously took time out of their busy schedules to spend hours sharing their knowledge and recollections of their time at the helm of FEMA. Madhu Beriwal, the CEO of Innovative Emergency Management, provided access to documents and her staff that prepared the Hurricane Pam exercise, while Greg Peters, a contract employee at the company, gave a fly's-eye view of what it was like to participate in that most unusual drill.

New Orleans engineer Walter Baudier provided tremendous insight into the design and building of the city's levee system, as well as the underpinning political philosophy that led to the construction of these structures. Colonel Pete Schneider of the Louisiana National Guard showed tremendous patience as he ran down all manner of details and photographs and set up perhaps a dozen interviews. Bob Mann and Andy Kopplin of the Louisiana governor's office spent hours explaining in minute detail the days that followed Katrina's landfall. Numerous people in Baton Rouge and New Orleans bent over backward to help make this book a true account, even as they coped with a disaster that had consumed their city and their state.

The Federal Protective Service produced for interviews agents and officials who were among the first federal representatives on the ground in Mississippi and Louisiana; they provided invaluable information about important events. Sources inside the Department of Homeland Security, FEMA, the Senate Committee on Homeland Security and Government Affairs, and the House Select Bipartisan Committee to Investigate Preparation for and Response to Hurricane Katrina also provided many documents and depositions to us, including the Senate staff interviews of Matthew Broderick, and Secretary Michael Chertoff's written replies to senators' questions. Representative Tom Davis, the chairman of the House committee, in particular deserves special recognition for ruling that all documents gathered in the investigation should reside in the public domain.

Several other people inside FEMA, the Department of Homeland Security, Congress, the White House, and the state of Louisiana provided us with valuable insight and information but requested that they not be publicly acknowledged.

The following is a sampling of some of the events and source material, including White House documents, that were referred to directly or indirectly in the book.

Books

Platt, Rutherford H. *Disasters and Democracy: The Politics of Extreme Natural Events*. Washington, D.C.: Island Press, 1999.

Sheets, Bob, and Jack Williams. *Hurricane Watch: Forecasting the Deadliest Storms on Earth*. New York: Vintage Books, 2001.

Steinberg, Ted. *Acts of God: The Unnatural History of Natural Disaster in America*. New York: Oxford University Press, 2000.

Witt, James Lee. *Stronger in the Broken Places: Nine Lessons for Turning Crisis into Triumph*. New York: Times Books, 2002.

Katrina Chronologies

Center for Cooperative Research. "Katrina Timeline."

Louisiana Department of Wildlife and Fisheries. "Activity Report on Hurricane Katrina."

Louisiana State Police. "Hurricane Katrina Timeline of Events."

Office of the Governor, State of Louisiana. "Overview of Governor Kathleen Babineaux Blanco's Actions in Preparation for and Response to Hurricane Katrina."

Task Force Pelican. "Hurricane Katrina Chronology of Significant Events."

United States Senate, Committee on Homeland Security and Government Affairs. "Situational Awareness: The Day of Landfall."

Academic Papers

Carafano, James Jay, and David Heyman. "DHS 2.0: Rethinking the Department of Homeland Security." The Heritage Foundation and the Center for Strategic and International Studies, Washington, D.C., 2004.

Ellig, Jerry. "Learning from the Leaders: Results-Based Management at the Federal Emergency Management Agency." Mercatus Center, George Mason University, Fairfax, Va., March 29, 2000.

Roberts, Patrick S. "Reputation and Federal Emergency Preparedness Agencies, 1948–2003." Department of Politics, University of Virginia, Charlottesville, Va., September 2, 2004.

U.S. Department of Homeland Security and
Federal Emergency Management Agency

"DHS/FEMA Initial Response Hotwash." Royal Sonesta Hotel, New Orleans, La., December 13–14, 2005.

"How Terrorists Might Exploit a Hurricane." Department of Homeland Security, Information Analysis and Infrastructure Protection, September 15, 2004.

"Initial National Response Plan." Department of Homeland Security, September 30, 2003.

"National All-Hazards Exercise Schedule." Federal Emergency Management Agency, February 2004.

"National Planning Scenarios: Created for Use in National, Federal, State, and Local Homeland Security Preparedness Activities." Department of Homeland Security, April 2005.

"National Preparedness Guidance Homeland Security Presidential Directive 8: National Preparedness." Department of Homeland Security, April 27, 2005.

"National Response Plan." Department of Homeland Security, December 2004.

"A Performance Review of FEMA's Disaster Management Activities in Response to Hurricane Katrina." Department of Homeland Security, Office of Inspector General, Office of Inspections and Special Reviews, March 2006 (OIG-06-32).

"A Review of the Top Officials 3 Exercise." Department of Homeland Security, Office of Inspector General, Office of Inspections and Special Reviews, November 2005 (OIG-06-07).

State of Louisiana

Blanco, Governor Kathleen. Correspondence.

Bottcher, Denise. E-mail messages.

"City of New Orleans Emergency Management Plan 2004."

"Commodity Status by Site," Camp Beauregard, La., Operational Staging Area. August 27, August 29, and September 4, 2005.

Kopplin, Andy. E-mail messages.

Ryder, Terry. E-mail messages.

"Southeast Louisiana Catastrophic Hurricane Plan," plus annexes, July 2004 through September 2005.

U.S. Army Corps of Engineers

Annual Inspection of Completed Works, 2004.

Interagency Performance Evaluation Task Force. Field survey data, presentations, reports.

Lake Pontchartrain and Vicinity Hurricane Protection Project. Design memoranda for the 17th Street, London Avenue, and Orleans Avenue outfall canal projects.

U.S. Government Accountability Office (Formerly General Accounting Office)

"Emergency Preparedness and Response: Some Issues and Challenges Associated with Major Emergency Incidents." Statement of William O. Jenkins, Jr., director, Homeland Security and Justice Issues, February 23, 2006.

"Hazard Mitigation: Proposed Changes to FEMA's Multihazard Mitigation Programs Present Challenges." September 2002.

"Hurricane Katrina: GAO's Preliminary Observations Regarding Preparedness, Response, and Recovery." Statement of David M. Walker, comptroller general of the United States, March 8, 2006.

U.S. Congress

Disaster Assistance Act of 1970 (PL 91-606).

Robert T. Stafford Disaster Relief and Emergency Assistance Act (PL 93-288).

Homeland Security Act of 2002 (PL 107-296).

Hearings before the House of Representatives Select Bipartisan Committee to Investigate Preparation for and Response to Hurricane Katrina: September 22 and 27, 2005; October 3, 19, and 27, 2005; November 2 and 9, 2005; December 6, 7, and 14, 2005.

Deposition of FEMA director Michael Brown before the House of Representatives Select Bipartisan Committee to Investigate Preparation for and Response to Hurricane Katrina, February 11, 2006.

"A Failure of Initiative: The Final Report of the House Select Bipartisan

Committee to Investigate the Preparation for and Response to Hurricane Katrina," February 15, 2006.

Hearings before the U.S. Senate Committee on Homeland Security and Government Affairs: September 14 and 28, 2005; October 6 and 20, 2005; November 2 and 9, 2005; December 8 and 15, 2005; January 17, 24, 30, and 31, 2006; February 1, 2, 6, 9, 10, 13, and 15, 2006.

Statement of Richard A. Falkenrath, visiting fellow, the Brookings Institution, before the United States Senate Committee on Homeland Security and Governmental Affairs, January 26, 2005.

"Hurricane Katrina: A Nation Still Unprepared. The Final Report of the U.S. Senate Committee on Homeland Security and Governmental Affairs," May 2, 2006.

Daily Videoconference Call Transcripts

Transcripts from FEMA, the states, and other federal agencies. August 25, 26, 27, 28, 29, 30, and 31, 2005; September 1, 2, and 4, 2005.

Videoconference call summaries. September 1, 2, 3, 4, 5, and 13, 2005.

The White House (Including White House Homeland Security Council Documents)

Sunday, August 28, 12:32 P.M.—DHS Advisory: Buses not in use, should be moved to high ground. Surge predicted to exceed twenty feet and levees to be breached.

Sunday, August 28, 1:07 P.M.—White House receives overview regarding capabilities of National Guard units from Louisiana, Alabama, Mississippi, and Florida.

Monday, August 29, 6:52 A.M.—Department of Defense briefs White House regarding capabilities of Civil Support.

Monday, August 29, 10:58 A.M.—Kirstjen Nielsen, special assistant to the president and senior director for preparedness and response, advises federal agencies that the White House homeland security committee will be available twenty-four hours a day through the duration of Hurricane Katrina. Bethany Nichols and Dan Kaniewski are identified as additional White House staff monitoring Katrina.

Tuesday, August 30, 12:02 A.M.—HSOC reports Marty Bahamonde's report after a helicopter overflight of New Orleans.

Tuesday, August 30, 8:13 A.M.—DHS watch officer e-mails White House and others that a two-hundred-foot levee breach is being assessed.

Tuesday, August 30, 10:23 A.M.—DHS watch officer e-mails White House maps identifying locations of breached levees.

Tuesday, August 30, 11:18 A.M.—Nielsen e-mails Red Cross and acknowledges several federal partners have expressed a lack of situational awareness and are having problems getting logistics issues resolved.

Tuesday, August 30, 11:50 A.M.—FEMA requests evacuation of 15,000 to 20,000 people from the Louisiana Superdome.

Tuesday, August 30, 11:51 A.M.—DHS watch officer advises White House that martial law has reportedly been declared in Jefferson and Orleans parishes.

Tuesday, August 30, 2:08 P.M.—DHS watch officer advises White House of distinction between the terms "martial law" and "law enforcement emergency."

Tuesday, August 30, 9:00 P.M.—Memo from Secretary Chertoff distributed to cabinet activates the National Response Plan and names Michael Brown as principal federal official.

Wednesday, August 31, 2:00 A.M.—HSOC reports that Superdome needs to be evacuated; population is 12,000 to 15,000 people.

Wednesday, August 31, 5:47 A.M.—HSOC reports that waters are rising due to a three-hundred-foot breach in the 17th Street Canal levee. Without a fix, flooding will not stop until it reaches lake level.

Thursday, September 1, 1:00 A.M.—"Commodity Status" report lists locations and commodity supplies.

Thursday, September 1, 5:50 A.M.—HSOC reports that the New Orleans Police Department has suspended search-and-rescue efforts and is focusing on securing the city from lawlessness. Pipeline from Plaquemines Parish is leaking an estimated 240 barrels of oil a day.

Thursday, September 1, 11:24 A.M.—Nielsen complains that information arriving at the White House homeland security committee from the HSOC is stale.

Thursday, September 1, 1:48 P.M.—DHS watch officer advises White House that the New Orleans Police Department reports that a National Guardsman was shot in a Superdome bathroom after an altercation with an evacuee.

Thursday, September 1, 2:37 P.M.—Flyover pictures sent to White House show the magnitude of the damage.

Thursday, September 1, 2:47 P.M.—Hostage situation at Tulane Hospital reported.

Thursday, September 1, 6:00 P.M.—Availability of generators and military rations are insufficient due to overwhelming demand.

Thursday, September 1, 6:14 P.M.—National Guard is deployed to assist with law and order. Significant flooding continues in Jefferson, Orleans, and St. Bernard parishes. 17th Street Canal levee breach is being repaired. Food and water air drops are taking place through the affected area.

Thursday, September 1, 7:24 P.M.—E-mail trail begins with Richard Davis at the White House homeland security committee asking for specific operational response plans for attending to hospitals.

Thursday, September 1, 10:19 P.M.—Transportation Security Administration personnel report trouble maintaining order at Louis Armstrong International Airport.

Thursday, September 1, 10:50 P.M.—Dan Ostergaard at DHS advises Richard Davis at White House that the response to Katrina is a national disgrace.

Friday, September 2, 5:44 A.M.—DHS "Briefing Points" report that Federal Protective Service officers have walked the perimeter of the Convention Center, and there are approximately 1,000 people there. It also says, "New Orleans Officers on scene and tactically prepared."

Friday, September 2, 12:44 P.M.—DHS notifies the White House that the correct population figure for the New Orleans Convention Center is 25,000, according to FEMA. It adds that limited food and water are available.

"The Federal Response to Hurricane Katrina: Lessons Learned." The White House, February 23, 2006.

Newspaper and Magazine Articles

Andersen, Martin Edwin. "Local Officials Howl at DHS Emergency Management Plan." *Congressional Quarterly*, August 8, 2003.

Arndorfer, Bob. "Area Roots Run Deep for State Emergency Chief Craig Fugate." *Gainesville Sun*, October 22, 2005.

Bageant, Joe. "Driving on the Bones of God, You and I May Get Smoked, but the Fat Cats Will Still Dine on Peacock Tongues." Joebageant.com, August 23, 2004.

Ball, Jeffrey, Ann Zimmerman, and Gary McWilliams. "Rita's Wrenching Exodus; Texans Snarl the Interstates While Carless Wait for Buses; Some Give Up and Turn Back." *Wall Street Journal*, September 23, 2005.

Block, Robert. "Documents Reveal Extent of Fumbles on Storm Relief." *Wall Street Journal*, September 13, 2005.

———. "FEMA Points to Flaws, Flubs in Terror Drill." *Wall Street Journal*, October 31, 2003.

———. "Identity Crisis: Hurricane Tests Emergency Agency at Time of Ferment; Now Under Homeland Security, FEMA Has Lost Clout, Managers on Ground Say; Terrorist with 145 MPH Winds." *Wall Street Journal*, August 16, 2004.

———. "U.S. Had Plan for Crisis Like Katrina; A 2004 Exercise Produced an Evacuation Strategy; It Wasn't Ready in Time." *Wall Street Journal*, September 19, 2005.

Block, Robert, and Amy Schatz. "Storm Front: Local and Federal Authorities Battle to Control Disaster Relief; Florida Beat Back Washington During Hurricane Wilma; A Video-Conference Coup; Mr. Fugate Seizes 300 Phones." *Wall Street Journal*, December 8, 2005.

Block, Robert, Amy Schatz, Gary Fields, and Christopher Cooper. "Power Failure: Behind Poor Katrina Response, a Long Chain of Weak Links; Changing Structure of FEMA, Emphasis on Terrorism Contributed to Problems; A Shortage of Helicopters." *Wall Street Journal*, September 6, 2005.

Boyd, Gerald M. "A Disaster Agency's Image Disaster." *New York Times*, January 6, 1984.

Braun, Stephen, and Ralph Vartabedian. "The Politics of Flood Control, Levees Weakened as New Orleans Board, Federal Engineers Feuded." *Los Angeles Times*, December 25, 2005.

Bryce, Robert. "The Fab Four." Salon.com, June 16, 1999.

"Christmas Mail by FEMA Chief Found Improper." *Washington Post*, June 3, 1985.

Clarke, David. "Mike Brown: A Cool Man in the Hot Seat." *Congressional Quarterly*, March 20, 2003.

Cooper, Christopher. "A City's Stragglers Depend on Kindness of Dr. Brobson Lutz; Man About French Quarter Moves Bodies, Treats Ills; Giving Viagra to the Cops." *Wall Street Journal*, September 16, 2005.

———. "Misinformation Slowed Federal Response to Katrina." *Wall Street Journal*, September 30, 2005.

———. "Old-Line Families Escape Worst of Flood and Plot the Future; Mr. O'Dwyer at His Mansion, Enjoys Highball with Ice; Meeting with the Mayor." *Wall Street Journal*, September 8, 2005.

Cooper, Christopher, and Jeff D. Opdyke. "Cost to Remove Katrina's Dead Stirs Criticism." *Wall Street Journal*, November 4, 2005.

Cooper, Christopher, and Dionne Searcey. "In Katrina's Wake; Some Hold-outs Leave, Others Stay as Authorities Urge Evacuation." *Wall Street Journal*, September 9, 2005.

Garland, Susan. "If Disaster Reigns, FEMA Holds the 'Umbrella.'" *Christian Science Monitor*, December 17, 1981.

Glasser, Susan B., and Michael Grunwald. "Department's Mission Was Undermined from Start." *Washington Post*, December 22, 2005.

Grunwald, Michael, and Susan B. Glasser. "FEMA, Brown Lost All the Turf Wars; Homeland Security Kept Bleeding Agency." *Washington Post*, December 23, 2005.

Hsu, Spencer S., and Steve Hendrix. "Hurricanes Katrina and Rita Were Like Night and Day." *Washington Post*, September 25, 2005.

Kirkpatrick, David D., and Scott Shane. "Ex-FEMA Chief Tells of Frustration and Chaos." *New York Times*, September 15, 2005.

Kurtz, Howard. "FEMA Chief, 6 Aides Defy Hill Subpoena." *Washington Post*, December 13, 1984.

———. "FEMA Transferred Branch Chief Whose Complaints Sparked Probes." *Washington Post*, October 26, 1984.

———. "FEMA's Director's Stars Followed Brief Hitches; Promotions Came in State Military Reserves." *Washington Post*, June 11, 1985.

———. "Noncompetitive Award of Contract for Training Manual Faces Probes; Influential Republicans Contacted FEMA Official." *Washington Post*, February 13, 1985.

———. "Retired Military Policeman Troop into Highly Paid Agency Jobs." *Washington Post*, February 3, 1985.

———. "U.S. Paid for FEMA Chief's Attendance at a Fund-Raiser; Consulting Firm Billed Government." *Washington Post*, October 25, 1984.

Kurtz, Howard, and Pete Earley. "Hill Panel Probes FEMA Official; Agency Funds Said Used for Residence." *Washington Post*, August 1, 1984.

———. "No. 3 FEMA Official Quits Amid Charges of Misusing Funds." *Washington Post*, August 4, 1984.

Lipowicz, Alice. "Interim Plan Details Coordination of Federal Response to Emergencies." *Congressional Quarterly*, October 10, 2003.

Lipton, Eric. "National Security Chief Vows He Is Fixing What Hurricanes Showed Was Broken." *New York Times*, October 25, 2005.

————. "White House Knew of Levee's Failure on Night of Storm." *New York Times*, February 10, 2006.

Loven, Jennifer. "White House Falls out of Step." Associated Press, September 6, 2005.

Marshall, Bob, John McQuaid, and Mark Schleifstein. "For Centuries, Canals Kept New Orleans Dry. Most People Never Dreamed They Would Become Mother Nature's Instrument of Destruction." *Times-Picayune* (New Orleans), January 29, 2006.

Mowbray, Rebecca. "Vertical Evacuation High on Risk; Hotels Urged Not to Take in Guests During Hurricanes." *Times-Picayune* (New Orleans), May 24, 2005.

Russakoff, Dale. "U.S. Trying to Revive A-Plant That State, County Believe Is Dying." *Washington Post*, May 6, 1984.

Sawyer, Kathy, and Howard Kurtz. "Chief Denies Intentional Wrongdoing; Giuffrida Tells House Panel That Recent Probes Have Been 'Soul-Searing.'" *Washington Post*, March 5, 1985.

Shane, Scott, and Eric Lipton. "Stumbling Storm-Aid Effort Put Tons of Ice on Trips to Nowhere." *New York Times*, October 2, 2005.

Starks, Tim. "Fixing FEMA: A Flurry of Ideas to Address Autonomy, Control and Purpose." *Congressional Quarterly*, April 27, 2006.

Stein, Jeff. "Top DHS Emergency Official Matthew Broderick Resigns." *Congressional Quarterly*, March 2, 2006.

Sullivan, Eileen. "Chertoff Rejects Claims That Poor Hurricane Response Linked to FEMA Being in DHS." *Congressional Quarterly*, April 12, 2006.

————. "White House Still Searching for New FEMA Director." *Congressional Quarterly*, February 14, 2006.

Terhune, Chad, Kris Hudson, and Ann Carrns. "Texas, Louisiana Brace for a Devastating Blow; Evacuees Cram Highways to Flee Hurricane Rita; New Floods in New Orleans." *Wall Street Journal*, September 24, 2005.

Wakabayashi, Daisuke. "Rita Evacuees Hunt for Open Shelters Across Texas." Reuters, September 22, 2005.

Weinraub, Bernard. "Civil Defense Agency: 'Trying to Do Something.'" *New York Times*, April 8, 1982.

Zimmerman, Ann, and Valerie Bauerlein. "At Wal-Mart, Emergency Plan Has Big Payoff." *Wall Street Journal*, September 12, 2005.

Acknowledgments

It took more than sources and a Patton-style editor to drive this work to completion under a schedule that at times seemed impossibly rigorous. Our wives, Remi and Donna, put up with us for months while we ignored them, blew off our responsibilities, and demurred on the household chores. Our sons, Jack and Ethan, also had to make do without their fathers, sometimes for long stretches, and we thank them for being understanding, forgiving, and so grown up about it all.

This book would be no more than a jumble of notes without the unwavering support of Jerry Seib, the *Wall Street Journal*'s Washington bureau chief, who proclaimed himself behind this endeavor from day one, and never once deviated from that. There's no doubt that we tested the limits of his seemingly boundless patience, but if he was on full boil, he never let on. Jerry's support was instrumental, rock steady, and genuine. We are tremendously grateful for it.

Others took up the slack for us around the office as we pursued our obsession, most notably Winston Wood, one of the Washington bureau's news editors, who recognized early on that our appetite was rapacious for all things Katrina. As we worked on the manuscript, he ensured that we stayed up with current events by pushing a flood of breaking news reports our way. Reporter John McKinnon kept the White House beat from melting down in our absence and graciously shouldered more than his fair share of the spot news as we ran down the last strands of reporting. Todd Shuster and Esmond Harmsworth served as our agents in every sense of the word and more than earned their keep with their zealous pursuit of our interests. Their integrity is beyond peer.

Sebastian Abbot, a Harvard grad student, helped us because he wanted to, providing us with vital research assistance, constructing timelines, and accepting nothing but a club sandwich and a Coke in return. Similarly, Moira Whelan not only was a cheerleader for the project but used her natural charm to convince a few Department of Homeland Security officials and congressional staffers that their suspicion of reporters was valid but shouldn't apply to us. David Wallace-Wells of Times Books saved us many hours of work by tirelessly tracking down and cataloging the photographs we needed for this book.

Eileen Sullivan of *Congressional Quarterly* and Lara Jakes Jordan of the Associated Press shared documents, tips, and notes with us, and were a huge help in our research. Jim Lewis, a journalist and a wonderful novelist, opened his heart and his house in Texas, when we visited there. Norma Driver in Alabama had to put up with millions of phone calls, e-mails, and faxes. Dr. Brobson Lutz provided a place to stay in the French Quarter, as well as wine, beautiful food, and a gorgeous, sun-filled courtyard in which to work. Peter Baker of the *Washington Post* and Peter Wallsten of the *Los Angeles Times*, authors both, provided repeated, soothing predictions that this thing we loosely referred to as a manuscript would one day magically transform itself into something worth reading.

There are others who played vital roles in our endeavor but who for various reasons would prefer to remain anonymous. Still we couldn't have done much without the help and guidance of BL, JM, JL, MM, and BK.

And finally, Paul Golob, the editorial director of Times Books, kept a steady hand on the tiller and gave us something we could be both proud of and truly call our own. He is firm without being pedantic. He has an ear for the internal cadence of a sentence and an eye for the tiny details that form the mosaic of a rich narrative. His unswerving dedication to order added the perfect amount of rigor into what at times seemed like a hopelessly chaotic writing exercise. Such attributes shouldn't be rare in a business like this, but they are. And we are extremely fortunate to have happened upon him.

Index

ABOUT THE AUTHORS

CHRISTOPHER COOPER is a national political correspondent for *The Wall Street Journal* and a former White House correspondent for the paper. Before joining the *Journal,* he was a political reporter for *The Times-Picayune* of New Orleans.

ROBERT BLOCK covers the Department of Homeland Security for *The Wall Street Journal* and is a former foreign correspondent who has reported on terrorism and war from Europe, Africa, and the Middle East.

Both authors live in Washington, D.C.